DATE DUE

#47-0108 Peel Off Pressure Sensitive

Bloom's Major Literary Characters

Hester Prynne

Edited and with an introduction by
Harold Bloom
Sterling Professor of the Humanities
Yale University

CHELSEA HOUSE
P U B L I S H E R S
A Haights Cross Communications Company
Philadelphia

©2004 by Chelsea House Publishers, a subsidiary of
Haights Cross Communications.

A Haights Cross Communications Company

Introduction © 2004 by Harold Bloom.

Printed and bound in the United States of America.

10 9 8 7 6 5 4 3 2 1

Library of Congress Cataloging-in-Publication Data applied for.

ISBN 0-7910-7884-1

Contributing editor: Pamela Loos

Cover design by Keith Trego

Cover: Library of Congress, LC-USZC4-4290

Layout by EJB Publishing Services

Chelsea House Publishers
1974 Sproul Road, Suite 400
Broomall, PA 19008-0914

www.chelseahouse.com

Contents

HAROLD BLOOM

The Analysis of Character

"Character," according to our dictionaries, still has as a primary meaning a graphic symbol, such as a letter of the alphabet. This meaning reflects the word's apparent origin in the ancient Greek character, a sharp stylus. *Charactēr* also meant the mark of the stylus' incisions. Recent fashions in literary criticism have reduced "character" in literature to a matter of marks upon a page. But our word "character" also has a very different meaning, matching that of the ancient Greek *ēthos*, "habitual way of life." Shall we say then that literary character is an imitation of human character, or is it just a grouping of marks? The issue is between a critic like Dr. Samuel Johnson, for whom words were as much like people as like things, and a critic like the late Roland Barthes, who told us that "the fact can only exist linguistically, as a term of discourse." Who is closer to our experience of reading literature, Johnson or Barthes? What difference does it make, if we side with one critic rather than the other?

Barthes is famous, like Foucault and other recent French theorists, for having added to Nietzsche's proclamation of the death of God a subsidiary demise, that of the literary author. If there are no authors, then there are no fictional personages, presumably because literature does not refer to a world outside language. Words indeed necessarily refer to other words in the first place, but the impact of words ultimately is drawn from a universe of fact. Stories, poems, and plays are recognizable as such because they are human utterances within traditions of utterances, and traditions, by achieving authority, become a kind of fact, or at least the sense of a fact. Our sense that literary characters, within the context of a fictive cosmos, indeed are fictional personages is also a kind of fact. The meaning and value of every character in a successful work of literary representation depend upon our ideas of persons in the factual reality of our lives.

Literary character is always an invention, and inventions generally are indebted to prior inventions. Shakespeare is the inventor of literary character as we know it; he reformed the universal human expectations for the verbal imitation of personality, and the reformation appears now to be permanent and uncannily inevitable. Remarkable as the Bible and Homer are at representing personages, their characters are relatively unchanging. They age within their stories, but their habitual modes of being do not develop. Jacob and Achilles unfold before us, but without metamorphoses. Lear and Macbeth, Hamlet and Othello severely modify themselves not only by their actions, but by their utterances, and most of all through *overhearing themselves*, whether they speak to themselves or to others. Pondering what they themselves have said, they will to change, and actually do change, sometimes extravagantly yet always persuasively. Or else they suffer change, without willing it, but in reaction not so much to their language as to their relation to that language.

I do not think it useful to say that Shakespeare successfully imitated elements in our characters. Rather, it could be argued that he compelled aspects of character to appear that previously were concealed, or not available to representation. This is not to say that Shakespeare is God, but to remind us that language is not God either. The mimesis of character in Shakespeare's dramas now seems to us normative, and indeed became the accepted mode almost immediately, as Ben Jonson shrewdly and somewhat grudgingly implied. And yet, Shakespearean representation has surprisingly little in common with the imitation of reality in Jonson or in Christopher Marlowe. The origins of Shakespeare's originality in the portrayal of men and women are to be found in the *Canterbury Tales* of Geoffrey Chaucer, insofar as they can be located anywhere before Shakespeare himself, Chaucer's savage and superb Pardoner overhears his own tale-telling, as well as his mocking rehearsal of his own spiel, and through this overhearing he is emboldened to forget himself, and enthusiastically urges all his fellow-pilgrims to come forward to be fleeced by him. His self-awareness, and apocalyptically rancid sense of spiritual fall, are preludes to the even grander abysses of the perverted will in Iago and in Edmund. What might be called the character trait of a negative charisma may be Chaucer's invention, but came to its perfection in Shakespearean mimesis.

The analysis of character is as much Shakespeare's invention as the representation of character is, since Iago and Edmund are adepts at analyzing both themselves and their victims. Hamlet, whose overwhelming charisma has many negative components, is certainly the most comprehensive of all literary characters, and so necessarily prophesies the labyrinthine complexities of the will in Iago and Edmund. Charisma, according to Max Weber, its first codifier, is primarily a natural endowment, and implies a primordial and idiosyncratic power over nature, and so finally over death. Hamlet's uncanniness is at its most suggestive in the scene of his long dying, where the audience, through the mediation of Horatio, itself is compelled to meditate upon suicide, if only because outliving the prince of Denmark scarcely seems an option.

Shakespearean representation has usurped not only our sense of literary character, but our sense of ourselves as characters, with Hamlet playing the part of the largest of these usurpations. Insofar as we have an idea of human disinterestedness, we tend to derive it from the Hamlet of Act V, whose quietism has about it a ghostly authority. Oscar Wilde, in his profound and profoundly witty dialogue, "The Decay of Lying," expressed a permanent insight when he insisted that art shaped every era, far more than any age formed art. Life imitates art, we imitate Shakespeare, because without Shakespeare we would perish for lack of images. Wilde's grandest audacity demystifies Shakespearean mimesis with a Shakespearean vivaciousness: "This unfortunate aphorism about art holding the mirror up to Nature is deliberately said by Hamlet in order to convince the bystanders of his absolute insanity in all art-matters." Of *Hamlet*'s influence upon the ages Wilde remarked that: "The world has grown sad because a puppet was once melancholy." "Puppet" is Wilde's own deconstruction, a brilliant reminder that Shakespeare's artistry of illusion has so mastered reality as to have changed reality, evidently forever.

The analysis of character, as a critical pursuit, seems to me as much a Shakespearean invention as literary character was, since much of what we know about how to analyze character necessarily follows Shakespearean procedures. His hero-villains, from Richard III through Iago, Edmund, and Macbeth, are shrewd and endless questers into their own self-motivations. If we could bear to see Hamlet, in his unwearied negations, as another hero-villain, then we would judge him the supreme analyst of the darker recalcitrances in the selfhood. Freud followed the pre-Socratic Empedocles, in arguing that character is fate, a frightening doctrine that maintains the fear that there are no accidents, that overdetermination rules us all of our lives. Hamlet assumes the same, yet adds to this argument the terrible passivity he manifests in Act V. Throughout Shakespeare's tragedies, the most interesting personages seem doom-eager, reminding us again that a Shakespearean reading of Freud would be more illuminating than a Freudian exegesis of

Shakespeare. We learn more when we discover Hamlet in the Freudian Death Drive, than when we read *Beyond the Pleasure Principle* into *Hamlet*.

In Shakespearean comedy, character achieves its true literary apotheosis, which is the representation of the inner freedom that can be created by great wit alone. Rosalind and Falstaff, perhaps alone among Shakespeare's personages, match Hamlet in wit, though hardly in the metaphysics of consciousness. Whether in the comic or the modern mode, Shakespeare has set the standard of measurement in the balance between character and passion.

In Shakespeare the self is more dramatized than theatricalized, which is why a Shakespearean reading of Freud works out so well. Character-formation after the passing of the Oedipal stage takes the place of fetishistic fragmentings of the self. Critics who now call literary character into question, and who proclaim also the death of the author, invariably also regard all notions, literary and human, of a stable character as being mere reductions of deeper pre-Oedipal desires. It becomes clear that the fortunes of literary character rise and fall with the prestige of normative conceptions of the ego. Shakespeare's Iago, who wars against being, may be the first deconstructionist of the self, with his proclamation of "I am not what I am." This constitutes the necessary prologue to any view that would regard a fixed ego as a virtual abnormality. But deconstructions of the self are no more modern than Modernism is. Like literary modernism, the decentered ego came out of the Hellenistic culture of ancient Alexandria. The Gnostic heretics believed that the psyche, like the body, was a fallen entity, mechanically fashioned by the Demiurge or false creator. They held however that each of us possessed also a spark or pneuma, which was a fragment of the original Abyss or true, alien God. The soul or psyche within every one of us was thus at war with the self or pneuma, and only that sparklike self could be saved.

Shakespeare, following after Chaucer in this respect, was the first and remains still the greatest master of representing character both as a stable soul and a wavering self. There is a substance that endures in Shakespeare's figures, and there is also a quicksilver rendition of the unsettling sparks. Racine and Tolstoy, Balzac and Dickens, follow in Shakespeare's wake by giving us some sense of pre-Oedipal sparks or drives, and considerably more sense of post-Oedipal character and personality, stabilizations or sublimations of the fetish-seeking drives. Critics like Leo Bersani and René Girard argue eloquently against our taking this mimesis as the only proper work of literature. I would suggest that strong fictions of the self, from the Bible through Samuel Beckett, necessarily participate in both modes, the sublimation of desire, and the persistence of a primordial desire. The mystery of Hamlet or of Lear is intimately invested in the tangled mixture of the two modes of representation.

Psychic mobility is proposed by Bersani as the ideal to which deconstructions of the literary self may yet guide us. The ideal has its pathos, but the realities of literary representation seem to me very different, perhaps destructively so. When a novelist like D. H. Lawrence sought to reduce his characters to Eros and the Death Drive, he still had to persuade us of his authority at mimesis by lavishing upon the figures of *The Rainbow* and *Women in Love* all of the vivid stigmata of normative personality. Birkin and Ursula may represent antithetical and uncanny drives, but they develop and change as characters pondering their own pronouncements and reactions to self and others. The cost of a non-Shakespearean representation is enormous. Pynchon, in *The Crying of Lot 49* and *Gravity's Rainbow*, evades the burden of the normative by resorting to something like Christopher Marlowe's art of caricature in *The Jew of Malta*. Marlowe's Barabas is a marvelous rhetorician, yet he is a cartoon alongside the troublingly equivocal Shylock. Pynchon's personages are deliberate cartoons also, as flat as comic strips. Marlowe's achievement, and Pynchon's, are beyond dispute, yet they are like the prelude and the postlude to Shakespearean reality. They do not wish to engage with our hunger for the empirical world and so they enter the problematic cosmos of literary fantasy.

No writer, not even Shakespeare or Proust, alters the available stock that we agree to call reality, but Shakespeare, more than any other, does show us how much of reality we could encounter if only we retained adequate desire. The strong literary representation of character is already an analysis of character, and is part of the healing work of a literary culture, which implicitly seeks to cure violence through a normative mimesis of ego, *as if it were stable*, whether in actuality it is or is not. I do not believe that this is a social quest taken on by literary culture, but rather that we confront here the aesthetic essence of what makes a culture *literary*, rather than metaphysical or ethical or religious. A culture becomes literary when its conceptual modes have failed it, which means when religion, philosophy, and science have begun to lose their authority. If they cannot heal violence, then literature attempts to do so, which may be only a turning inside out of the critical arguments of Girard and Bersani.

I conclude by offering a particular instance or special case as a paradigm for the healing enterprise that is at once the representation and the analysis of literary character. Let us call it the aesthetics of being outraged, or rather of successfully representing the state of being outraged. W.C. Fields was one modern master of such representation, and Nathanael West was another, as was Faulkner before him. Here also the greatest master remains Shakespeare, whose Macbeth, himself a bloody outrage, yet retains our imaginative sympathy precisely because he grows increasingly outraged as he experiences the equivocation of the fiend that lies like truth. The double-natured promises and the prophecies of the weird sisters finally induce in Macbeth an apocalyptic version of the stage actor's anxiety at missing cues, the horror of a phantasmagoric stage fright of missing one's time, of always reacting too late. Macbeth, a veritable monster of solipsistic inwardness but no intellectual, counters his dilemma by fresh murders, that prolong him in time yet provoke him only to a perpetually freshened sense of being outraged, as all his expectations become still worse confounded. We are moved by Macbeth, however estrangedly, because his terrible inwardness is a paradigm for our own solipsism, but also because none of us can resist a strong and successful representation of the human in a state of being outraged.

The ultimate outrage is the necessity of dying, an outrage concealed in a multitude of masks, including the tyrannical ambitions of Macbeth. I suspect that our outrage at being outraged is the most difficult of all our affects for us to represent to ourselves, which is why we are so inclined to imaginative sympathy for a character who strongly conveys that affect to us. The Shrike of West's *Miss Lonelyhearts* or Faulkner's Joe Christmas of *Light in August* are crucial modern instances, but such figures can be located in many other works, since the ability to represent this extreme emotion is one of the tests that strong writers are driven to set for themselves.

However a reader seeks to reduce literary character to a question of marks on a page, she will come at last to the impasse constituted by the thought of death, her death, and before that to all the stations of being outraged that memorialize her own drive towards death. In reading, she quests for evidences that are strong representations, whether of her desire or her despair. Such questings constitute the necessary basis for the analysis of literary character, an enterprise that always will survive every vagary of critical fashion.

Editor's Note

My introduction emphasizes Hester's centrality as the inaugural heroine of the Protestant will in American prose fiction.

D.H. Lawrence—magnificent novelist, story-writer, and poet—expresses visionary outrage at *his* Hester, who is a "devil," one of those "leprous-white, seducing, spiritual women" who had driven Lawrence wild, and whom he, in return, had driven quite crazy.

In a very different perspective, Edward Stone sees Hester as a woman of the Old World struggling to retain her identity in the New, while Charles Feidelson instead resorts to images of secularized symbolism.

Austin Warren, my favorite critic of the New England literary tradition, admires Hester's tenacity while deploring her poor judgment in having loved the weakling, Dimmesdale.

In Walter Shear's judgement, Hawthorne simultaneously adopts both a High Romantic (Emersonian) stance towards Hester, and a sentimental view, in which she is a figure of pathos.

Preston Browning regards Hester as a heroine of what I would call the American religion, post-Protestant and allowing for secular sainthood.

Historically, Michael Colacurcio links Hester Prynne to the heroic Ann Hutchinson, defiant antagonist of those male Puritans who could not accept her illumination by the Inner Light.

Nina Baym finds in Hawthorne's narrative emphasis an ongoing male confusion about what constitutes a woman's strength, after which Lois Cuddy also applies current feminist thought on the ambivalent bond between Hester and Pearl, mother and daughter.

Thomas Hardy usefully is contrasted to Hawthorne by Janis Stout, who discovers elements of male anxiety in the portraits both of Hester and of Hardy's Tess.

Monica Elbert conveys an accurate sense of Hawthorne's unresolved tensions towards Hester, while Leland Person concludes this volume by exploring some of the analogues between Hester and slave mothers.

HAROLD BLOOM

Introduction

Of all the principal female characters in our national literature, Hester Prynne is clearly the central figure. American male novelists, except for Hawthorne and James, have not been able to represent American women with the force and vivacity that have marked the English tradition that goes from Samuel Richardson's Clarissa Harlowe through E. M. Forster's Schlegel sisters in *Howards End*. In our century, the women portrayed by Faulkner, Hemingway, and Fitzgerald are generally less vivid than the men, with a few significant exceptions. James's heroines, from Isabel Archer on, have a clear family resemblance to aspects of Hawthorne's Hester. If we have a national heroine of our version of the Protestant will in America, then it must be Hester Prynne, and yet Hester, though Hawthorne's triumph, yields only grudgingly to our criticism. She is larger than her book, admirable as *The Scarlet Letter* certainly is, because she incarnates more paradoxes and even contradictions than Dimmesdale does, let alone Chillingworth or the visionary Pearl. Hopelessly old-fashioned critic that I am, I do not regard achieved literary characters as so many marks upon the page, or as metaphors for racial, gender, and class differences. The extraordinary Hawthornian imagination, wandering between mimetic realism and high romance, gave us an overwhelming personality and puzzling moral character in the sensual and tragic Hester, who is at once the ideal object of Hawthorne's desire and a troubled projection of Hawthorne's authorial subjectivity, cast out from him but never definitively. Strong writers of romance are both subject and object of their own quests, and there is a profound sense in which Hester is as much a representation of Hawthorne's deep inwardness as Clarissa is Richardson's vision of his own inmost self.

As many critics tell us, Hester Prynne is primarily a sexual being, a truth about her that scarcely can be overemphasized. As a truth, it possesses terrible pathos, for her heroic sexuality has yielded her two impossible men, her Satanic husband Chillingworth and her inadequate lover Dimmesdale, each of them admirably named. Hester has Pearl, a few poor memories of Dimmesdale, and mostly her own pride to sustain her. Her sexuality has been balked, yet constitutes the core of her resistance to her Puritan persecutors. It constitutes also a considerable part of her strong appeal to Hawthorne and to his readers. What matters most about Hester is the vital intensity of her being, her frustrated promise of more life, which is the Hebraic sense of the Blessing. There are a number of valid ways of explaining Hester's charismatic quality, both in and out of the pages of *The Scarlet Letter*, but the most accurate, I am convinced, is to see her charisma as implicit sexual power.

Critics have found both Puritan and Emersonian strands in Hester, and her uneasy religion indeed is a highly contradictory blend of Calvinism and of Emerson's American religion of Self-reliance. Her daughter Pearl is something wilder, but then Pearl belongs almost wholly to the representational order of high romance. Hester's inconsistencies have exercised critics, but the wonder is that there are not many more of them in someone so tormented by an insanely, even obscenely moralistic society, which is to make a judgment that Hawthorne the novelist certainly would have repudiated. Perhaps it might be fairer to say that the strains in Hester uncover some of the strains in Hawthorne, whose creative drive ensues from a temperament more dialectical even than that of his grudging and involuntary heir, Henry James. Hawthorne has something of the same relationship to Calvinism as his truest precursor, Edmund Spenser, who harmonized antithetical elements with a freedom not available to American romance. It is a kind of aesthetic miracle that *The Scarlet Letter* could be written at all, in a cultural situation as belated as Hawthorne's, one that enables *The Marble Faun* and *The House of the Seven Gables* far more readily than Hawthorne's higher achievement in the best of the tales and *The Scarlet Letter*.

Hester's relation to the personality of Anne Hutchinson has been widely studied, but is bound to remain problematical, because the deepest aspect of the relation is that she does not develop into a second Anne Hutchinson. We sense that the movement of sexual power into an antinomian context is what Hester and Mrs. Hutchinson share, but

Hawthorne partly evades such a movement in his Hester. He will not let her prophesy, and will not quite prophesy for her. This makes the book spiritually irritating to some readers, particularly at the present time, but undoubtedly helps create its aesthetic strength, since the reader becomes ever more convinced that there is more to Hester than the storyteller is willing to unfold. We want her to say more, to do more, and yet we understand the appropriateness of the way the book both arouses such desires and refuses to gratify them. Hester does not run away from her story, but she runs off with it. We are left not caring much about Dimmesdale, Chillingworth, and Pearl, because they are not adequate to Hester's greatness, nor are we. Critics who chide Hester for her self-deceptions and her moral inconsistencies always sound as silly to me as the endless heaps of scholars who denounce Shakespeare's Falstaff. Hester does not contain us as Falstaff and Rosalind, Hamlet and Cleopatra contain us, but Hester always precedes us as the most representative fictive portrait of an American woman. She cannot hold together her incompatible impulses, and yet she survives an outrageously dreadful societal and erotic context that ought to have driven her either to madness or to suicide. It is absurd for any critic not to learn from her, while speculating again as to the sources of her extraordinary strength of being.

Hester sends us back to Hawthorne, despite his subtlest efforts to evade an identity with her, efforts that profoundly influenced James's similar evasions in regard to Isabel Archer. Isabel's recoil from Goodwood's aggressive sexuality has no parallel in Hester, who would have enveloped Goodwood had he been available to her, and if he could have been endowed by his author with a few touches of what after all is massively present in poor Dimmesdale, spiritual awareness. There was an overt separation in Hawthorne's consciousness between sexual power and the quest of the Protestant will for its own autonomy and dignity, and that separation is painfully repeated in Hester's mind. But the great artist in Hawthorne knew more, and we receive a sense throughout the novel that Hester is working through, not to an impossible integration, but to a stance prophetic of something evermore about to be, a possible sublimity of a changed relationship between men and women. Since that relationship would require a coherent social sanction, it could not achieve the full autonomy of the American religion of Self-reliance, but then even the theologian of our religion, Emerson himself, refrained from extending his vision into the sexual domain, except in certain poems.

Hester, as critics acknowledge, is herself an artist, and her embroidery has its own affinities to Hawthorne's mixed mode of novel and romance, as well as to the outward show of Puritan Boston in *The Scarlet Letter*. But I think she fails her art, which may be part of the cost of Hawthorne not failing his, and it may be that Hester's compromised condition at the book's close is the consequence of being sacrificed by the author as a substitute for himself. Even as Hester devotes herself to the sufferings of other women, she has yielded to Puritan society's initial judgment upon her. In doing so, she certainly has abandoned much of value in her own passional stance, and we can be tempted into an admiring anger against Hawthorne for having diminished her. And yet the "Conclusion" is not the book, though how else Hawthorne could have concluded one scarcely knows. Hester does not break, and we can believe Hawthorne's affirmation that her own free will prevails, but it becomes a very negative will indeed. The alternative presumably would have been for Hawthorne to have converted the book from romance to tragedy, but that he would not do. Hester was not to be a female version of Melville's Ahab, dying in Promethean and Gnostic defiance of a tyrannical universe, darting a final harpoon into the sanctified flesh of a merely demiurgical creation. Instead Hester submits, but only in part, and with sublime trust in the coming revelation of a woman yet to be.

What if Hawthorne had made of Hester not an embroiderer but a romancer, a writer of narrative, whose "rich, voluptuous, Oriental" nature had ensued in twice-told tales? Since Hawthorne grants Hester extraordinary vitality but inadequate articulation, it might seem as though my question is inappropriate to what is, after all, Hawthorne's Hester. Still, Hester is always telling herself, and Pearl, fictions about her situation, and her refusal to forsake her role, in the "Conclusion," is a stubborn extension of her will-to-power over her own story. Chillingworth and Pearl are well content to be figures of romance, and Dimmesdale finally falls back into the marvelous also, though in the saddest way. Hester forces Hawthorne out of romance and into the psychological novel, which is a mark of her relative freedom and of her author's curious bondage, his inability to make his strongest character conform to his moral expectations. Hester deceives others, and for a time herself, but she does not allow Hawthorne to deceive himself. He might have preferred to see her as a dark woman of romance but in her he did not create either another masochist, as he did with Dimmesdale, or another sadist, as with Chillingworth. We ought never to forget that Dimmesdale fails Hester yet once more, at the novel's conclusion, when she goes up to the scaffold to join him at his insistence, but goes very reluctantly and against her true will. Inadequate as Dimmesdale is to her, she still wants him, and until he dies her impulses remain totally healthy. She does not deny her vitalism; Hawthorne defrauds her, for the sake of his art.

No one who lives in Hawthorne's Puritan Boston could hope to defeat it, and Hawthorne thought better than allowing Hester to try so impossible a project. Yet he lavished upon Hester all his innermost resources of vital apprehension, while denying her the preternatural strength that would have turned his novel into the Promethean mode that he rejected. I begin to doubt that any American novelist, female or male, is going to transcend Hester Prynne as a representation of the irreconcilable demands placed upon an American woman, even in an age supposedly no longer Puritan. Feminism, in its latest phase, struggles with the lasting residuum of Puritan values, while remaining deeply contaminated by them. It may even be that current literary feminism is destined to become our new or newest Puritanism, imposing uniform ideals upon intellectual women, by again refusing any alliance between their sexuality and their potential antinomianism. Hester will then abide as the image condensed into the most powerful single sentence of Hawthorne's book: "The scarlet letter had not done its office." No societal emblem will perform a definitive judgment upon Hester, nor will she be contained by any program, however belatedly it would do justice to her. Richardson's Clarissa achieved her formidable strength, too strong even for the daemonic Lovelace, by her unmediated relationship to the Protestant God, who purified her will until only dying to this life was possible for her. Hawthorne celebrates his version of the Protestant will in Hester, but he has no way open to the Puritan God, and would not wish one, even if it were available to him, or to Hester. Dimmesdale finds the way back to God, but hardly out of strength, as Clarissa did. Hester is very strong, certainly too strong for Dimmesdale, and finally too strong even for Hawthorne. It is a very dialectical moment when Hawthorne condenses into a single sentence both Hester's stance towards life and her grand effect upon his own art: "It was only the darkened house that could contain her."

D.H. LAWRENCE

Nathaniel Hawthorne and "The Scarlet Letter"

Nathaniel Hawthorne writes romance.

And what's romance? Usually, a nice little tale where you have everything As You Like It, where rain never wets your jacket and gnats never bite your nose and its always daisy-time. *As You Like It* and *Forest Lovers*, etc. *Morte D' Arthur*.

Hawthorne obviously isn't this kind of romanticist: though nobody has muddy boots in the *Scarlet Letter*, either.

But there is more to it. *The Scarlet Letter* isn't a pleasant, pretty romance. It is a sort of parable, an earthly story with a hellish meaning.

All the time there is this split in the American art and art-consciousness. On the top it is as nice as pie, goody-goody and lovey-dovey. Like Hawthorne being such a blue-eyed darling, in life, and Longfellow and the rest such sucking doves. Hawthorne's wife said she "never saw him in time." which doesn't mean she saw him too late. But always in the "frail effulgence of eternity."

Serpents they were. Look at the inner meaning of their art and see what demons they were.

You *must* look through the surface of American art, and see the inner diabolism of the symbolic meaning. Otherwise it is all mere childishness.

That blue-eyed darling Nathaniel knew disagreeable things in his inner soul. He was careful to send them out in disguise.

From *Studies in Classic American Literature*. © 1923 by Thomas Seltzer, Inc.

Always the same. The deliberate consciousness of Americans so fair and smooth-spoken, and the under-consciousness so devilish. *Destroy! destroy! destroy!* hums the under-consciousness. *Love and produce! Love and produce!* cackles the upper consciousness. And the world hears only the Love-and-produce cackle. Refuses to hear the hum of destruction underneath. Until such time as it will *have* to hear.

The American has got to destroy. It is his destiny. It is his destiny to destroy the whole corpus of the white psyche, the white consciousness. And he's got to do it secretly. As the growing of a dragon-fly inside a chrysalis or cocoon destroys the larva grub, secretly.

Though many a dragon-fly never gets out of the chrysalis case: dies inside. As America might.

So the secret chrysalis of *The Scarlet Letter*, diabolically destroying the old psyche inside.

Be good! Be good! warbles Nathaniel. *Be good, and never sin! Be sure your sins will find you out.*

So convincingly that his wife never saw him "as in time."

Then listen to the diabolic undertone of *The Scarlet Letter*.

Man ate of the tree of knowledge, and became ashamed of himself.

Do you imagine Adam had never lived with Eve before that apple episode? Yes, he had. As a wild animal with his mate.

It didn't become "sin" till the knowledge-poison entered. That apple of Sodom.

We are divided in ourselves, against ourselves. And that is the meaning of the cross symbol.

In the first place, Adam knew Eve as a wild animal knows its mate, momentaneously, but vitally, in blood-knowledge. Blood-knowledge, not mind-knowledge. Blood-knowledge, that seems utterly to forget, but doesn't. Blood-knowledge, instinct, intuition, all the vast vital flux of knowing that goes on in the dark, antecedent to the mind.

Then came that beastly apple, and the other sort of knowledge started.

Adam began to look at himself. "My hat!" he said. "What's this? My Lord! What the deuce!—And Eve! I wonder about Eve."

Thus starts KNOWING. Which shortly runs to UNDERSTANDING, when the devil gets his own.

When Adam went and took Eve, *after* the apple, he didn't do any more than he had done many a time before, in act. But in consciousness he did something very different. So did Eve. Each of them kept an eye on what they were doing, they watched what was happening to them. They wanted to KNOW. And that was the birth of sin. Not *doing* it, but KNOWING about it. Before the apple, they had shut their eyes and their minds had gone dark.

Now, they peeped and pried and imagined. They watched themselves. And they felt uncomfortable after. They felt self-conscious. So they said, "The *act* is sin. Let's hide. We've sinned."

No wonder the Lord kicked them out of the Garden. Dirty hypocrites.

The sin was the self-watching, self-consciousness. The sin, and the doom. Dirty understanding.

Nowadays men do hate the idea of dualism. It's no good, dual we are. The Cross. If we accept the symbol, then, virtually, we accept the fact. We are divided against ourselves.

For instance, the blood *hates* being KNOWN by the mind. It feels itself destroyed when it is KNOWN. Hence the profound instinct of privacy.

And on the other hand, the mind and the spiritual consciousness of man simply *hates* the dark potency of blood-acts: hates the genuine dark sensual orgasms, which do, for the time being, actually obliterate the mind and the spiritual consciousness, plunge them in a suffocating flood of darkness.

You can't get away from this.

Blood-consciousness overwhelms, obliterates, and annuls mind-consciousness.

Mind-consciousness extinguishes blood-consciousness, and consumes the blood.

We are all of us conscious in both ways. And the two ways are antagonistic in us.

They will always remain so.

That is our cross.

The antagonism is so obvious, and so far-reaching, that it extends to the smallest thing. The cultured, highly-conscious person of to-day *loathes* any form of physical, "menial" work: such as washing dishes or sweeping a floor or chopping wood. This menial work is an insult to the spirit. "When I see men carrying heavy loads, doing brutal work, it always makes me want to cry," said a beautiful, cultured woman to me.

"When you say that, it makes me want to beat you," said I, in reply. "When I see you with your beautiful head pondering heavy thoughts, I just want to hit you. It outrages me."

My father hated books, hated the sight of anyone reading or writing.

My mother hated the thought that any of her sons should be condemned to manual labour. Her sons must have something higher than that.

She won. But she died first.

He laughs longest who laughs last.

There is a basic hostility in all of us between the physical and the mental, the blood and the spirit. The mind is "ashamed" of the blood. And the blood is destroyed by the mind, actually. Hence pale-faces.

At present the mind-consciousness and the so-called spirit triumphs. In America supremely. In America, nobody does anything from the blood. Always from the nerves, if not from the mind. The blood is chemically reduced by the nerves, in American activity.

When an Italian labourer labours, his mind and nerves sleep, his blood acts ponderously.

Americans, when they are *doing* things, never seem really to be doing them. They are "busy about" it. They are always busy "about" something. But truly *immersed* in *doing* something, with the deep blood-consciousness active, that they never are.

They *admire* the blood-conscious spontaneity. And they want to get it in their heads. "Live from the body," they shriek. It is their last mental shriek. *Co-ordinate*.

It is a further attempt still to rationalize the body and blood. "Think about such and such a muscle," they say, "and relax there."

And every time you "conquer" the body with the mind (you can say "heal" it, if you like) you cause a deeper, more dangerous complex or tension somewhere else.

Ghastly Americans, with their blood no longer blood. A yellow spiritual fluid.

The Fall.

There have been lots of Falls.

We *fell* into *knowledge* when Eve bit the apple. Self-conscious knowledge. For the first time the mind put up a fight against the blood. Wanting to UNDERSTAND. That is to intellectualize the blood.

The blood must be *shed*, says Jesus.

Shed on the cross of our own divided psyche.

Shed the blood, and you become mind-conscious. Eat the body and drink the blood, self-cannibalizing, and you become extremely conscious, like Americans and some Hindus. Devour yourself, and God knows what a lot you'll know, what a lot you'll be conscious of.

Mind you don't choke yourself.

For a long time men *believed* that they could be perfected through the mind, through the spirit. They believed, passionately. They had their ecstasy in pure consciousness. They *believed* in purity, chastity, and the wings of the spirit.

America soon plucked the bird of the spirit. America soon killed the *belief* in the spirit. But not the practice. The practice continued with a sarcastic vehemence. America, with a perfect inner contempt for the spirit and the consciousness of man, practises the same spirituality and universal love and KNOWING all the time, incessantly, like a drug habit. And inwardly gives not a fig for it. Only for the *sensation*. The pretty-pretty *sensation* of love, loving all the world. And the nice fluttering aeroplane *sensation* of knowing, knowing, knowing. Then the prettiest of all sensations, the sensation of UNDERSTANDING. Oh, what a lot they understand, the darlings! So good at the trick, they are. Just a trick of self-conceit.

The Scarlet Letter gives the show away.

You have your pure-pure young parson Dimmesdale.

You have the beautiful Puritan Hester at his feet.

And the first thing she does is to seduce him.

And the first thing he does is to be seduced.

And the second thing they do is to hug their sin in secret, and gloat over it, and try to understand.

Which is the myth of New England.

Deerslayer refused to be seduced by Judith Hutter. At least the Sodom apple of sin didn't fetch him.

But Dimmesdale was seduced gloatingly. Oh, luscious Sin!

He was such a pure young man.

That he had to make a fool of purity.

The American psyche.

Of course the best part of the game lay in keeping up pure appearances.

The greatest triumph a woman can have, especially an American woman, is the triumph of seducing a man: especially if he is pure.

And he gets the greatest thrill of all, in falling.—"Seduce me, Mrs. Hercules."

And the pair of them share the subtlest delight in keeping up pure appearances, when everybody knows all the while. But the power of pure appearances is something to exult in. All America gives in to it. *Look* pure!

To seduce a man. To have everybody know. To keep up appearances of purity. Pure!

This is the great triumph of woman.

A. The Scarlet Letter. Adulteress! The great Alpha. Alpha! Adulteress! The new Adam and Adama! American!

A. Adulteress! Stitched with gold thread, glittering upon the bosom. The proudest insignia.

Put her upon the scaffold and worship her there. Worship her there. The Woman, the Magna Mater. *A.* Adulteress! Abel!

Abel! Abel! Abel! Admirable!

It becomes a farce.

The fiery heart. *A.* Mary of the Bleeding Heart. Mater Adolerata! *A.*

Capital *A*. Adulteress. Glittering with gold thread. Abel! Adultery. Admirable!

It is, perhaps, the most colossal satire ever penned. *The Scarlet Letter*. And by a blue-eyed darling of a Nathaniel.

Not Bumppo, however.

The human spirit, fixed in a lie, adhering to a lie, giving itself perpetually the lie.

All begins with *A*.

Adultress. Alpha. Abel, Adam. *A*. America.

The Scarlet Letter.

"Had there been a Papist among the crowd of Puritans, he might have seen in this beautiful woman, so picturesque in her attire and mien, and with the infant at her bosom, an object to remind him of the image of Divine Maternity, which so many illustrious painters have vied with one another to represent; something which should remind him, indeed, but only by contrast, of that sacred image of sinless Motherhood, whose infant was to redeem the world."

Whose infant was to redeem the world indeed! It will be a startling redemption the world will get from the American infant.

"Here was a taint of deepest sin in the most sacred quality of human life, working such effect that the world was only the darker for this woman's beauty, and more lost for the infant she had borne."

Just listen to the darling. Isn't he a master of apology?

Of symbols, too.

His pious blame is a chuckle of praise all the while.

Oh, Hester, you are a demon. A man *must* be pure, just that you can seduce him to a fall. Because the greatest thrill in life is to bring down the Sacred Saint with a flop into the mud. Then when you've brought him down, humbly wipe off the mud with your hair, another Magdalen. And then go home and dance a witch's jig of triumph, and stitch yourself a Scarlet Letter with gold thread, as duchesses used to stitch themselves coronets. And then stand meek on the scaffold and fool the world. Who will all be envying you your sin, and beating you because you've stolen an advantage over them.

Hester Prynne is the great nemesis of woman. She is the KNOWING Ligeia risen diabolic from the grave. Having her own back. UNDERSTANDING.

This time it is Mr. Dimmesdale who dies. She lives on and is Abel.

His spiritual love was a lie. And prostituting the woman to his spiritual love, as popular clergymen do, in his preachings and loftiness, was a tall white lie. Which came flop.

We are so pure in spirit. Hi-tiddly-i-ty!

Till she tickled him in the right place, and he fell.

Flop.

Flop goes spiritual love.

But keep up the game. Keep up appearances. Pure are the pure. To the pure all things, etc.

Look out, Mister, for the Female Devotee. Whatever you do, don't let her start tickling you. She knows your weak spot. Mind your Purity.

When Hester Prynne seduced Arthur Dimmesdale it was the beginning of the end. But from the beginning of the end to the end of the end is a hundred years or two.

Mr. Dimmesdale also wasn't at the end of his resources. Previously, he had lived by governing his body, ruling it, in the interests of his spirit. Now he has a good time all by himself torturing his body, whipping it, piercing it with thorns, macerating himself. It's a form of masturbation. He wants to get a mental grip on his body. And since he can't quite manage it with the mind, witness his fall—he will give it what for, with whips. His will shall *lash* his body. And he enjoys his pains. Wallows in them. To the pure all things are pure.

It is the old self-mutilation process, gone rotten. The mind wanting to get its teeth in the blood and flesh. The ego exulting in the tortures of the mutinous flesh. I, the ego, I *will* triumph over my own flesh. Lash! Lash! I am a grand free spirit *Lash!* I am the master of my soul! *Lash! Lash!* I am the captain of my soul. *Lash!* Hurray! "In the fell clutch of circumstance," etc., etc.

Good-bye Arthur. He depended on women for his Spiritual Devotees, spiritual brides. So, the woman just touched him in his weak spot, his Achilles Heel of the flesh. Look out for the spiritual bride. She's after the weak spot.

It is the battle of wills.

"For the will therein lieth, which dieth not—"

The Scarlet Woman becomes a Sister of Mercy. Didn't she just, in the late war. Oh, Prophet Nathaniel!

Hester urges Dimmesdale to go away with her, to a new country, to a new life. He isn't having any.

He knows there is no new country, no new life on the globe to-day. It is the same old thing, in different degrees, everywhere. *Plus ça change, plus c'est la même chose.*

Hester thinks, with Dimmesdale for her husband, and Pearl for her child, in Australia, maybe, she'd have been perfect.

But she wouldn't. Dimmesdale had already fallen from his integrity as a minister of the Gospel of the Spirit. He had lost his manliness. He didn't see the point of just leaving himself between the hands of a woman, and going away to a "new country," to be her thing entirely. She'd only have despised him more, as every woman despises a man who has "fallen" to her: despises him with her tenderest lust.

He stood for nothing any more. So let him stay where he was and dree out his weird.

She had dished him and his spirituality, so he hated her. As Angel Clare was dished, and hated Tess. As Jude in the end hated Sue: or should have done. The women make fools of them, the spiritual men. And when, as men, they've gone flop in their spirituality, they can't pick themselves up whole any more. So they just crawl, and die detesting the female, or the females, who made them fall.

The saintly minister gets a bit of his own back, at the last minute, by making public confession from the very scaffold where she was exposed. Then he dodges into death. But he's had a bit of his own back, on everybody.

"'Shall we not meet again?' whispered she, bending her face down close to him. 'Shall we not spend our immortal life together? Surely, surely we have ransomed one another with all this woe! Thou lookest far into eternity with those bright dying eyes. Tell me what thou seest!'"

"'Hush, Hester—hush,' said he, with tremulous solemnity. 'The law we broke!—the sin here so awfully revealed! Let these alone be in thy thoughts. I fear! I fear!'"

So he dies, throwing the "sin" in her teeth, and escaping into death.

The law we broke, indeed. You bet!

Whose law?

But it is truly a law, that man must either stick to the belief he has grounded himself on, and obey the laws of that belief. Or he must admit the belief itself to be inadequate, and prepare himself for a new thing.

There was no change in belief, either in Hester or in Dimmesdale or in Hawthorne or in America. The same old treacherous belief, which was really cunning disbelief, in the Spirit, in Purity, in Selfless Love, and in Pure Consciousness. They would go on following this belief, for the sake of the sensationalism of it. But they would make a fool of it all the time. Like Woodrow Wilson, and the rest of modern Believers. The rest of modern Saviours.

If you meet a Saviour, to-day, be sure he is trying to make an innermost fool of you. Especially if the saviour be an UNDERSTANDING WOMAN, offering her love.

Hester lives on, pious as pie, being a public nurse. She becomes at last an acknowledged saint, Abel of the Scarlet Letter.

She would, being a woman. She has had her triumph over the

individual man, so she quite loves subscribing to the whole spiritual life of society. She will make herself as false as hell, for society's sake, once she's had her real triumph over Saint Arthur.

Blossoms out into a Sister-of-Mercy Saint.

But it's a long time before she really takes anybody in. People kept on thinking her a witch, which she was.

As a matter of fact, unless a woman is held, by man, safe within the bounds of belief, she becomes inevitably a destructive force. She can't help herself. A woman is almost always vulnerable to pity. She can't bear to see anything *physically* hurt. But let a woman loose from the bounds and restraints of man's fierce belief, in his gods and in himself, and she becomes a gentle devil. She becomes subtly diabolic. The colossal evil of the united spirit of Woman. WOMAN, German woman or American woman, or every other sort of woman, in the last war, was something frightening. As every *man* knows.

Woman becomes a helpless, would-be-loving demon. She is helpless. Her very love is a subtle poison.

Unless a man believes in himself and his gods, *genuinely*: unless he fiercely obeys his own Holy Ghost; his woman will destroy him. Woman is the nemesis of doubting man. She can't help it.

And with Hester, after Ligeia, woman becomes a nemesis to man. She bolsters him up from the outside, she destroys him from the inside. And he dies hating her, as Dimmesdale did.

Dimmesdale's spirituality had gone on too long, too far. It had become a false thing. He found his nemesis in woman. And he was done for.

Woman is a strange and rather terrible phenomenon, to man. When the subconscious soul of woman recoils from its creative union with man, it becomes a destructive force. It exerts, willynilly, an invisible destructive influence. The woman herself may be as nice as milk, to all appearance, like Ligeia. But she is sending out waves of silent destruction of the faltering spirit in men, all the same. She doesn't know it. She can't even help it. But she does it. The devil is in her.

The very women who are most busy saving the bodies of men, and saving the children: these women-doctors, these nurses, these educationalists, these public-spirited women, these female saviours: they are all, from the inside, sending out waves of destructive malevolence which eat out the inner life of a man, like a cancer. It is so, it will be so, till men realize it and react to save themselves.

God won't save us. The women are so devilish godly. Men must save themselves in this strait, and by no sugary means either.

A woman can use her sex in sheer malevolence and poison, while she is *behaving* as meek and good as gold. Dear darling, she is really snow-white in her blamelessness. And all the while she is using her sex as a she-devil, for the endless hurt of her man. She doesn't know it. She will never believe it if you tell her. And if you give her a slap in the face for her fiendishness, she will rush to the first magistrate, in indignation. She is so *absolutely* blameless, the she-devil, the dear, dutiful creature.

Give her the great slap, just the same, just when she is being most angelic. Just when she is bearing her cross most meekly.

Oh, woman out of bounds is a devil. But it is man's fault. Woman never *asked*, in the first place, to be cast out of her bit of an Eden of belief and trust. It is man's business to bear the responsibility of belief. If he becomes a spiritual fornicator and liar, like Ligeia's husband and Arthur Dimmesdale, how *can* a woman believe in him? Belief doesn't go by choice. And if a woman doesn't believe in a *man*, she believes, essentially, in nothing. She becomes, willy-nilly, a devil.

A devil she is, and a devil she will be. And most men will succumb to her devilishness.

Hester Prynne was a devil. Even when she was so meekly going round as a sick-nurse. Poor Hester. Part of her wanted to be saved from her own devilishness. And another part wanted to go on and on in devilishness, for revenge. Revenge! REVENGE! It is this that fills the unconscious spirit of woman to-day. Revenge against man, and against the spirit of man, which has betrayed her into unbelief. Even when she is most sweet and a salvationist, she is her most devilish, is woman. She gives her man the sugar-plum of her own submissive sweetness. And when he's taken this sugar-plum in his mouth, a scorpion comes out of it. After he's taken this Eve to his bosom, oh, so loving, she destroys him inch by inch. Woman and her revenge! She will have it, and go on having it, for decades and decades, unless she's stopped. And to stop her you've got to believe in yourself and your gods, your own Holy Ghost, Sir Man; and then you've got to fight her, and never give in. She's a devil. But in the long run she is conquerable. And just a tiny bit of her wants to be conquered. You've got to fight three-quarters of her, in absolute hell, to get at the final quarter of her that wants a release, at last, from the hell of her own revenge. But it's a long last. And not yet.

"She had in her nature a rich, voluptuous, oriental characteristic—a taste for the gorgeously beautiful." This is Hester. This is American. But she repressed her nature in the above direction. She would not even allow herself the luxury of labouring at fine, delicate stitching. Only she dressed her little sin-child Pearl vividly, and the scarlet letter was gorgeously embroidered. Her Hecate and Astarte insignia.

"A voluptuous, oriental characteristic—" That lies waiting in American women. It is probable that the Mormons are the forerunners of the coming real America. It is probable that men will have more than one wife, in the coming America. That you will have again a half-oriental womanhood, and a polygamy.

The grey nurse, Hester. The Hecate, the hellcat. The slowly-evolving voluptuous female of the new era, with a whole new submissiveness to the dark, phallic principle.

But it takes time. Generation after generation of nurses and political women and salvationists. And in the end, the dark erection of the images of sex-worship once more, and the newly submissive women. That kind of depth. Deep women in that respect. When we have at last broken this insanity of mental-spiritual consciousness. And the women *choose* to experience again the great submission.

"The poor, whom she sought out to be the objects of her bounty, often reviled the hand that was stretched to succour them."

Naturally. The poor hate a salvationist. They smell the devil underneath.

"She was patient—a martyr indeed—but she forbore to pray for her enemies, lest, in spite of her forgiving aspirations, the words of the blessing should stubbornly twist themselves into a curse."

So much honesty, at least. No wonder the old witch-lady Mistress Hibbins claimed her for another witch.

"She grew to have a dread of children; for they had imbibed from their parents a vague idea of something horrible in this dreary woman gliding silently through the town, with never any companion but only one child."

"A vague idea!" Can't you see her "gliding silently?" It's not a question of a vague idea imbibed, but a definite feeling directly received.

"But sometimes, once in many days, or perchance in many months, she felt an eye—a human eye—upon the ignominious brand, that seemed to give a momentary relief, as if half her agony were shared. The next instant, back it all rushed again, with a still deeper throb of pain; for in that brief interval she had sinned again. Had Hester sinned alone?"

Of course not. As for sinning again, she would go on all her life silently, changelessly "sinning." She never repented. Not she. Why should she? She had brought down Arthur Dimmesdale, that too-too snow-white bird, and that was her life-work.

As for sinning again when she met two dark eyes in a crowd, why of course. Somebody who understood as she understood.

I always remember meeting the eyes of a gypsy woman, for one moment, in a crowd, in England. She knew, and I knew. What did we know? I was not able to make out. But we knew.

Probably the same fathomless hate of this spiritual-conscious society in which the outcast woman and I both roamed like meek-looking wolves. Tame wolves waiting to shake off their tameness. Never able to.

And again, that "voluptuous, oriental" characteristic that knows the mystery of the ithyphallic gods. She would not betray the ithyphallic gods to this white, leprous-white society of "lovers." Neither will I, if I can help it. These leprous-white, seducing, spiritual women, who "understand" so much. One has been too often seduced, and "understood." "I can read him like a book," said my first lover of me. The book is in several volumes, dear. And more and more comes back to me the gulf of dark hate and *other* understanding, in the eyes of the gypsy woman. So different from the hateful white light of understanding which floats like scum on the eyes of white, oh, so white English and American women, with their understanding voices and their deep, sad words, and their profound, *good* spirits. Pfui!

Hester was scared only of one result of her sin: Pearl. Pearl, the scarlet letter incarnate. The little girl. When women bear children, they produce either devils or sons with gods in them. And it is an evolutionary process. The devil in Hester produced a purer devil in Pearl. And the devil in Pearl will produce—she married an Italian Count—a piece of purer devilishness still.

And so from hour to hour we ripe and ripe.

And then from hour to hour we rot and rot.

There was that in the child "which often impelled Hester to ask in bitterness of heart, whether it were for good or ill that the poor little creature had been born at all."

For ill, Hester. But don't worry. Ill is as necessary as good. Malevolence is as necessary as benevolence. If you have brought forth, spawned, a young malevolence, be sure there is a rampant falseness in the world against which this malevolence must be turned. Falseness has to be bitten and bitten, till it is bitten to death. Hence Pearl.

Pearl. Her own mother compares her to the demon of plague, or scarlet fever, in her red dress. But then plague is necessary to destroy a rotten, false humanity.

Pearl, the devilish girl-child, who can be so tender and loving and *understanding*, and then, when she has understood, will give you a hit across the mouth, and turn on you with a grin of sheer diabolic jeering.

Serves you right, you shouldn't be *understood*. That is your vice. You shouldn't want to be loved, and then you'd not get hit across the mouth. Pearl will love you: marvellously. And she'll hit you across the mouth: oh, so neatly. And serves you right.

Pearl is perhaps the most modern child in all literature.

Old-fashioned Nathaniel, with his little-boy charm, he'll tell you what's what. But he'll cover it with smarm.

Hester simply *hates* her child, from one part of herself. And from another, she cherishes her child as her one precious treasure. For Pearl is the continuing of her female revenge on life. But female revenge hits both ways. Hits back at its own mother. The female revenge in Pearl hits back at Hester, the mother, and Hester is simply livid with fury and "sadness," which is rather amusing.

"The child could not be made amenable to rules. In giving her existence a great law had been broken; and the result was a being whose elements were perhaps beautiful and brilliant, but all in disorder, or with an order peculiar to themselves, amidst which the point of variety and arrangement was difficult or impossible to discover."

Of course the order is peculiar to themselves. But the point of variety is this: "Draw out the loving, sweet soul, draw it out with marvellous understanding; and then spit in its eye."

Hester, of course, didn't at all like it when her sweet child drew out her motherly soul, with yearning and deep understanding: and then spit in the motherly eye, with a grin. But it was a process the mother had started.

Pearl had a peculiar look in her eyes: "a look so intelligent, yet so inexplicable, so perverse, sometimes so malicious, but generally accompanied by a wild flow of spirits, that Hester could not help questioning at such moments whether Pearl was a human child."

A little demon! But her mother, and the saintly Dimmesdale, had borne her. And Pearl, by the very openness of her perversity, was more straight-forward than her parents. She flatly refuses any Heavenly Father, seeing the earthly one such a fraud. And she has the pietistic Dimmesdale on toast, spits right in his eye: in both his eyes.

Poor, brave, tormented little soul, always in a state of recoil, she'll be a devil to men when she grows up. But the men deserve it. If they'll let themselves be "drawn," by her loving understanding, they deserve that she shall slap them across the mouth the moment they *are* drawn. The chickens! Drawn and trussed.

Poor little phenomenon of a modern child, she'll grow up into the devil of a modern woman. The nemesis of weak-kneed modern men, craving to be love-drawn.

The third person in the diabolic trinity, or triangle, of the *Scarlet Letter*, is Hester's first husband, Roger Chillingworth. He is an old Elizabethan physician with a grey beard and a long-furred coat and a twisted shoulder. Another healer. But something of an alchemist, a magician. He is a magician on the verge of modern science, like Francis Bacon.

Roger Chillingworth is of the old order of intellect, in direct line from the mediæval Roger Bacon alchemists. He has an old, intellectual belief in the dark sciences, the Hermetic philosophies. He is no Christian, no selfless aspirer. He is not an aspirer. He is the old authoritarian in man. The old male authority. But without passional belief. Only intellectual belief in himself and his male authority.

Shakspere's whole tragic wail is because of the downfall of the true male authority, the ithyphallic authority and masterhood. It fell with Elizabeth. It was trodden underfoot with Victoria.

But Chillingworth keeps on the *intellectual* tradition. He hates the new spiritual aspirers, like Dimmesdale, with a black, crippled hate. He is the old male authority, in intellectual tradition.

You can't keep a wife by force of an intellectual tradition. So Hester took to seducing Dimmesdale.

Yet her only marriage, and her last oath, is with the old Roger. He and she are accomplices in pulling down the spiritual saint.

"Why dost thou smile so at me—" she says to her old, vengeful husband. "Art thou not like the Black Man that haunts the forest around us? Hast thou not enticed me into a bond which will prove the ruin of my soul?"

"Not thy soul!" he answered with another smile. "No, not thy soul!"

It is the soul of the pure preacher, that false thing, which they are after. And the crippled physician—this other healer—blackly vengeful in his old, distorted male authority, and the "loving" woman, they bring down the saint between them.

A black and complementary hatred, akin to love, is what Chillingworth feels for the young, saintly parson. And Dimmesdale responds, in a hideous kind of love. Slowly the saint's life is poisoned. But the black old physician smiles, and tries to keep him alive. Dimmesdale goes in for self-torture, self-lashing, lashing his own white, thin, spiritual saviour's body. The dark old Chilling-worth listens outside the door and laughs, and prepares another medicine, so that the game can go on longer. And the saint's very soul goes rotten. Which is the supreme triumph. Yet he keeps up appearances still.

The black, vengeful soul of the crippled, masterful male, still dark in his authority: and the white ghastliness of the fallen saint! The two halves of manhood mutually destroying one another.

Dimmesdale has a "coup" in the very end. He gives the whole show away by confessing publicly on the scaffold, and dodging into death, leaving Hester dished, and Roger as it were, doubly cuckolded. It is a neat last revenge.

Down comes the curtain, as in Ligeia's poem.

But the child Pearl will be on in the next act, with her Italian Count and a new brood of vipers. And Hester greyly Abelling, in the shadows, after her rebelling.

It is a marvellous allegory. It is to me one of the greatest allegories in all literature, *The Scarlet Letter*. Its marvellous under-meaning! And its perfect duplicity.

The absolute duplicity of that blue-eyed *Wunderkind* of a Nathaniel. The American wonder-child, with his magical allegorical insight.

But even wonder-children have to grow up in a generation or two.

And even SIN becomes stale.

EDWARD STONE

The Antique Gentility of Hester Prynne

One soon sees that the edifice of the scaffold in the Boston market place is an important device in the structural symmetry of *The Scarlet Letter*: not only is it represented as the stage for the initial, central, and final letter-revelation scenes, but Hester herself comes in time to feel that it is the "whole orb" of her life, "the one point that gave it unity." Actually, she exaggerates its importance; for she is never in a position, as is the reader, to observe that another device gives her life another, less theatrical, unity. That device is her coat of arms. Hawthorne has in fact worked the theme of "gentility" carefully into his fable to two closely interrelated ends, one close to his heart, the other invaluable to the symmetry of his major characterization: (1) in general, he can remind his own age that here and there the "ivy, lichens, and wallflowers" of Old World culture once bloomed on these flinty shores; (2) in particular, he can effectively invest one of their dear dead number with heraldry as the most prominent of the characteristics of that noble gentility that keeps her head high in life and consecrates her fame in the grave. Gentility—aristocracy, nobility—in one form or other is in fact prominent among the "symbolical intricacies" which Matthiessen sees opening out every time we read *The Scarlet Letter*.[1]

From *Philological Quarterly* 36, no. 1 (January 1957). © 1957 by The State University of Iowa.

I

When these Puritans came to the wilderness that was North America, Hawthorne's sense of history insists, they came trailing clouds of the familied antiquity that was their English home, and the sombre austerity of their way of life in the new land was for a brief time held in balance by a traditional aristocracy. This fact Hawthorne takes such pains to demonstrate that the historian in him seems to vie with the romancer. Particularly in that richly documentary chapter "The Governor's Hall" is the reader made aware of the charm of that Old World heritage. The sunshine falling aslant the stucco and the broken-glass fragments of the front of Governor Bellingham's mansion invests the building with a "brilliancy [that] might have befitted Aladdin's palace," and the serving-man there wears the blue coat traditional to "the old hereditary halls of England." The interior of the mansion the Governor has planned "after the residences of gentlemen of fair estate in his native land": its entire furniture, Elizabethan or pre-Elizabethan or heirloom, all transported from his paternal home in England; the pewter tankard, its froth of ale still on it; the family portraits with their armor and "stately ruffs and robes of peace"—all this is not a new civilization but an old one uprooted and transplanted.

Prominent in the mansion is the suit of mail that Bellingham has had made in London, "so highly burnished as to glow with white radiance, and scatter an illuminaton everywhere about upon the floor": it bespeaks a time-honored institution of Old World culture—the soldiery. It was the aristocratic valor this armor suggests that lived on into American history, into the Niagara campaign, in the gallant "I'll try, sir" of the anonymous republican soldier—a phrase that moved his chronicler-associate of the Salem Custom House a generation later to reflect that "If, in our country, valor were rewarded by heraldic honor, this phrase ... would be the best and fittest of all mottoes for the General's shield of arms." The original Puritan soldiery, Hawthorne reminds us in "The Procession," won their spurs in the Low Countries and elsewhere in Europe; they were gentlemen and even sought to perpetuate the nobility of their Old World calling in some sort of College of Arms or Knights Templars.

As for their civilian counterparts, the Bradstrees, Endicotts, Dudleys, and Bellinghams of that early time had so naturally magisterial a demeanor, "the mother country need not have been ashamed to see these foremost men of an actual democracy adopted into the House of Peers, or made the Privy Council of the sovereign." To these, add the first Puritan clergy, for it is the patriarchal old Reverend Mr. Wilson, "nurtured at the rich bosom of the English Church" who marvels tolerantly at little Pearl's outlandishly rich raiment, reflecting that he has seen "just such figures, when the sun has been shining through a richly painted window, and tracing out the golden and crimson images across the floor." "But," he muses, "that was in the old land."[2] And in the "gorgeous folds" of Mistress Hibbins's "rich velvet" gown that the townspeople shrink from on Election Day, in the "great magnificence, ... triple muff, ... broidered stomacher, ... and ... gold-headed cane" that this ancient lady wears, is there not, along with necromancy, a strong suggestion of the majesty of the sovereign within fifty years of whose time, Hawthorne reminds us, all of these people flourished? In short, the pages of the nostalgic author, like the floor of the Governor's mansion, are virtually aglow with symbols of Old World aristocracy.

But their disappearance, alas, is already imminent. Thus the children of the Puritans are spoken of as not so much playing as engaging in "what passed for play with those sombre little urchins"; the country-fair, village green sports such as wrestling matches and buckler-and-broadsword exhibitions are broken off by the severe town beadle of the New World;[3] in the garden that looks out from Bellingham's majestic mansion, cabbages triumphantly thrive where the "rude and immature attempt at shrubbery" does not; indeed, directly beneath the hall window of his Old World installation, "as if to warn the Governor that this great lump of vegetable gold was as rich an ornament as New England would offer him," hangs a huge pumpkin. There is more than meets the eye in the tableau of the ruined Hester looking through the Governor's window at this ruined garden!

II

Now this theme of Old World gentility fighting a losing fight against the rough air and temper of the New World moves early and importantly into the plot when Hester stands alone above the curious throng assembled to witness the publication of her infamy. In fact, it is only in the light of her own origins that the pathos of Hester's situation can be fully grasped. Indeed, Hawthorne deliberately portrays her as looking out from a position that is not only physically but figuratively as well a *"miserable eminence"*; for "the decayed house of gray stone, with a poverty-stricken aspect" that was her paternal home in the Old England village re-emerges in the sorrowing young woman's mind's eye as "retaining a half-obliterated shield of arms over the portal, in token of antique gentility." It is this recollection that privately heightens her present ignominy ("Lilies that fester ..."); but by the same token it is this "native" "combative energy of her character" that by implication goes into the making of the pride, however wrongful,—the noblesse oblige, almost—with which she bears herself in the hostile gaze of the townspeople. Poor as she is, she seeks out the poor as "objects of her bounty"; to vituperation she makes no reply; forgiveness and prayer (humility) struggle unsuccessfully against an aristocratic stubbornness.

At this point the reader is encouraged to interpret as an inter-weaving of Hawthorne's two themes the fact that Hester earns her livelihood with the same instrument used to elaborate the bright stigma she wears; for just as it is her characteristic pride that keeps her from depression and surrender (as well, to be sure, as from repentance), so it is the characteristic panoply of her own native culture that calls her needlework into being: "Deep ruffs, painfully wrought bands, and gorgeously embroidered gloves, were all deemed necessary to the official state of men assuming the reins of power; and were readily allowed to individuals dignified by rank or wealth, even while sumptuary laws forbade these and similar extravagances to the plebeian order. In the array of funerals, too,—whether for the apparel of the dead body, or to typify it, by manifold emblematic devices of sable cloth and snowy lawn, the sorrow of the survivors—there was a frequent and characteristic demand for such labor as Hester Prynne could supply." All the public ceremonies, in short, of this traditionless land "and all that could give majesty to the forms in which a new government manifested itself to the people, were, as a matter of policy, marked by a stately and well-conducted ceremonial, and a sombre, but yet a studied magnificence."

Despite her fall from grace, however, Hester actually at no time loses either her heraldic arms or what they symbolize—her gentility: for there is a kind of studied magnificence in this "curiously embroidered" letter as well as disdain. In fact, by his use of this very symbol Hawthorne may be seen with a painstaking and poetic irony transmuting her Old World armorial bearings into a new, wilderness form. Note that only initially is this proudly adorned letter identified with her ignominy. Even at the start not everyone makes this identification: the Governor's bond-servant, not aware of its purpose, admits Hester to the mansion ironically because he is *impressed* by the glittering symbol, but also "perhaps judging from the decision of her air ... that she was a great lady in the land." Indeed, as the years pass, its original reference becomes dim and we see it beginning to acquire a kind of heraldic significance: "... many people said that it meant Able; so strong was Hester Prynne, with a woman's strength."[4] By the time of Hester's voluntary return from abroad at the end, it has completely lost its stigmatic meaning and has become "a type of something to be sorrowed over, and looked upon with awe, yet with reverence too." Eventually Hester achieves the fame of a confidante, almost (though Hawthorne warns against its possibility) of the prophetess of the "new truth" to be revealed to mankind.

It is, therefore, consistent with the aristocracy of both the Old England and the New England Hester that the simple slab of slate above her grave bears, not the infamy that she originally feared would be her only monument, but a device, "a herald's wording of which might serve for a motto ... of our now concluded legend ... 'ON A FIELD, SABLE, THE LETTER A, GULES.'" In brief, Hester does *not* merely *acquire* a heraldry by death: she *reclaims* in death the aristocracy that was her birthright and whose half-obliterated Old World face she in effect *restores*—her fall notwithstanding—by her bearing in life. It is, to be sure, as much an alteration as a restoration—the emblem of passion, of "the gorgeously beautiful" rests on the sable simplicity of Puritan dress; but it stands, as Hawthorne has it, in the midst of other "monuments carved with armorial bearings"—in brief, in a company where it belongs.

III

Although this striking heraldic motto closes out the book and Hester's life, Hawthorne has already extended his story in time by virtue of the future he has sketched in for Pearl. By so doing he has attempted to round out the story of the Old World's struggle to keep its identity in voluntary exile. Significantly, the means he employs to accomplish this are the same as those employed in interpreting Hester's character: the investing of the child with attributes of Old World aristocracy, and eventually with a heraldry of her own.

The illustriousness of her future does not rest primarily on the solidity (and perhaps implausibility) of the great fortune she inherits: it has been carefully prepared for. Like Hester, she ends *not* so much by *acquiring* distinction as by coming into *her own*. As an infant, even, she was perfectly formed and faultlessly beautiful, "worthy to have been brought forth in Eden,"[5] a fit "plaything of the angels," for all that Hester's transgression has visited a "disorder" upon the child's personality. It is very much the daughter of the woman imperiously gaining entrance to the Governor's mansion who dauntlessly routs the canting urchins in their path that day. It is she who spies the few roses struggling amidst the New World cabbages and pumpkins and cries for one, whose regality so impresses the Reverend Mr. Wilson, and who in effect reminds Hester of her gentility as well as her infamy when Hester flings the letter down in the forest. Eventually, then, when to her recluse mother, as we are told, letters come from abroad "with armorial seals upon them, though of bearings unknown to English heraldry," Pearl can be seen retrieving her birthright as an inhabitant of another (and, by implication, more fitting) land.[6]

Yet further. In the bleak, unlovely wilderness we eventually find Hester "embroidering a baby-garment, with such a lavish richness of golden fancy as would have raised a public tumult, had any infant, thus apparelled, been shown to our sober-hued community." These trappings of antique gentility, we recall, Old Wilson had once recognized and approved; so, doubtless, will others "in another land." And so on, Hawthorne seems to be saying, *per saecula saeculorum....*

Hester's illustrious ignominy has been perpetuated in death with the bearings of her character. Yet Fate may be said to have done her memory this ironic disservice, that the distinguished armorial company in whose midst she rests obstructs posterity's view of the first native heraldry of the New World. For, finding in his native land "no shadow, no antiquity, no mystery, no picturesque and gloomy wrong," Hawthorne reached back across the centuries and created his own.

NOTES

1. I wish to acknowledge here the valuable suggestions Professors John C. Gerber and Austin Warren contributed to the writing of this essay.

2. The few rose bushes and apple trees in the Bellingham garden are attributed to "the Reverend Mr. Blackstone," not only described as "the first settler of the peninsula," but offered by the legend-hungry romancer as "that half-mythological personage, who rides through our early annals, seated on the back of a bull."

3. In the story Hawthorne wrote in 1836, it will be remembered, Endicott and his followers break up the Maypole ceremonies at Merrymount and convert the pagan bride and groom into good Puritans.

4. Compare the "Admirable, or anything rather than Adulteress" interpretation of the earlier conception of Hester in "Endicott and the Red Cross."

5. Note that her mother, on emerging from prison, is spoken of, like Milton's Eve, as having "the world before her."

6. Another, and perhaps equal, possibility is that just as the stain of her mother's sin can never fully leave her, so the heraldic arms that Pearl acquires by marriage can never be as good as those of English heraldry.

CHARLES FEIDELSON, JR.

The Scarlet Letter

*T**he Scarlet Letter* is a moral tale in a Christian setting, but the imaginative method of the book is not distinctively moral or religious. It is distinctively historical, and historical in a rather complex way. The issues of the story and the experiences of individual characters are projected in the peculiar terms of a specific epoch; Hester Prynne, the people of Boston, Dimmesdale, Chillingworth, and Pearl are shaped by and give shape to the meaning of their time. Yet the epoch is not simply "Puritan." It is also more generally "modern," despite the provincial locale and the idiosyncratic culture through which it is rendered. In many respects, Puritan manners and morals here become a modern instance, a test case of life in the "new" (that is, post-medieval) world. And this modern life was Hawthorne's as well as the life of his characters. The author of *The Scarlet Letter* looks back through time, but he exists in historical continuity with the world he describes. The book is most profoundly historical because it is not only *about* but also *written out of* a felt historical situation.

We need not suppose that Hawthorne had any theoretical idea of "modernity" (he had few theories of any kind, and none of much interest). What he had was the nineteenth-and twentieth-century experience of radical solitude, which he sought to encompass by externalizing it, taking it as his imaginative subject. Possibly his twelve years in the lonely chamber at Salem,

From *Hawthorne Centenary Essays*, edited by Roy Harvey Pearce. © 1964 by Ohio State University Press.

for which he could "assign no reasonable why and wherefore," were
motivated less by a desire for privacy than by an impulse to dramatize his
spiritual isolation. He could escape it only by publicly acknowledging and
expressing it. In any case, this was a characteristic maneuver of his literary
imagination—as he put it, to render in "the style of a man of society" what
would otherwise be "the talk of a secluded man with his own mind and
heart." Yet "to open an intercourse with the world" in this way was not
enough if the world was really a non-world, a society of isolatoes, as his
experience drove him to depict it. Nor could he simply assert in the face of
his experience that a "magnetic chain of humanity" was always open to the
loving heart. The only adequate ground he had for communication and for
faith in human community was paradoxical: alienation as a historical datum.
Hawthorne turned to American history, the history of alienation, as the basis
of his communion. What isolatoes had in common, their magnetic chain, was
precisely the spiritual history of their isolation. Hawthorne became the
historian of the historically disinherited.

The Puritans conceived alienation as the cause and consequence of sin,
and up to a point it is so represented in *The Scarlet Letter*. Hester's pride of
self is the essential crime within her crime and the essential aberration within
her later secret heterodoxy. Much the same might be said of Dimmesdale and
Chillingworth. But if alienation is equivalent to sin in the perspective of
Hawthorne's seventeenth-century Boston, and if Hawthorne himself never
wholly abandons that perspective, he also pictures a Puritan society that
positively fosters an alienated individualism. Hester Prynne, her lover, and
her husband are as much sinned against as sinning in their social isolation;
they have been thrown back upon themselves by an inorganic community, a
culture that substitutes external law for immediate relations. And if this is so,
if the Puritan mind itself is in one sense guilty of the crime it abhors, in a
further sense the book does not deal with crime as such but with a moral
predicament, a style of thought. Though Hawthorne often echoes the
Puritan language of moral reprobation, and though he often turns round and
condemns the Puritans themselves for lack of humanitarian sympathy, he is
always fully aware of a historical context for these moral stances—a world
view that molds the Puritan consciousness as well as his own.

These people have experienced a disintegration of God's world into
God-and-nature, a collapse of the secular world into nature-and-man, a
fragmentation of the human world into community-and-individual, and a
division of the private world into body-and-mind. Obviously there is nothing
novel about such disjunctions in the long history of Christian theology and
morals; but in the universe of *The Scarlet Letter* they have taken on a primacy
that is striking and new. This disjunctive structure has become a

metaphysical presupposition, a reality to be assumed rather than an actuality to be deplored. Moral existence is no longer a pursuit of the Good; it is experience in the goods and evils of a dichotomous world. The official creed of Massachusetts Congregationalism is one configuration of that world—an attempt to find coherence by making the most of disjunction. Hester, Dimmesdale, and Chillingworth devise and suffer other versions of the modern consciousness, worlds of profounder terror and hope. The imagination of Hawthorne, partaking of the condition it projects in the book, moves through the pages in a speculative, inquisitive, experimental mood. Like his characters—but on a much larger scale, since his vision is more inclusive—Hawthorne seeks the center of a world where centers do not hold.

His symbolic method, though he himself was among the first to complain of it, is thoroughly in keeping with his historical premise. If the stuff of actuality is thin in his fiction, it is because he renders an actuality consumed from within, attenuated by a problematic reality that feeds upon it. In *The Scarlet Letter*, people know themselves by means of revelatory "images" that inform mind and body, and they apprehend other human beings as powerful "shapes" impinging upon them. Nature is portentous, the everyday scene is starkly structured, and a dream-figure like Mistress Hibbens walks the streets. While this atmospheric "significance" recalls the medieval allegorical universe, it disintegrates instead of supporting the substance of things. The voices of God and Devil are heard in human discourse, and "Providence" presides over the action; but the supernatural voices are the riddles of natural man, and the providential design is something to be discovered, not assumed. The immanent Word has become completely immanent; the only sacramental form is the empty vessel of the letter *A*, whose content alters and grows with time. Correspondingly, the images inherent in the social scene and private experience are fugitive and multivalent. The author collects alternative interpretations; his tone shifts; his opinions are contradictory; his knowledge of fact is often uncertain. Beneath the measured speech and ceremonial behavior of the Boston theocracy is a vast realm of the publicly unsaid and even unsayable—the esoteric community of Hester, Dimmesdale, and Chillingworth. The demands for utterance that punctuate *The Scarlet Letter* ("Speak out the name!"—"What does this ... letter mean?") are unanswerable theoretically as well as practically; for outside the official consensus no one knows exactly what to call himself or how to construe the significance of the central symbol.

Yet Hester Prynne, who is officially cast down into the underground world of "secrets," comes closest to positive vision and speech, as she comes closest to the substance of fictional character. Deprived of a public voice and reduced to a gray shadow, Hester lives out the problematic situation that everyone in the book knowingly or unknowingly experiences. Deliberately living it out, she emerges on the other side of it. She converts disinheritance into freedom, isolation into individuality, excommunication into a personal presence that is actual and communicable. To do this without denying the negative burden of history—her own and that of her time—is her moral achievement. It is analogous to Hawthorne's aesthetic achievement in the book as a whole. He must undergo his story if he is to tell it at all; *The Scarlet Letter* is imposed upon him, much as the letter itself is imposed upon Hester. But his narration is active; and out of the negative world that he inherits he constructs an image of positive human enterprise.

II

In "The Custom-House: Introductory to 'The Scarlet Letter,'" Hawthorne has nothing explicit to say about such matters as the modern consciousness; indeed, the essay at first seems designed to have as little as possible to do with the story it introduces. But Hawthorne's stance here is wholly consonant with his method in *The Scarlet Letter*; his preface functions as a modest suggestion of the nature of his art.

Reality in "The Custom-House" is history—history in various forms that play upon one another, deny and reinforce each other, until a dense historical world surrounds us. It is a history that moves in chronological sequence from past to present to future, but it also endures. It is unchanging and changing, active and decadent, predetermined and indeterminate, vacuous and full of meaning. Above all, it is both private and public—a reality experienced individually and socially. Though the scarlet letter is discovered at the climax of a personal narrative, it is a public emblem apparently signifying some "rank, honor, and dignity, in by-past times" (appropriately, the letter and its attendant documents are found amid the archives of the Customs, "materials of local history"). Conversely, the symbol communicates its social meaning only to the inner sense of the lonely Hawthorne, not to his analytic and rational public mind, and the documents are "not official, but of a private nature," written by an eighteenth-century predecessor "in his private capacity." When Hawthorne places the letter against his breast, two dimensions of history come into contact. This is a moment of social revelation on the one hand and self-discovery on the other:

> ... It strangely interested me. My eyes fastened themselves upon the old scarlet letter, and would not be turned aside. Certainly, there was some deep meaning in it, most worthy of interpretation, and which, as it were, streamed forth from the

mystic symbol, subtly communicating itself to my sensibilities, but evading the analysis of my mind.

While thus perplexed, ... I happened to place it on my breast. It seemed to me ... that I experienced a sensation not altogether physical, yet almost so, as of burning heat; and as if the letter were not of red cloth, but red-hot iron.

It is not primarily a moment of conscience, for Hawthorne carefully avoids any explicit reference to the theme of adultery or even to the idea of sin. As a single letter, the most indeterminate of all symbols, and first letter of the alphabet, the beginning of all communication, Hester's emblem represents a potential point of coherence within a manifold historical experience.

There is another Hawthorne in "The Custom-House," one who is not inclined to take such apocalyptic moments very seriously. He is an image largely projected by style—frank, good-humored, a man of feeling, but urbane, sharp-eyed, something of an ironist. This cultivated and self-assured gentleman is somewhat complacent; and he belongs to a stable, secure public world of ready categories and easy communication. We might call him the Cosmopolitan. As readers, we quickly identify ourselves with him; we are all gentlemen together. Salem, the Custom House and its denizens, the Surveyor himself with his literary ambitions, are the objects of our sophisticated interest. We are capable of reflecting that Hester Prynne, though she may have been an angel on earth for some of her contemporaries, was probably a mere "intruder and ... nuisance" for others. We accede to the game while our whimsical author spins his tale of mysterious documents and grandly offers to show them to us. This is the social situation that Hawthorne invokes at the very beginning of his essay, when he assures us that he will speak as a man in company addressing "a kind and apprehensive, though not the closest friend." He is a strong exponent of propriety, ensconced in a conventional but comfortable mid-world where the private man and the social forms may come into easy relation. He neither would give unseemly publicity to intimate matters nor (since he will be only the "editor, or very little more," of *The Scarlet Letter*) would he give intimacy to public matters. He would speak in such a way as not to violate "either the reader's rights or his own."

In the part of his mind that always greatly distrusted whatever he had written, Hawthorne obviously wanted to relieve the "gloom" of his book by a jaunty preface. As the Cosmopolitan, he is untouched by the experiences through which he has passed. He views his "autobiographical impulse" as a kind of harmless seizure, and at the end of his discourse he still speaks as from a secure position outside of time. He tells the story of a "well balanced" man in an essentially secure comic world; though he is thrown out of office, no real harm can come to him. But this self-projection is essentially dramatic; and in the essay as a whole, the Cosmopolitan turns out to be the least important of Hawthorne's roles. He is relatively naïve and imperceptive; he maintains his balance by excluding some unpleasant truths.

Throughout the opening paragraphs we feel the presence of an uneasy person within the suave personage who confronts us. Though he arrives at a reassuring formula, we can see him casting about for "the truth" of the matter—his "true relation with his audience," his "true reason for assuming a personal relation with the public," his "true position as editor." Within the gentlemanly consensus that he presupposes, there are factors that pull apart. He reveals them with startling clarity, if only to deny them. On the one hand, there is "the inmost Me behind its veil," the state of alienation when "thoughts are frozen and utterance benumbed." On the other hand, there is a dream of total interrelation, "the one heart and mind of perfect sympathy; as if the printed book ... were certain to find out the divided segment of the writer's own nature, and complete his circle of existence by bringing him into communion with it." The secure Hawthorne who is content with a social self and a conventional society, who is so much at home in history that he can ignore its tensions, is haunted by an alter ego whose "circle of existence" is painfully incomplete, for whom history is the vain pursuit of total communion by an isolated self.

This malaise is mainly represented through another self-projection, the Surveyor of the Customs, who mediates between the Cosmopolitan and the historical visionary brooding over the scarlet letter. True to his title, the Surveyor makes it his business to "watch and study," to measure his colleagues, himself, and the house they inhabit. He is at once a solitary man, a self-appointed surveyor whose public office is hardly more than a title, and a social man, very much a creature of the "customs" he surveys. Inquisitive but tentative, he wanders through the building or stands aside and observes his fellow officers. He enters into the narrative voice in much the same spirit of inquiry: careless of contradiction, he adopts various perspectives with equal feeling, as though to make an inventory of the possibilities of life. Like the Cosmopolitan, the Surveyor never disappears from view or lapses into silence; at the end of the essay, he is still addressing us. But only in the climactic moment of communion with the letter, when he is transformed, do we see a potential author of *The Scarlet Letter* or a ground on which he can take his stand.

The ground of the Custom House is shaky—not only because Salem has outlived its time, but also because time still moves on. There are two aspects of social history here, to which we are introduced by the long sentence that leads us up the wharf to a "spacious edifice of brick" and down "the track of ... years" from the old days of bustling commerce to the present era of decay. The house, a stage for mere mock-activity, the "formalities of office" zealously pursued by the custom officials, is also Uncle Sam's going concern. Though Salem, in comparison with other ports, is fast asleep, there are still merchants here, "men of traffic" whose names Hawthorne tells over. There are days when "affairs move onward" and a bustle disturbs the torpid old retainers. There is even a "man of business" among them. The house itself, as opposed to its functionaries, often represents a commercial and political life full of action and change. The past counts for nothing in Uncle Sam's work. His old records are thrown aside as "rubbish," and the labor that went into them is wholly lost. What counts is the future. Uncle Sam changes his garments, from Whig to Democrat and back again, striking terror into the hearts of those who look for passivity and permanence. His emblem, the national eagle displayed over the entrance to the Custom House, signifies destruction as well as protection. It is the emblem of a "struggling world" that is wholly unstable and immediate, always building the future out of its own dissolution.

On the other hand, there is old and forever unfinished business in the Custom House, work that will never begin again. The building was "originally projected ... with an idea of subsequent prosperity destined never to be realized," and a large room on the second floor, still unpaneled and unplastered, testifies to an arrest of time. The occasional activities of the customs are always "for the time being": they are present moments without a future, hollow re-enactments of the past. This quality of fixation characterizes the "permanent" officials as they sit in their row of old-fashioned chairs tilted against the wall. They live in a changeless present, keeping their "accustomed" places and ritualistically repeating their old yarns. The Collector, the most experienced of them all, is the most static; he stands on his past as on a pedestal. His life, like theirs, was once full of changes and chances; it was futuristic, like the world of affairs that now surrounds them. But it became *a past* life precisely by stopping short in a permanent present, a "new lease of existence" that negates the movement of existence and even death. The past, as embodied in these old men, is time that has ceased to act and to evolve new content—time denatured. Therefore they retain none of the substance of their earlier lives and seem to have learned nothing at all from their long experience. The Inspector, who has spent all his adult years in the Custom House, is an utterly mindless animal, for without time man ceases to be; his memory is a parody of memory, a long vista of dinner tables ranged behind the dinner of the day.

Just as the futurism of Uncle Sam has nothing behind it and emerges from a dissolving present, so the past of the Custom House officers is history that has come to nothing in a static present. A problematic duality of traditionalism and futurism lies beneath the positive surface of the Custom House world, and there is a certain emptiness within the apparent substance of that world, whether it be backward-looking or forward-looking. This is a very different social milieu from the one projected through the style of the Cosmopolitan. The world of the Surveyor is not a sustaining medium, a rich present; it is vitiated by chronological time, which either comes to a dead halt or abdicates before the putative future.

The Surveyor is very much aware of his own chronology: once a writer at the Old Manse, he is now Surveyor of the Revenue whose "prophetic instinct" tells him that another "change of custom" is in store for him. Back of his sojourn in the Old Manse lie the temporal depths of Salem, his "native place"; beyond his eventual discharge from office lies the time at which he will be a writer again, six months later, and beyond that a further future when he will be "a citizen of somewhere else." His sympathies point in both directions; the intrinsic duality of the Custom House world reappears in him. He is an activist and a decadent, a futurist and a traditionalist.

As an exponent of healthy change, he delights in the Custom House as a place of new experience for himself. Though his return to Salem has brought him back to his own earliest past and to the past of his race, his position there is a decided change from his more recent life. He has been wholly converted from a writer to "a man of affairs," and his name emblazoned on boxes of merchandise will go where no title page would ever carry it. In this perspective, his previous literary career becomes unreal— becomes, indeed, a traffic in "unrealities." For the futurist Surveyor, literature is not only an archaic activity, out of date in Uncle Sam's new world, but doubly insubstantial, since it is associated with his own outmoded self. It also pertains to the side of him that continues to dabble in the social past, foolishly trying, amid "the materiality of ... daily life," to go back into another age and create "the semblance of a world out of airy matter." Literature ceases to be suspect only when it ceases to be past-centered and embraces "the reality of the flitting hour." When the Surveyor bids us farewell, he speaks as the realistic author of "A Rill from the Town-Pump," and the flitting hour is carrying him on to other realities. The Custom House "lies like a dream behind me"; Salem is now "no portion of the real earth, but an overgrown village in cloud-land"; and he foresees the time when "the great-grandchildren of the present race" will conceive of him (quite properly) as a "scribbler of bygone days" known only to the village antiquary.

What had brought him to the Custom House, however, was not a quest for new experience but a "strange, indolent, unjoyous attachment" to his birthplace and to the old Salem behind the new one. He has a "home-feeling with the past," a sense of more reality in it than in "the present phase of the town" or his own actual existence. The "earnest and energetic men" who founded his family and helped establish Salem have greater moral validity, "both good and evil," than the activists of the dissolving present. If his relation to them is profitless, it is because their reality annihilates his present life, just as the old active life of the custom officers has terminated in a rigid posture, an empty form. The traditionalist decays because he is fixed; with "oyster-like tenacity" he "clings to the spot where his successive generations have been imbedded." He feels his past as a doom. And if he is a writer, his role is as much diminished in his own eyes by his ancestors' contempt as by the condescension of his readers' great-grandchildren. The old Puritans looking over his shoulder see the future (any change from their pattern) as necessarily decadent; and for them literature, which is wholly a thing of the future, is mere idleness. The backward-oriented mind of the Surveyor can only share their view of himself. As a degenerate "writer of story-books," he takes a feeble vengeance upon them for their tyranny over him: his triviality is their punishment, and he even undertakes, "as their representative," to enter a jocular apology for their sins.

In sum, the chronological world is a trap. If the Surveyor welcomes the Custom House as a "change of diet," he knows all the while that it is a stagnant place, thoroughly detrimental to manly character and to his literary powers. It will change him into permanence ("make me permanently other than I had been"). And if he chooses, with equal paradox, to regard the stagnation as a "transitory life" and look toward "a new change of custom," what can he have in view? Merely an opportunity to "recall whatever was valuable in the past"—in the aesthetic life that his futurism always belittles. Not surprisingly, a literary and intellectual torpor overcomes him. Though he mainly blames it on the inactive, dependent, static life of the customs, which destroys his sense of actuality, his impotence is equally a result of the surrounding practical activity, "actual circumstance," in which his traditionalism can see nothing of value. The two aspects of his world meet only to negate each other; the personal existence of the Surveyor is canceled out by the negative world he surveys.

Superficially at home in the Custom House, the Surveyor is truly in the alienated condition that the Cosmopolitan mentions and blithely passes over: his "thoughts are frozen and utterance benumbed." In his moonlit room late at night—between darkness and daylight, past and future—he longs for a more productive meeting of "the Imaginary" and "the Actual," personal vision and the public world. In utter solitude, he can conceive of perfect communion between a private imagination oriented toward the past and a public actuality oriented toward the future. But he can go no further in his role of Surveyor. Each factor refuses to "imbue itself with the nature of the other," and his midnight sessions come to nothing. He is finally content with a *modus vivendi* that simplifies his problem without solving it. He finds himself completely caught up in a futurist society; Providence, in the guise of a change of administration, saves him from his impasse. In a sudden flurry of activity, he is defined as the active man despite his apparent passivity. With his head cut off and his sensibility thereby simplified, he sits down to prepare the "Posthumous Papers of a Decapitated Surveyor." He looks back only with tolerant amusement; parodies the backward-looking documents of Surveyor Pue, whose own "mental part" had survived the centuries; and deplores the "stern and sombre aspect" of *The Scarlet Letter*, in which there are unfortunate traces of his personal "turmoil" in the past.

Yet he notes the odd fact that he was very happy while writing *The Scarlet Letter*. The author of that book, who is quite another person, lurks within the Surveyor of the Customs, just as the latter haunts the Cosmopolitan. Indeed, the moment of revelation when Hawthorne confronts the letter is what the Surveyor is vainly trying to recapture in his moonlit room. This revelation is not a "transcendence." Hawthorne, the potential Author, is as partial to the past as the Surveyor (in the end) is to the future. He returns not only to the "sunless fantasies" of New England legend but also to his literary "habits of bygone days." And he is as solitary as the Surveyor, finally, is sociable. It is in a "deserted chamber of the Custom-House" that his mind returns to its "old track" and he receives his charge from the ghost of Mr. Pue. Traditionalist and solitary, he is thoroughly immersed in the chronological condition. But he does not succumb to chronological determinism, the past that always threatens to come upon him as a doom and fixate him in an empty present. He turns it about, conceives it as an enduring past contained in and latently possessed by the present, as the scarlet letter is "present" beneath the dead records and illusory contemporary world of the Custom House. Nor does he accept the barren role of alienated imagination, reduced to a sluggish "fancy" by the senseless archives of the customs. He converts his solitude into self-pursuit, an active state, which is identical with pursuit of the "deep meaning" of the scarlet letter.

He had earlier felt a similar sense of duration in contemplating the statuesque Collector. Viewed with "affection," the old general seemed to lose his fixity and become the living vessel of a still-living past. Yet in this case, the would-be Author could only arrive at loose generalizations; he could not find his way through the ruins of time to the "real life" that he supposed to exist within the old man's memory. The scarlet letter is a different case because it not only gives Hawthorne a token of duration but also includes him, alienated as he is, in the enduring reality it radiates. Coming to him in solitude, it is relevant to the meaning of his solitude; and he, poring over it, is saved from solitude. He is in communion; he belongs in the succession of Hester Prynne, who first wore the letter, and of Surveyor Pue, on whose mind it was so deeply branded. In a roundabout way, he has found "the divided segment of ... [his] own nature," completed his "circle of existence."

If he is redeemed, he is also invested with a mission. Leaving behind his colleagues "seated ... at the receipt of custom," he has been summoned "like Matthew ... for apostolic errands." His mission is not to preach but to act— to appropriate the universe of discourse now open to him and thereby to "interpret" the reality of consciousness that "stream[s] forth from the mystic symbol." In *The Scarlet Letter*, the *A* will hang over the entire story, as in its greatest scene a portentous *A* hangs over and illuminates the persons of the drama: Hester, Pearl, and Dimmesdale on the scaffold, Chillingworth below them, and the surrounding town of Boston. Each of these five figures—for the Puritan town is an agent, not a mere setting—will acquire meaning from the universal center but reconstruct the meaning in a particular way. Thus the sphere of the book (which is full of references to "spheres" and "circles") will be progressively redefined as the emblematic letter is approached and shines out from one side or another. In this large sense, *The Scarlet Letter* will be the icon of a creative mind at work, not merely suffering or resting in its inheritance but actively seizing upon the history that made it. And something analogous to this, translated into moral terms, will be the dominant theme of the book—the major meaning derived from and projected upon the central symbol.

III

The book begins with a vignette of the people of Boston—a single sentence set off in a paragraph by itself: "A throng of bearded men, in sad-colored garments and gray, steeple-crowned hats, intermixed with women, some wearing hoods, and others bareheaded, was assembled in front of a wooden edifice, the door of which was heavily timbered with oak, and studded with iron spikes." Just as Hawthorne gazes at the symbolic letter, seeking the meaning in it, they stand "with their eyes intently fastened on the iron-clamped oaken door," out of which Hester Prynne will come with the letter on her bosom. In effect, the prison door is their avenue to the meaning of the symbol; and these colorless men and women, though they stand outside the prison, have all the demeanor of prisoners. Any Utopian colony, Hawthorne declares, will soon find it necessary "to allot a portion of the virgin soil as a cemetery, and another portion as the site of a prison"; but these people embrace the necessity. Though they are "founders of a new colony," they have based it upon the oldest facts of human experience— crime and death. Though they would cultivate "human virtue and happiness," they have no faith in any direct approach to this end. The jail and its companion-place, the burial ground, are their proper meeting houses; the scaffold, situated "nearly beneath the eaves of Boston's earliest church," is the center of the society. Not once in the book is a church physically described or a scene actually staged within it. Their true religious exercise is the contemplation of Hester, their scapegoat and counterpart, set up before them on the scaffold. Even as they denounce her, they are fascinated by her as an emblem of the world they inhabit.

The ceremony in the market place is genuinely religious, not merely perverse, but it is oblique. The ministers do not urge Hester to seek divine support but only to suffer her punishment, repent her transgression, and name another sinner. If there were some "Papist among the crowd of Puritans," this woman taken in adultery might recall to his mind the contrasting "image of Divine Maternity." But the Puritans invoke no such image to relieve the horror before them; on the contrary, their faith positively depends on discovering a "taint of deepest sin in the most sacred quality of human life." They would honor a transcendent God who enters this world mainly as law-giver and executioner. His mercy appears through his justice, his love through his power. His incarnation is the impress of his abstract supernatural code, which primarily reveals the evils of flesh and the universality of sin. As administrators of the code, the ministers and magistrates on the balcony have no concrete human existence for themselves or others, and they have no perception of the concrete reality of Hester on the scaffold. "Sages of rigid aspect," standing in God's holy fire, they are blind to the "mesh of good and evil" before them. They see only the abstract Adulteress. As when Hester later views her image in Governor Bellingham's breastplate, she is "absolutely hidden behind" the "exaggerated and gigantic" abstraction that engrosses her accusers.

If they were merely self-righteous and sadistic, these Bostonians would be much less formidable. They are impressive because their doctrinaire moralism has a metaphysical basis: they purge their town in token of a universe where only God is really pure and only purity is of any account. Hawthorne does full justice to the moral seriousness, the strength of character, and the practical ability that their way of thinking could foster. He affirms that the Puritan society "accomplish[ed] so much, precisely because it imagined and hoped so little." And in various ways his Puritans, though eccentric, are old-fashioned folk, not radical innovators. In comparison with the "heartlessness" of a later era of sophisticated moral tolerance, the punishment inflected on Hester, however cruel, is dignified by moral principle. In comparison with later democratic irreverence, the respectfulness and loyalty of the Massachusetts citizens to their leaders are still close to the feudal virtues. In comparison with their genteel descendants, the merciless harpies of the market place still have a moral as well as physical substance, "a boldness and rotundity," that derives from the old England they have put behind them.

But in all fundamental respects Hawthorne's Puritans are both problematic and unprecedented. They are men responding to an extreme intellectual predicament by extreme measures, and their predicament is one with their disseverance from the old world. The pompous forms and dress of their great public occasions, like the aristocratic menage of Governor Bellingham, are nostalgic and imitative, not characteristic. The old order vaguely survives in their consciousness because they stand at the beginning of a new epoch, but it survives much as memories of King James' court flit through the mind of the Reverend Mr. Wilson. It is true that Europe sometimes figures in the book as "newer" than the Puritan colony: the "other side of the Atlantic" is a place of intellectual and social emancipation, to which Dimmesdale and Hester might flee and to which Pearl betakes herself at the end. But Europe is a refuge because, whether old or new, feudal or modern, it signifies no struggle of consciousness, no necessity to reckon with the foundations of the new era. New England is the place where men must confront the founding questions of their time, which are set forth in the topography, the intellectual landscape, of *The Scarlet Letter*.

Above them stretches the heaven of supernatural revelation, where "any marked event, for good or evil," is prefigured in "awful hieroglyphics." The physical heavens are also spiritual, a medium of the divine word. But no civilized society was ever so directly in contact with brute nature. The settlement is encircled by the teeming "Western wilderness" on one side and the open sea on the other. Though the townsmen studiously abjure this "wild, heathen Nature ..., never subjugated by human law, nor illumined by higher truth," it invades their prison-fortress. Savage Indians and even more savage sailors are a familiar sight in their streets. And physical nature is equivocal in relation to man. While it reduces him to "animal ferocity," it also sanctions "human nature," the life of feeling, and the virtues of the heart. The possibility of a humanistic naturalism lurks in the wild rosebush growing out of "the deep heart of Nature" beside the prison door. The possibility becomes actual in the person of Hester Prynne on the scaffold and later in her cottage on the outskirts of the town between the sea and the forest. What is more, Hester represents a positive individualism, alien to Puritan society but capable of creating a human community of its own. By her refusal to play out her appointed role on the scaffold, she becomes doubly an outcast from Boston; and yet, standing there in all her concrete individuality, she seems to claim a general truth, a concrete universality. She tacitly challenges the abstract city of their abstract God.

The challenge is momentous because she activates problems that their rationale is designed to anticipate and lay to rest. And similar questions rise to the surface, make themselves manifest, in ironic turns of the Puritan mind and behavior. Hawthorne persistently describes the spiritual abstraction of these people in terms of inanimate physical nature. The "rigid aspect" of the sages on the balcony corresponds to "the grim rigidity that petrifie[s] the bearded physiognomies" of the congregation in the market place. These are "iron men," as Hester later says; their creed is an "iron framework," aptly reflected in the "iron-clamped oaken door" on which their eyes are fixed and in the "contrivance of wood and iron," the pillory, that stands on the scaffold. It is as though their aspiration toward abstract super-natural truth has ironically brought them around to an abstract natural automatism, a world of law that is closer to the inorganic forms of stone, metal, and dead timber than to the mind of God. On the other hand, the ferocity of the women in the market place is as lawless and as natural as the lust they denounce, and it complements the rigid natural law that dominates their men. For all of them, "civilized life" consists of putting nature into prison; but the prison itself, the "black flower" of their town, partakes of the subhuman nature they contemn and obsessively scrutinize. The black flower blossoms apace, as Chillingworth observes. Meanwhile, natural affection, the red flower, lives on, unwanted and disclaimed, in the heart of Mr. Wilson and in the potential "heart of the multitude." Two voices of that heart, one of personal sympathy and one of faith in natural virtue, arise unaccountably amidst the chorus of reprobation. They are barely individualized, simply a young wife with a child and "a man in the crowd," but they testify to a community of individuals within this authoritarian society. The official "community" depends on a consensus of power and submission, a free election of individuals chosen to suppress individuality. But the scene in the market place, with elevated individual dignitaries opposed to a shapeless "throng" below, intimates a latent failure within the Puritan social system. The way is open for the "multitude" to gain shape through respect for its own multiple individuality. Puritanism contains and secretly invites its opposite, as it contained Anne Hutchinson from whose footsteps the wild rose bush may have sprung.

In this sense, the Puritans of *The Scarlet Letter* are deeply involved in the dialectic of modern freedom. They themselves are creatures of the early modern era with which Hawthorne explicitly associates Hester—that moment when "the human intellect, newly emancipated, ... [took] a more active and a wider range than for many centuries before." In Europe, "men of the sword [have] overthrown nobles and kings," and "men bolder than these [have] overthrown and rearranged ... the whole system of ancient prejudice, wherewith was linked much of ancient principle." The mind of Hawthorne's Puritans is a negative version of this same libertarianism, which has cut loose the secular world from God, mankind from nature, and individual men from universal Man. In them, freedom appears as *deprivation*: a world removed from God and definable only in terms of that distance—a mankind at war with nature and able to create value out of it only by denying its intrinsic value, as God denies the value of man—and an individual alienated from humanity, who can rehabilitate himself only by self-annihilation before an external public law. In their prison-worship, the Puritans define modern liberty as a fearful freedom, and they make the most of fear, the terror of deprivation, in order to regain an idea of universal law, however abstract, unnatural, and inhuman. What dogs them, and confronts them in the person of Hester, is the other face of freedom—an affirmative individualism, humanism, and naturalism. The proscribed individual regenerates their society; they unwittingly are moved, for good and evil, by the nature they vilify; and a multiform, emergent divinity speaks in the forest or shows his features in Hester's elf-child.

By and large, in the course of the book, the Puritan version of the modern consciousness gives way to this positive version. Hester comes to dominate the landscape not only as a character in the eyes of the reader but also as an agent of transvaluation for her contemporaries. The natural affections of the "multitude," oriented toward her, escape from the abstract law of the ministers and magistrates. The final scene in the market place is very different in tonality from that of the first three chapters. There is variety, color, and movement in the picture; the darting figure of the antinomian Pearl weaves through the crowd. And yet we are reminded that "the blackest shade of Puritanism" still lies in the future and that its effect will linger on for two centuries. The populace gathered for this New England holiday are intent on the sign of sin and once more condemn Hester to "moral solitude." The climactic death of Dimmesdale in utter self-negation recalls the basic negativity of the Puritan vision which underlies the solemn procession of dignitaries and his own eloquent sermon on God's work in Massachusetts. For, given Hawthorne's historical method, he can have no intellectual right, and indeed no desire, to represent a complete and irreversible transformation of Puritan orthodoxy. It is the Puritan mind that proposes his subject, postulates the scarlet letter; he can move beyond this negative frame of reference only by keeping it in view. If the letter were not potentially more than a doom and a sign of doom, he could not turn back upon it and repossess it; but if it did not continue to have power to burn, he would not be trying to discover its meaning.

IV

Emerging from the prison, Hester forthwith rejects the "Puritanic code of law" that has put her there. The town beadle, with sword and staff, officially draws her toward the door; but "on the threshold," we are told, "she repelled him, by an action marked with natural dignity and force of character, and stepped into the open air, as if by her own free-will." There is more than bravado in her action, though she is full of shame and uncertain of her ground. She walks out of the prison as representative of an ideal pointedly opposed to "the righteous Colony of the Massachusetts, where iniquity is dragged out into the sunshine." She is converting the isolation of a criminal into the free self-determination of an individual, and she is pitting her "natural" dignity and force against the abstract dignity and force by which the Puritans attempt to annihilate nature. Similarly, the scarlet letter that she wears has been deliberately transformed into a "fitting decoration" for the natural individual. The "fertility and gorgeous luxuriance of fancy" manifested in her gold-embroidered letter, together with the "wild and picturesque peculiarity" of her gown, express both a "desperate recklessness"—what the Puritans condemn in her—and also a creative spirit—the other side of her "impulsive and passionate nature." Thus reinterpreted, the unholy flesh emphasized and stigmatized by the letter becomes a unique physical presence, a "lady-like ... state and dignity." The spell of the letter, "taking her out of the ordinary relations with humanity, and inclosing her in a sphere by herself," is not cast by Puritan law but by her own sense of its positive meaning; it "transfigure[s]" her into an individual because she has transfigured it into an emblem of individuality.

The naturalism and individualism dramatized by Hester in this scene point toward the "freedom of speculation" that Hawthorne later attributes to her—and beyond that to the scene with Dimmesdale in the forest, for which her "whole seven years of outlaw and ignominy ... [are] little other than a preparation." When she appears at Bellingham's mansion, she is "so conscious of her own right, that it seem[s] scarcely an unequal match between the public ... and a lonely woman, backed by the sympathies of nature." The effect of her estrangement, intended to mark her bondage to evil, has been "to set her free." Her liberated "intellect and heart" move through the world of her consciousness like "the wild Indian in his woods." Her appeal to Dimmesdale is calculatedly couched in the language of natural and personal "possibility." The forest-track leads to a point where all tracks disappear: "There thou art free!" The "broad pathway of the sea" opens out into a cosmopolitan civilization where freedom is taken for granted. Both betoken the individual's capacity for endless self-invention—the power to "begin all anew," to give up an old name and "make ... another."

Hawthorne remarks that Hester's judges, had they known of her free-thinking, "would have held [it] to be a deadlier crime than that stigmatized by the scarlet letter." But in fact Hester's sexual crime hardly exists for the reader as something distinct from her posture on the scaffold and her later philosophic libertarianism. Not that we are led to suppose she committed adultery for theoretical reasons; but we are interested in her deed mainly for thematic reasons. It contains the same sort of ambivalence as she imports into the idea of nature and the idea of the individual. The adultery of Hester and Dimmesdale, subverting the communal law, produces the only real community in the book. This is presumably her meaning when she says to Dimmesdale that "what [they] did had a consecration of its own." The proof of the consecration is precisely in the communion they attained by ignoring the sacrosanct community: "We felt it so! We said so to each other!" Pearl, dressed to personify the scarlet letter, stands between her parents to form "an electric chain" binding them together. She is the immanent word they have freely created. A similar dream of personal immediacy, according to Chillingworth, was what led him to marry Hester. The wrong against her that he confesses is his sin against this dream, the "false and unnatural relation" of a merely external marriage. The wrong that he feels was done to him, as he hints, is not so much possible exposure to public dishonor as a personal affront for which he will seek a personal revenge. Ironically, then, these three members of an adulterous triangle commune more profoundly in their dissociation and even in their antagonism than do any of the spokesmen of society. The monolithic state surrounding them is not only ignorant of their secret but also unacquainted with the kind of relation, the intimate good and evil, that they experience. In this sense, it is the official society, much more than Hester, that is excluded from the "common nature" of men.

Yet Hester's "freedom"—the creative nature, the individuality, and the antinomian community she represents—is inherently dialectical. In order that the letter may be "transformed into something that should speak a different purport," she must feel it as "too deeply branded" for anyone to remove. A prevailing image for her situation throughout the book is that of a lonely being encircled by "a thousand unrelenting eyes ... concentred at her bosom." Though she is separated from these observers as by a great void—whether a "magic circle of ignominy" or a self-generated circle of freedom—her meaning depends on her "intense consciousness" of what she means to them. The values associated with her have no existence except as transformations of Puritan values. And her self-effacing role after she is released from her prison term, her apparent humility and public conformity, indicates that her business is not an external battle against the established order but an internal struggle to assimilate that order by translating it into her own language. Her consciousness becomes the stage of a lifelong dialogue between the voice of Puritan negation and the voice of that positive freedom which is evinced by the very fact of her lively consciousness.

The process begins while she is still on the scaffold. When she summons up "phantasmagoric forms" from the past in order to escape from the "cruel weight and hardness of ... reality," the past leads her back to the crushing present, the inescapeable product of all she has been; but her identity is being dramatized all the while in the energy of her thought and the vividness with which she conceives the entire present moment, including herself. This dialectical vocation is what keeps her in Boston, despite the fact that she might easily follow the path she later offers to Dimmesdale, into the forest or over the sea. Her self-respect is bound up with her shame, her freedom with her bondage: "her sin, her ignominy, [are] the roots which she [has] struck into the soil." Her perennial gray costume, resembling a prison uniform, expresses the annihilation of self that the scarlet letter is intended to inflict; it has "the effect of making her fade personally out of sight and outline." Yet simultaneously she is "brought ... back from this twilight indistinctness" by the embroidered letter, her handiwork, which "reveal[s] her under the moral aspect of its own illumination."

Therefore the movement of her experience—the freedom she enacts, as distinguished from the absolute, ideal freedom she sometimes proposes— is tormented, difficult, full of doubt. Hester's agony of consciousness is greater than the particular agony of her shame, the "penance" imposed by Puritan law (just as the exercise of her consciousness, the enactment of her freedom, is the only redemption she will ever know). She moves back and forth between aberrant extremes; and in her very effort to conceive a *via media*, she falls into traps of thought.

Almost immediately after her release from prison, Hawthorne notes a kind of tergiversation—"something doubtful, something that might be deeply wrong"—in her attitude toward her sufferings. She cannot adopt the Puritan rationale of sin, penance, and repentance without an oblique assertion of her own self-determining and passionate nature. She imagines herself as proceeding through humiliation and ostracism to a triumphant state of saint-like purity; and the persistence of her "rich, voluptuous, Oriental ... taste for the gorgeously beautiful" is revealed by the very severity with which she chastens it. On the other hand, her latent idea that what makes for "sin" can also make for good is confused and perverted by a Puritanical concept of evil. From the beginning she has had some notion of a communion of sinners. The passionate nature that in one sense alienates criminals from the community of law can serve in another sense to unite them in sympathy: "... Would that I might endure his agony, as well as mine!" At a later stage, she acts on her belief that the "link of mutual crime" establishes mutual responsibility between persons who have "cast off all duty towards other human beings." But the communion of sinners, seen in a Puritan perspective, becomes a communion of sin. When a sympathetic eye (perhaps Dimmesdale's) falls upon the scarlet letter and makes her feel "as if half of her agony were shared," she conceives the moment as a renewal of evil affection, not a transmutation of evil into good. Unable to surrender her faith in final union with her lover, but pre-occupied with the Puritan view of their love as wholly evil, she is driven to picture a communion of the damned, "a joint futurity of endless retribution." She struggles against the "sympathetic knowledge of ... hidden sin" that the letter gives her, for it seems to imply a world of common sin rather than a community of sympathy. Her only recourse is to repress her vision of reunion with Dimmesdale—"bar it in its dungeon"—and try to "believe that no fellow-mortal [is] guilty like herself."

The terrible phenomenon of Chillingworth objectifies and confirms Hester's vision of an evil communion. He foresees and tells her of the perverse "sympathy," the sudden shudder of recognition, by which he will know her lover through the affinity of sin for sin. Doubtless he is present in her mind when the "electric thrill" of the scarlet letter seems to reveal to her a multitude of companions in evil. When she seeks him out again to reaffirm her loyalty to Dimmesdale, the letter burns ironically in token of her relation to Chillingworth, who has become a devil in a world that he envisages as wholly devilish. The bond that she swore with Chillingworth, as she now perceives, was the devil's bond: her sympathetic assumption of Dimmesdale's agony has brought about a perverse intimacy of fiend and victim that mocks her idea of passion self-redeemed in love. Chillingworth destroys her faith in the potential good of the letter she wears, leaving only the mark of universal sin, "the truth of red-hot iron," and a natural world "quickened to ... evil purpose." The question whether Dimmesdale should be exposed becomes unimportant, for in any case "there is no good" for him or anyone concerned. The path of her speculation is now a "dismal maze." As Chillingworth turns away from her, she revels in her hate of him, accepting the inverted reality that he represents. Seven years of penance not only have "wrought out no repentance" but also have destroyed the new sense that she was trying to lend to the word.

In the wake of her interview with Chillingworth, Hester for the first time denies that the scarlet letter has any meaning at all. If informing Pearl of the Puritan meaning of the symbol is "the price of the child's sympathy," it is more than she is willing to pay. For she has good reason to distrust any purported meeting ground between the sign of evil and human good; and she is turning toward a conception of unmitigated freedom, which she sets forth in the forest scene that immediately follows. She asks Dimmesdale to believe that he has left his sin far behind him, superseded by a "penitence ... sealed and witnessed by good works." Going further, she conjures away the very idea of penitence, tossing the scarlet letter aside: "The past is gone! ... See! With this symbol, I undo it all, and make it as it had never been!" The wilderness around them responds with favorable auguries; the "mystery" of nature, the ambivalent joy-and-sorrow in which her whole history once seemed to center, has been resolved into a single "mystery of joy." Hester is still thinking in these terms as she comes into the market place for the final scene. She contemplates wearing the letter "freely and voluntarily" but with secret disdain and the intention of discarding it forever—"in order to convert what had so long been agony into a kind of triumph." Her attitude is strikingly opposed to her dialectical self-conversion and triumph in her first appearance in the market place; she has solved her problem by cutting the knot.

Yet her dialectical stance persists insofar as she is still trying to find a morality in freedom, not merely to enjoy the sensation of being free. And along her way there have been indications that nature and the individual, fully liberated, become impoverished and disoriented; liberation is ultimately as nihilistic as the presumption of guilt. Taken in either sense, "the scarlet letter [has] not done its office." Thus Hester's "freedom of speculation," though theoretically sanctioned by natural freedom, is in practice contrary to nature. Her personality and appearance are reduced to a "bare and harsh outline," and she is deprived of "passion and feeling" by her independence of mind. The cold abstractness of her free thinking isolates her as much as the public proscription that set her free. Nature, the only ground for her thought, suffers a reversal of meaning and becomes a "wild and ghastly scenery" that "image[s] ... the moral wilderness" of her speculations. This is the way she pictures herself while waiting for Dimmesdale in the forest. The "dark labyrinth" of liberty is hard to distinguish from the "dismal maze" of deviltry in which Chillingworth left her. Having discarded the letter, seeing only evil in its "stern and severe, but yet ... guardian spirit," she has entered upon another realm where values dissolve into nothingness. Her dream of an open future with Dimmesdale is ominously preceded and shadowed by the image of their first encounter in the dim wood. They meet as ghosts, awe-stricken at each other and at themselves. It is a true communion of individuals: "... the crisis flung back to them their consciousness, and revealed to each heart its history and experience.... The soul beheld its features in the mirror of the passing moment." But the hands they extend to one another are "chill as death" and barely convince them of their "actual and bodily existence."

If the world exemplified in Chillingworth, though it has the substance of evil, is ultimately without good, the world of absolute freedom is finally without substance, without "truth." It is the example of Dimmesdale that brings this home to Hester and thereby helps to restore her intellectual balance. For in her conversation with him she is fighting against this realization as much as she is combatting the claims of the scarlet letter. She denies that his private life, cut off from public truth, is "falsehood ... emptiness ... death." His public reputation, according to her, is a function of his private substance, and both demonstrate his real holiness. The private communion with friend or enemy that he desperately imagines as a last resort is for her the solution of his problem. Re-established in his benign relation with her and cognizant of his malign relation with Chillingworth, he will be part of a world of personal good and evil that is more substantial than the external Puritan forms for which he yearns. But Dimmesdale, though he agrees to strike out for freedom with her, never accepts her contention that private freedom is more real than public order. The Election Sermon is on his mind as he returns from the forest; and when he passes Hester in the procession, he is "unattainable in his worldly position," far removed from the personal communion of "their mutual world." His voice from the church, telling unmistakably of a personal anguish, nevertheless speaks in the language of impersonal authority. As she stands at the foot of the scaffold listening to him, she is recalled from her dissolving private dream to the solid coherence of social reality: "There was a sense within her ... that her whole orb of life, both before and after, was connected with this spot [the scaffold], as with the one point that gave it unity."

Still, the coercive social reality that rushes back in the final chapter is not Hester's proper home. It is one dimension of her personal universe, and it exists for her only in relation to her own naturalistic freedom. The scaffold is the center of her orb of life because the letter which society once imposed and she voluntarily assumed on that spot is the center of her dialectical consciousness. Through all her gradations of attitude this problematic center is implied as a reference point; it is the potential focus of her experience. It is also a very actual idea for her—one that she contemplates through the ever-present figure of Pearl. Hester is everywhere accompanied by the thought of her daughter, that "lovely and immortal flower" growing out of the "rank luxuriance of a guilty passion." By dressing Pearl as a personification of the scarlet letter, identifying "the object of her affection" with "the emblem of her guilt," she images the convertibility of terms like guilt and love, affection and passion. This concept of metamorphosis, though it is her own, at first puzzles her almost as much as it does the Puritan elders to whom she later propounds it. How can the "badge of shame" be "capable of being loved"? And how can such love fail to be merely a disguise for unrepentant lust? Her affection will quicken her torment, she tells them; she will be chastened by her sense of the distance between her feeling for Pearl and the shameful deed that brought Pearl into being. What is more apparent, however, is that she has introduced the positive idea of a quickening power into the negative Puritan concept of passionate human nature. The elders have reason to be startled. A direct consequence of this bold intellectual step is her confident "power to do, and power to sympathize," which lead the Puritan populace to reinterpret the "A" as "Able." The "unearthly ray" of the embroidered letter in the sick-chamber is cast by a "warm and rich" earthliness that she does not seek to hide.

As Hester embraces Dimmesdale at his death on the scaffold, she speaks in this dialectical mode. The other side of their common suffering for earthly love, the suffering that is all Dimmesdale now wants to feel or remember, is an "immortal life together." They have "ransomed one another"; if their "woe" implies the evil of passion, their passion reappears as redeeming affection. By a similar logic, Hester is drawn back to Boston at the end and lives out her days with the scarlet letter on her bosom. Here is "real life," for here is the locus of sin, sorrow, and penitence. But the letter is taken up—in a phrase recalling her first appearance in the book—"of her own free will." And her penitence is "yet to be"—for her it will always be unfinished. It can only be conceived and made manifest as a perennial conversion of the stuff of sin and sorrow into positive freedom—the creativity, individuality, and sympathetic community of natural men.

V

In response to Hester's plea, the dying Dimmesdale delivers the most eloquent Puritan statement in the entire book. Though he is lying in her arms, he rejects her faith in their eternal union and maintains that in their love, far from redeeming one another, they "violated [their] reverence each for the other's soul." Sin alone should be in their thoughts, and salvation lies in the torture inflicted by an angry God. Dimmesdale displays his stigmatic letter to the multitude as a token of complete self-abnegation, or rather of a self finally rediscovered in "triumphant ignominy." How did such a man ever come to wander "beyond the scope of generally received laws"?—and why, having wandered, was he not for the rest of his life "safer within the line of virtue, than if he had never sinned at all"? On the one hand, as we are told, his was "a sin of passion, not of principle"; and, on the other hand, as he himself declares and as Hawthorne often repeats, he lacks the courage of his convictions. But in this book passion itself is a principle, and moral cowardice is a symptom of moral embarrassment. In effect, Dimmesdale is as much a creature of his age as Hester and his fellow Puritans: he is a victim (until his final moments) of the divided universe in which they find opposite ways to live. His existence has been contorted into an "inextricable knot"—his simultaneous desire to repent and incapacity to do so—because he entertains conflicting interpretations of his deed. If his final sense of the letter he wears is unequivocal, for most of his career he has worn it as the very mark of equivocation, the sign of two voices warring within him.

His conflicts are more completely internal than Hester's: in him, the disjunctive world is registered as alienation from self. We first encounter him as "a being who [feels] himself quite astray and at a loss in the pathway of human existence, and ... only ... at ease in some seclusion of his own." Moreover, his manner suggests a profound uneasiness even in his solitude— a combination of "nervous sensibility and a vast power of self-restraint." His devotees associate his isolation with intellectual elevation, a "purity of thought" that gives him "the speech of an angel." But in this first scene he is dramatically isolated as much by his sensibility as by his intellectual purity. He responds to the voice of feeling in Hester's silence: "Wondrous strength and generosity of a woman's heart!" Under the scrutiny of Chillingworth, his inner division appears as an alienation of mind and body, of his "spiritual" being and his "strong animal nature," of his "soul" and "the hot passion of his heart." Unlike Hester, who even in despair preserves some of her individual integrity, her concrete presence at once mental and physical, Dimmesdale falls apart. He is of all men the one "whose body is the closest conjoined, and imbued, and identified ... with the spirit," but only to express the body's demand for dominion over the spirit and simultaneously the spirit's utter rejection of that claim. This is the condition signified by his psychosomatic letter and deliberately fostered by Chillingworth.

In one aspect he knows himself as "a true priest, a true religionist," whose inner peace depends on the "iron framework" of his creed. His subjective correlative to the prison-world of Boston is a "constant introspection" by which he seeks to keep his sin in sight and thereby to rise above it. In accordance with the Puritan paradox, he would convert his flesh to spirit by dwelling upon the total disparity of his "sinful" natural body and his intelligent mind. As he marches in the procession, he almost seems to have achieved his goal of "purity." The entire world of sight and sound has ceased to exist for him; he is pure thought. But, all the while, his very striving for selfhood implies a different valuation of himself from any that his Puritan creed would allow. By subjectifying his punishment, making himself at once prisoner and judge, he demonstrates an esteem for his own individuality even while denouncing the natural man within him. And he is fully aware, in certain moods, that the idea of the unique individual counts for as much to him as the ideal of purification. He perplexes Mr. Wilson by declaring it a wrong to "the very nature of woman to force her to lay open her heart's secrets in such broad daylight, and in presence of so great a multitude." In discussion with Chillingworth, he holds that forced confession is not only wrong but impossible in principle; there is no public language for private secrets; and even voluntary confession may be impossible to some "by the very constitution of their nature" or by reason of a desire to redeem evil through good works. These arguments for individual value are not merely self-justification but evidence of a sense of self that brings him close to Hester's naturalism. When Hester at the Governor's mansion explains the meaning she attaches to Pearl, Dimmesdale thoroughly understands and seconds her revision of the idea of evil.

His own sermons illustrate the "truth in what Hester says," for his burden of sin and sorrow gives vitality and efficacy to his words. Like the embroidered letter and the letter doubly "endowed with life" by Pearl, Dimmesdale's "Tongue of Flame" is energized by the earthly passion that his Puritanical self despises. He speaks the language of doctrine, but there is an emotional language of "tone and cadence" interwoven with "the direct purport of the words." Coming back from the midnight vigil in which he renews his sin, he preaches more powerfully than ever before; and he writes his masterpiece, the Election Sermon, with strength acquired from Hester in the diabolic wilderness. The extraordinary communicative power of these sermons must be weighed against his retreat from public confession and his consequent self-contempt. The kind of truth he achieves as the greatest preacher of his time is precisely what makes him an "untrue man" in his own Puritan eyes. His heart speaks immediately to "the great heart of mankind"; he establishes a "sinful brotherhood." In this sense, he has already made confession, and from this standpoint mere self-humiliation would be a perverted "repentance." The very anguish he suffers because of his moral failure by orthodox standards contributes to his moral success as "the voice ... of suffering humanity."

But he always comes round to "the contrast between what I seem and what I am." Not being the pure spirit that his congregation think they see and hear, and not having shown himself in the guise of a worthless sinner, he conceives himself to be nothing at all. And he is right, according to Hawthorne, to the extent that he claims the identity of a Puritan minister; the only reality in him is his awareness of his unreality. To the extent that he claims identity as Hester's lover, he is equally insubstantial. This is Pearl's reproach: "Thou wast not bold!—thou wast not true!" Though "false to God and man" in his professional role, he has enjoyed a momentary truth of another sort on the scaffold at midnight and in the depths of the forest. He has known the reality of "sympathy" that he expresses in the poignant undersong of his sermons. Unable to go further and declare for personal freedom as the ground of sympathy—unwilling to stand in the market place at noon as he stood at midnight—he is "false" once more. Whether as minister or as lover, he can only look forward to the truth of Judgment Day, when "the dark problem of this life [will be] made plain."

If he does not actually wait until Judgment Day, but finally conceives and displays himself unambiguously as "the vilest ... of sinners," it is because he has undergone the experience of spiritual isolation to a far greater degree than Hester. As he tells her, "open ignominy" is what makes possible her "open triumph over ... evil." Since her shame is public, her transmutation of the shame is public, though she arrives at it by private processes. Her life, whatever phases of nihilism and despair she may pass through, is anchored in the society she would transform into sympathetic community. Therefore she is scarcely aware of Dimmesdale's basic problem. She does not perceive that by sparing him the isolation inflicted on her, by trying to preserve intact his individual dignity and freedom, she has actually isolated him completely. Even without the cruelties of Chillingworth, for which she feels responsible, Dimmesdale would have been tortured by a rootless subjectivism, a self-negating freedom. He comes to live in a solipsistic world of visions; in contrast to her train of images on the scaffold, his "spectral thoughts" have no termination in reality. We see him as a creature of the night, always "walking in the shadow of a dream." And this radically subjective world veers toward the deeper psyche; he makes acquaintance with perversities and blasphemies that never trouble Hester Prynne. The "dark transfiguration" that overcomes him for a moment in the forest is a symptom of what he knows to be potential in himself.

By the time Hester goes to meet Dimmesdale, determined to offer him the only truth she knows, he is no longer capable of assimilating individual freedom in the spirit in which she conceives it. She herself goes beyond the proper boundaries of her world by rejecting the letter entirely; but this access of freedom transforms her into an earth goddess, however dream-like and illusory. In him it works as a poison. The "profounder self" that she awakens in him desires "to do some strange, wild, wicked thing or other"; and the world about him, rendered wholly mutable, drifts toward the demon-ridden forest of Mistress Hibbens. He can only experience his liberation as a pact with the devil, a yielding "with deliberate choice ... to ... deadly sin." He has reached the nadir of freedom, a sense of "eternal alienation from the Good and True." At the same time, however, he has stepped over into another universe. By his conviction of mortal sin, he takes his place in the orthodox world where the reality of evil, the fact of alienation, is the very ground of civil and cosmic order. When Dimmesdale in the final scene moves toward the scaffold, he translates a personal existence that has become wholly insubstantial and subhuman into terms of a public world that can make sense of private devils. He is not only confessing a sin but also professing a truth that fulfils his consciousness of himself. He turns to Hester with a very pointed question: "Is not this better ... than what we dreamed of in the forest?"

Chillingworth can hardly believe that his victim has escaped him; and indeed there is only a difference in emphasis between the experience of evil that leads Dimmesdale to a vision of God and the vision of evil that leads Chillingworth to adopt the role of Satan. The minds of both these cultivated gentlemen, so long resident together, come to rest in the conviction of sin. The letter with which Dimmesdale involuntarily marks himself, and which he eventually displays in token of a reality founded on it, is the same that Chillingworth obsessively imagines and finally unveils with the wonder of a philosopher discovering the key to the universe. This is why the scaffold is the one place in the world where Dimmesdale could elude his pursuer: it is the locus of their similarity, where their difference must be established. Chillingworth once laid claim to it at midnight when his diabolic smile or scowl lingered on a darkness wherein "all things else were ... annihilated." Now, though defeated, he appropriately claims his place on the platform beside the man who has escaped him by passing through nothingness to the reality of God.

His former power over Dimmesdale also depended on other premises—ones that he shared with Hester (in a sense, Dimmesdale has escaped them both). Like Hester, though obviously in a parodic way, he appears from the beginning as a naturalist, individualist, and humanist. He arrives in Boston out of the wilderness, dressed in a mixture of "civilized and savage costume" and accompanied by an Indian. Usually solitary, this "individual, of singular aspect," wanders the borders of the settlement in search of natural medicines. Even after his hideous transformation, he can admire the "great elements" of personality and of natural good in Hester. These two are the secret free thinkers of Boston, a subversive pair at work within the rigid structure of Puritan ideology. Their secret community is intuitive, subrational—confirmed by the verbal bond they swear in Hester's prison cell, but initiated in a silent exchange of glances in the market place, where "all ... objects in the visible world [seem] to vanish, leaving only him and her." Their silent interview, while it is intensified by Hester's fear, anticipates the non-verbal, "sympathetic" mode of communication that is characteristic of Chillingworth throughout the book. As he tells Hester, he will abandon his public name not only out of pride but also "for other reasons"; actuated by the "strange secrecy in his nature" that Hester later counts upon, he is bent on "new interests" and a "new purpose" in a personal universe. Similarly, thought less deliberately, he abandons abstract, "geometrical" truth in order to "know" in a much more intimate way. He is not an inductive scientist; he proceeds by intuitive affinity. And though his first intent is to mock friendship by keeping Dimmesdale in ignorance, he is even more pleased by Dimmesdale's instinctive awareness of his hostile presence. For he dwells by choice in an underground world of immediate knowledge, an almost sexual "knowing." It is a perverse form of the world of Hester, who alone knows and seeks to know as much as he.

The perversity of Chillingworth lies in the peculiar way in which he combines Hester's sense of natural freedom and community with Dimmesdale's sense of the fact of evil. He envisages a communion of sinners like the one Young Goodman Brown beholds in the forest—united "by the sympathy of ... human hearts for sin." He himself is cast in the role of grand master of the secret order. The love he once sought with Hester is realized in the hate of his new relationships. His "human heart," no longer lonely, is expressed in the deeds of a "fiend." Shocked as he is when he sees this "frightful shape ... usurping the place of his own image," there is a fantastic logic in his transformation. To have "violated, in cold blood, the sanctity of a human heart" is not a gratuitous act if all hearts are wicked and all communion is anti-communion. It is the coherence of Chillingworth's vision that reduces Hester to despair, and the logic of Chillingworth is what gives him his power over Dimmesdale. For he sees that if good is impossible, a communion of "evil" is really a communion beyond good and evil. He intimates this to Hester when he first projects his plan: "... Elsewhere a wanderer, and isolated from human interests, I find here a woman, a man, a child, amongst whom and myself there exist the closest ligaments. No matter whether of love or hate; no matter whether of right or wrong!" Chillingworth imagines and takes his place in an amoral world of sheer power. He passes beyond the role of the perverse friend, "the Pitiless, ... the Unforgiving," to that of a supreme mechanist controlling the "engine" of Dimmesdale's life. As a black magician, he achieves his greatest feat not merely in promoting the wickedness of the enemy he embraces but in reducing Dimmesdale to the level of an inhuman natural phenomenon, a force overcome by a greater force. This is the union that Chillingworth finally accepts in lieu of his lost hope of love. When he declares, "Thou and thine, Hester Prynne, belong to me," he is Satan as the deity of mechanical power.

As such, he remains the villain of the piece, but he is also a kind of victim. His heterodox thought, as he himself comes to see, is dominated by Puritan concepts. When Hester tells him that he might yet re-establish good among them by forgiving the sin against himself, Chillingworth counters her appeal by falling back on the Puritan language of original sin and abstract wickedness. His world, where a "dark necessity" compels every "germ of evil" to grow into a "black flower," is the orthodox Puritan world but without the God against whom the Puritans measured it and by whose power they believed it might be saved as well as damned. His "old faith," in this truncated form, has been with him all along; it is, after all, the practical faith of a people whose town center is "the black flower of ... a prison" and who have surely "let the black flower blossom" in the case of Hester Prynne. Moreover, the amorality of Chillingworth, his world beyond right and wrong, derives from the negatively liberated, disjunctive world of Puritan theology. The rule of dark necessity, as he points out, would imply that human beings are "evil" only in a manner of speaking: "Ye that have wronged me are not sinful, save in a kind of typical illusion; neither am I fiend-like, who have snatched a fiend's office from his hands. It is our fate." What can one do but act? And in this perspective he cannot and does not claim any special power of action. His own force, his apparent freedom, is no less illusory than good and evil; for in a community of sheer power even the most powerful are determined by the blind forces of the universe, the purposeless workings of natural energy.

VI

The Puritan mind in *The Scarlet Letter* follows a logic of negative freedom. The antithetical good and evil of Puritan morality reflect a universe that is polarized into external relations on every level, so that good can be conceived only as an external order imposed by God on a fallen world, by man on a fallen nature, and by society on a fallen individual. Hester Prynne does not abandon that framework of thought but conceives and enacts a dialectical relation between evil and good based on a dialectical conversion of negative into positive freedom. She is creative in the face of destruction, and she is constantly making an idea of creativity—of individual value, organic community, and natural divinity—out of the tough negations of Puritan doctrine. Dimmesdale is torn apart, rendered insubstantial, by this dialectic, which gives substance to Hester even while it torments her. Unlike her, he experiences the ambiguity of freedom in a primarily negative form; and at the end of his life he commits himself to the negative Puritan rationale. Chillingworth, perverting both the Puritan vision and Hester's, takes evil as his good and thereby ultimately destroys the meaning of such terms as well as the meaning of liberation itself. His amoral world beyond good and evil is also beyond freedom, whether negative or positive.

In one way or another all these persons lay claim to the child that Hester clutches to her when she first appears on the scene. The Puritan elders would instruct Pearl "as to her soul, its present depravity, and future destiny." As the child of sin, she is their human archetype. Dimmesdale, pathetically treasuring the memory of her moments of affection for him, sees her as his hope of life, but infected with the doubtfulness of his hope. Looking at her with eyes accustomed to staring at himself, he cannot say whether one whose only "discoverable principle of being" is "the freedom of a broken law" may yet be "capable of good." Chillingworth, pursuing his amoral drive for power, is struck by Pearl's indifference to "human ordinances or opinions, right or wrong"; and he would use her, the embodiment of an amoral letter, as material for another such exercise of experimental power as he practices upon Dimmesdale. But the child evades them all, literally by skipping away and figuratively by eluding their conceptions of her. She partly evades even Hester, for whom she is identical with the moral dialectic within the embroidered letter. Pearl is not completely seized by any of the claims made on her—and from the reader's standpoint, she can never be fully grasped as a fictional "character"—because she represents something latent in all who observe her but incapable of being completely objectified in a single human form.

Pearl is the very principle of freedom, the essence of her time. She dances among the graves "like a creature that [has] nothing in common with a bygone and buried generation, nor own[s] herself akin to it." Since she seems to have been "made afresh, out of new elements," she "must perforce be permitted to live her own life, and be a law unto herself, without her eccentricities being reckoned to her for a crime." In this sense, Pearl's freedom is not a moral principle; she is prior to moral categories (though not, like Chillingworth, "beyond" them). The only good she affirms is the "boldness" of her "truth." And her truth consists wholly in her multiplicity, the "infinite variety" of her possibilities, the "many children" she intrinsically is. Hester looks in vain for "the master-word that should control this new and incomprehensible intelligence," for all the major terms of the book are applicable to it to some extent. Pearl is sheer energy, as Chillingworth perceives, and aware of her power; but her passionate, impulsive, capricious emotions are not primarily aggressive. She is by turns malicious and affectionate, as Hester and Dimmesdale discover, but never fully intimate in either way. Often she seems an entirely negative principle of "disorder," whose "freedom" is synonymous with the "broken law" that gave her birth. In her attitude toward other children, she accepts the role of "a born outcast." But more often she shrugs off all such Puritan concepts. Though she disclaims a heavenly father, she can deny that the Black Man will ever catch her, for her home is in the benign "wildness" of the "mother-forest." Yet even her naturalism is problematic: if she resembles a pagan nymph or dryad, her beauty and grace also suggest a prelapsarian child of Adam, a throwback to Eden before the fall.

For lack of a focus, a single "point of variety and arrangement," Pearl sometimes seems to disappear into a fluid, insubstantial ideality. She is attracted by the "visionary" counterpart that she finds in a pool on the shore, "beckoning the phantom forth, and—as it decline[s] to venture—seeking a passage for herself into its sphere of impalpable earth and unattainable sky." But she soon concludes that "either she or the image [is] unreal," and she craves reality as much as freedom. If her multiplicity tends to make her vague and indistinct, the "truth" in her tends away from the "remoteness and intangibility" of an "airy sprite" toward the substance of "a human child." Pearl's truth can become substantial, her freedom can become moral, only through a sacrifice of multiplicity—specifically, through the discipline of "grief." Her incarnation as "a noble woman," foreseen by Hester, will be a conversion of her "infinite variety" into human freedom by means of the suffering that is the sign of human limits. While this gives her definition, it will also open possibilities of a new kind, personal rather than impersonal, concrete rather than abstract. The "grief that [will] deeply touch her, and thus humanize," will "make her capable of sympathy." It will bring her into the sphere of free individuals in personal relationship.

So extreme is Pearl's sense of absolute freedom that all the drama of Dimmesdale's final agony is needed to complete her transformation. In some sense, of course, she must already have entered the human world, the world of sorrow, in order to feel his loss at all. Her earlier affection for him, the man with his hand over his heart, like her obsession with Hester's letter, indicates her nascent awareness of suffering and her correlative "humanization." But in the final episode she flits about the market place in utter independence and joy as though to affirm her infinitude for the last time. She must be drawn down to earth by a principle as strong as her own. Dimmesdale's "great scene of grief ... develop[s] all her sympathies," commits her to "human joy and sorrow," because he has reached an extreme of negation that counterbalances her libertarian extreme. Just as the kiss he asks from her is his last concession to the world of human relations that he rejects in his dying speech, so her bestowal of the kiss is her first act within the human world to which he has drawn her.

Since she becomes fully incarnate only in the final moments of the book, Pearl remains almost as abstract and schematic in her moral meaning as in her premoral multiplicity. We can seldom say with any confidence that she is actually experiencing either the limits or the possibilities of the concrete human life she represents. But Pearl "humanized," however abstractly, comes close to being what her mother sees in her—a symbol of Hester's own moral dialectic. She descends from a realm of total creativity into the middle world that Hester painfully reaches from below, from total self-negation and enslavement. This would seem to be the rationale of her behavior in the forest when Hester herself denies all limits and arrives at a project of absolute liberty. Like the pool on the shore, the forest brook that figures in this scene is a "boundary between two worlds"—between a visionary and a substantial (or human) existence. But it is also the spring of natural human life, where visionary freedom and actual bondage, joy and sorrow, are interdependent. Initially, Pearl can hear only the sad murmur of the little stream of natural life, and she dances off into ideal freedom and joy. When she returns to the boundary, however, she finds herself decisively relegated to the "shadowy and intangible" role of a watery "image." Having been exiled from the concrete world of human sympathy, she becomes poignantly aware of it. Even more, she becomes aware of the mixed world of man because of Hester's attempt to transcend it. By throwing away the scarlet letter, Hester has leveled the distinction between ideal and human freedom; there is no human world for Pearl to return to. Like a little prophetess, she summons her mother back to the reality of joy-and-sorrow that is guaranteed by sorrow: "Come thou and take it up!" She demands her place in a human group—"hand in hand, we three together." And once Hester has resumed the sign of suffering, Pearl kisses it in token of truth re-established.

Pearl has already expressed the positive side of Hester's truth by tracing a letter of grass upon herself, "freshly green instead of scarlet," in virtual answer to her own question as to what the letter means. As a "human child," she is a growing point of human experience, and she betokens a "oneness of ... being" in the parents who created her. This is her role, apparently assumed with some self-awareness, when she, Hester, and Dimmesdale form "an electric chain." It is validated when the celestial "A" shines down upon this archetypal trio: Pearl, "herself a symbol," is the human counterpart of the divine signature in the sky. Though the noonday light that suffuses the scene is like that of Judgment Day, it is not a visitation by an angry God; if it gives a new "moral interpretation to the things of this world," it does so by consecrating the emergent meaning of temporal life—in Dimmesdale, "with his hand over his heart"; in Hester, "with the embroidered letter glimmering on her bosom"; but especially in Pearl, "the connecting link between those two." And in this role Pearl is an aesthetic, as well as a moral, exemplar. She represents not only a secular morality but also a secularized symbolism. She recalls us once more to the distinctive imaginative medium of her author—the liberated modern consciousness that often dissolves, like Pearl, into a "vast variety of forms," but of which, again like Pearl, the imaginative structure of *The Scarlet Letter* is a "living hieroglyphic."

AUSTIN WARREN

The Scarlet Letter

I

In structure, *The Scarlet Letter* is rather a monody, like *Wuthering Heights* (its closest English analogue for intensity) or *The Spoils of Poynton* (with its thematic concentration), than like the massively rich and contrapuntal Victorian novel—say *Middlemarch* or *Bleak House*. And, conducted almost entirely in dialogues between two persons, or in tableaux, with something like the Greek chorus in the commenting community, it is also much nearer to a tragedy of Racine's than to the Elizabethan drama, of which the three-volumed Victorian novel was the legitimate successor.

This purity of method, this structural condensation and concentration, prime virtues of *The Scarlet Letter*, disturbed, while they obsessed, its author. He regretted not being able to intersperse the gloom of his novel by some chapters, episodes, or passages in a lighter mode. "Keeping so close to its point as the tale does, and diversified no otherwise than by turning different sides of the same idea to the reader's mind," he wrote his publisher, would, he feared, bore, disgust, or otherwise alienate the reader.

But the enduring power of the book lies in its "keeping so close to its point," lies in its method: looking at the "same idea" (the situation or theme) from "different sides." Hawthorne's phrase, "different sides," is not synonymous with the Jamesian "point of view," though there is a degree of

From *Connections*. © 1970 by The University of Michigan.

overlap. Hawthorne is the nineteenth-century omniscient author; and it is he who shows us the "different sides," now a character's public behavior, now the same character's private introspection; who presents two characters operating on each other; who gives us the shifting attitudes of the community to the actions of the central figures; who provides settings and symbols and generalizing comments. It is none the less true that the author does not flit from character to character. Each chapter has not only a center of interest, commonly indicated by its title, but tends to be seen through a single or central consciousness. As we remember the novel, the interpolations and other deviations fall away, and we retain the impression of a massive construction in terms of centers of interest and of consciousness.

The first eight chapters of the novel are seen through Hester's consciousness; even though the minister appears from time to time it is in his public capacity as her "pastor." The next four concern the minister, two of them close studies of "The Interior of a [Dimmesdale's] Heart." Hester again engages the next four. The Forest chapters represent the only real meeting, the only real converse between the two.

This is an eminently proper mode of telling the story. The two characters are joined by an act which occurred before the novel opens. They never meet again save twice, ritualistically, on the scaffold, and once, rituals dispensed with, in the Forest. Otherwise, these are tales of two isolated characters, isolated save for the attendant spirit of each—Pearl for Hester; for Dimmesdale, Chillingworth. Hester's story, as that of sin made public, must begin the novel; the telling of Dimmesdale's, as that of sin concealed, must be delayed till its effects, however ambivalently interpreted, begin to show. The last chapters must present both characters to our consciousness, even though Dimmesdale recedes into something like the public figure of the early chapters, lost in his double role of preacher and dying confessor.

The composition of the novel, deeply as it stirred Hawthorne, was creatively easy, for (as he wrote his publisher), "all being all in one tone, I had only to get my pitch and could then go on interminably." But this high, or deep, tragic pitch made him uncomfortable—as, I dare say, did Melville's praise of his *Mosses from an Old Manse*, in which the new friend, who was beginning to write *Moby Dick*, spoke of "the blackness in Hawthorne ... that so fixes and fascinates me," singling out from that collection "Young Goodman Brown," a piece "as deep as Dante." Hawthorne, waiving the question of his 'best,' preferred *The House of the Seven Gables* as "more characteristic" of him than *The Scarlet Letter*; and doubtless among his tales, too, he would have preferred the "more characteristic" to the 'best.' A critic may be pardoned if he prefers the 'best.'

And certainly *The Scarlet Letter* resumes, develops, and concentrates the themes which Hawthorne had already essayed in some of his chief and greatest short stories—"Roger Malvin's Burial," "The Minister's Black Veil," and, especially, "Young Goodman Brown": concealment of sin, penance, and penitence; the distinction between the comparatively lighter sins of passion and the graver sins of cold blood—pride, calculated revenge; the legacy of sin in making one detect, or suspect, it in others.

II

In reading Hawthorne's masterpiece, one should be careful to distinguish the 'story,' 'fable,' or 'myth' from the author's commentary. Even in his own lifetime, the now forgotten but good Boston critic, E. P. Whipple, wrote, acutely, that Hawthorne's "great books appear not so much created by him as through him. They have the character of revelations,—he, the instrument, being often troubled with the burden they impose upon his mind." *The Scarlet Letter* seems preeminently such a case. The 'myth' was a delivery; the commentary was an offering.

The novelist, whether the later James of the strict point of view constructions, or Jane Austen and E. M. Forster and Dostoevski, has an enviable 'dramatic' privilege. If his characters act out their willed destiny and utter the views appropriate to their characters, the novelist (who is also a nonwriter, a man whose divided self approves but in part of what his *personae* say and do) has the immunity of dissociating himself from a position which he can empathize or entertain but to which he does not wish to commit himself. Hawthorne could, if necessary, let his latent 'moral'—that of his powerfully presented 'myth'—go one way while he safeguarded his other self by uttering, in his own person, words of warning or reproof.

What the author says through his characters cannot 'legally' be quoted as his attitude; but, on the other hand, what he says as commentator must, almost equally, be regarded as not the view of his total self. As commentator, he may say what he thinks he believes or what is prudential. The blessed immunity and gift, thus, is to be able to give voice to all the voices in him, not, finally, attempting to suppress any of them—not, finally, feeling the need to pull himself together into the tight doctrinal consistency at which a theologian or philosopher must aim.

One cannot, in *The Scarlet Letter*, take 'proof-texts' out of their context or utterances away from their speakers. Hence, the 'moral' of the novel is not contained, as an eminent critic once asserted, in Hester's avowal to her "pastor" in the pagan Forest, that "What we did had a consecration of its own." Nor, since so many morals can be drawn from Dimmesdale's misery, are we to think that they can be summed up in the novelist's choice from among them, "Be true! Be true! Be true!" Because there are, in Hawthorne's phrase (doubtless half-ironic, half-satiric of Sunday School books and tracts), "many morals," the book has no 'moral.' At the least, half-true, and importantly true, is Henry James's conception that it was not as a 'moralist' that Hawthorne was drawn to his tales and novels of sin, that "What pleased him in such subjects was their picturesquesness, their rich duskiness of color, their chiaroscuro...."

Certainly, his literary fascination with sin was quite as much aesthetic and psychological as moral. As Henry, brother of William, so truly says of Hawthorne, "he cared for the deeper psychology." Such comparatives as "deeper" left suspended without what they are "deeper" than, I dislike; but I can't pretend, at least in this instance, not to know what is meant: deeper than analysis of manners, deeper than consciousness, deeper than normal normality—deeper also than 'univalent' judgments. Ambivalence and plurivalence are the "deeper psychology" open to the novelist even when, speaking in his own person, he too, casts a vote: I do not want to say a 'decisive vote,' since I doubt that, as commentator, his 'view' of his own work has any more authority than that of another critic: it may even have less.

<h1 style="text-align:center">III</h1>

Two of the characters in *The Scarlet Letter* certainly engaged Hawthorne in his 'deeper psychology,' and are richly developed.

About Hester, her creator had—as he did about his other brunettes, Zenobia and Miriam—ambivalent feelings. Twice, in *The Scarlet Letter*, he compares her to that seventeenth-century feminist Anne Hutchinson, whom, in *Grandfather's Chair*, his chronicle of New England history written for children, he calls, half or more than half ironically, "saintly"—that is, she who was regarded by many as saintly. 'Strong' women, whether sirens, seers, or reformers, were not, in his judgment, womanly.

For Hester, he provides some Catholic similitudes—the most striking in the description of her first appearance on the scaffold. "Had there been a Papist among the crowd of Puritans, he might have seen ... an object to remind him of Divine Maternity..." But it would have reminded him, indeed, "only by contrast, of that sacred image of sinless motherhood, whose infant was to redeem the world. Here ... the world was only the darker for this woman's beauty, and the more lost for the infant that she bore."

And, again: after seven years, Hester's life of charity gave her "scarlet letter the effect of the cross on a nun's breast." But Hawthorne draws back from taking the view which her life of self-abnegation might seem to entitle her to receive and him to take; for such a view would be based on Hester's Stoic pride and courage, not on her inner life of motive and thought. She has, to be sure, done penance, and done it with dignity—but she has done it with a *proud* dignity, for she is not penitent.

Her rich and luxuriant hair, though closely hidden by her cap, has not been cropped. Seven years after her act of adultery she still believes that what she and her lover did had "a consecration of its own." It is one of Hawthorne's shrewdest insights and axioms that "persons who speculate the most boldly often conform with the most perfect quietude to the external regulations of society. The thought suffices them...." And so Hester, outwardly penitent and charitable, allowed herself "a freedom of speculation which our forefathers, had they known of it, would have held to be a deadlier crime than that stigmatized by the scarlet letter." Some of these doubts and theorizings concerned the position of woman; and Hawthorne, antifeminist that he was, says of Hester that, her heart having lost its "regular and healthy throb," she "wandered without a clew in the dark labyrinth of mind...."

Hester has her femininities: her loyalty to her lover and to her child and the love of her craft ("Her Needle"). But her needle, like her mind, shows something awry. For Hawthorne bestows upon her—a kinswoman in this respect to Zenobia and Miriam—a "rich, voluptuous, Oriental characteristic." Despite her self-imposed penances of making "coarse garments for the poor"—gifts to those poor who often but revile and insult her, she allows her fancy and needleship free play in designing clothes for Pearl, her "elf-child."

Even more signally, she shows, in the badge of shame she herself wears—and that from her first appearance on the scaffold—a pride triumphing over her shame. It does not pass unnoticed by the women spectators at the scaffold: one remarks that the adulteress has made "a pride" out of what her judges meant for a punishment. And "at her needle," though clad in her gray robe of coarsest material, Hester still wears on her breast, "in the curiously embroidered letter, a specimen of her delicate and imaginative skill, of which the dames of a court might gladly have availed themselves...."

Appropriate as it is for the pious Bostonians to think Hester a witch, Hester has not signed with her own scarlet blood the Devil's book. Better, from an orthodox Puritan stance, that she had done so. But she has by-passed all that. She belongs in the Forest, where, in the one recorded conversation between the Pastor and his Parishioner, she meets Dimmesdale; she belongs in the Forest not because it is the Devil's opposing citadel to the Town but because she is pagan—as we might now say, because she is a 'naturalist.' To the Forest she belongs as does "the wild Indian." For years she "has looked from this estranged point of view at human institutions"—human, not merely Puritan—"criticizing all—with hardly more reverence than an Indian would feel for the clerical bands" (the prenineteenth century equivalent of the priest's collar), "the judicial robe, the pillory, the gallows, the fireside" (wedded, domestic, and familial bliss), "or the church."

"Like the wild Indian" (Hawthorne is in no danger of saying or thinking of the 'noble savage'), Hester has not judged men by their professional vestments or their status, nor institutions by virtue of their ideal rank in the hierarchy of some philosopher like Plato or Edmund Burke.

That her judgment was thus disillusioned was both good and bad: indeed, there are two seemingly contradictory truths both of which must be asserted and maintained. One is respect for persons in their representative capacities; for church, state, and university represent, with varying degrees of adequacy, the Ideas of holiness, civic virtue, and learning. The other is a dispassionately critical judgment which distinguishes between the personal and institutional representatives of the Ideas and the Ideas themselves. A third, doubtless, is the dispassionately critical judgment as to when particular persons and particular institutions so inadequately represent their respective Ideas as no longer to be sufferable—to require reform, expulsion, substitution; this is the Revolutionary judgment.

The difficulty of keeping these three truths—or even the first two of them—before one's mind in steady equipoise is as difficult as it is necessary. Hawthorne never attempted to formulate explicitly, even briefly, what I have just said; but such a conception seems clearly implicit in his characterization of Hester. Hester has been taught by shame, despair, and solitude; but, though they "had made her strong," that had "taught her much amiss."

Hester's exemplary conduct in the years which follow her first scene on the scaffold must be interpreted not as penitence but as stoicism, especially, a stoical disdain for the 'views' of society. She is bound to her Boston bondage partly by a kind of instinctive or romantic fatalism—not of the theological kind but fatalism of being bound to the place where she 'sinned' and to her lover. I put the word 'sinned' in quotes because Hester has not repented, not thinking that she has done anything of which she should repent. She still loves Dimmesdale, or at any event pities him, as weaker than herself; and, upon Dimmesdale's appeal to her, when (by her design and his accident) they meet in the Forest, that she advise him what to do, she is immediately purposeful and practical. Let him go into the forest among the Indians, or back to England, or to Europe. She is imperative: "Preach! Write! act! Do anything save to lie down and die!" Chillingworth's persecutions have made him too "feeble to will and to do"—will soon leave him "powerless even to repent! Up, and away!" And she arranges passage to England on a ship soon to leave Boston.

After Dimmesdale's death, Hester and Pearl disappear—Pearl, 'for good,' Hester, for many years. Yet Hester finally returns to Boston and to her gray cottage and her gray robe and her scarlet letter, for "Here had been her sin; her sorrow; and here was yet to be her penitence." The "yet to be," ambiguous in isolation, seems, in the rest of the penultimate paragraph, to mean that at the end of her life she did repent. In part, at least, this repentance was her renunciation of her earlier fanciful hope that she might be "the destined prophetess" of a new revelation, that of a sure ground for "mutual happiness" between man and woman. Here Hawthorne the myth-making creator and Hawthorne the Victorian commentator get entangled one with the other. Till the "Conclusion," the last few pages, Hester had remained, in ethics, a 'naturalist,' for whom 'sin,' in its Judaeo-Christian codification, had been a name or a convention. Now she is represented as comprehending that "no mission of divine and mysterious truth" can be entrusted to a woman "stained with sin, bowed down with shame, or even burdened with a life-long sorrow. The angel and apostle of the coming revelation must be a woman indeed, but lofty, pure, and beautiful, wise "through the ethereal medium of joy." Though this future "comprehension" is assigned to Hester, it is said in the voice of Hawthorne, the commentator, the husband of Sophia.

Whether applied to Hester specifically or to the mysterious new revelation to come—reminiscent of Anne Hutchinson, Mother Ann Lee, or Margaret Fuller, the pronouncement seems falsetto. Hawthorne's 'new revelation,' which seems (so far as I can understand it) not very new, is certainly not feminist but feminine and familial. Yet Hawthorne, I think, would allow Jesus His temptations and His sufferings: it is woman who is not permitted to be a *mater dolorosa*, whose nature is damaged, not illuminated and enriched, by sorrow.

Hester's voluntary return to the bleak cottage and the life of good works is intelligible enough without Hawthorne's 'revelation'—perhaps even without postulating her final penitence—which must mean her rejection of a naturalistic ethics, her acceptance of some kind of religious belief. Ghosts haunt the places where they died; college alumni return to the campuses where they spent, they nostalgically believe, the 'happiest years of their lives'; we all have 'unfinished business' which memory connects with the 'old home,' the town, the house, the room where we were miserable or joyful or, in some combination, both. There was a time, and there was a place, where, for whatever reason—perhaps just youth—we experienced, lived, belonged (if only by our *not belonging*).

Pearl, freed (like an enchanted princess) from her bondage, has married into some noble, or titled, European (not British) family and is now a mother; but Hester is not the grandmotherly type, nor to be fulfilled in the role of dowager, knowing, as she does, that—whatever the state of Continental ignorance or sophisticated indulgence—her pearls are paste, her jewels, tarnished. There can be no autumnal worldly happiness for her.

Without Christian faith, she must work out, work off, her Karma—achieve her release from selfhood.

IV

Hester's conceptions were altered by her experience; Dimmesdale's were not. Unlike her—and (in different and more professional fashion) the nineteenth-century agnostics Clough, Arnold, Leslie Stephen, and George Eliot—Dimmesdale was never seriously troubled by doubts concerning the dogmas of Christianity, as he understood them, and the ecclesiastical institution, the church, as he understood it. He was by temperament a "true priest": a man "with the reverential sentiment largely developed." Indeed, "In no state of society would he have been called a man of liberal views; it would always have been essential to his peace to feel the pressure of a faith about him, supporting, while it confined him within its iron framework."

Some aspects of Dimmesdale's rituals would seem to have been suggested by those of Cotton Mather, whom Barrett Wendell, in his discerning study, aptly called the "Puritan Priest." Though Mather's Diary was not published in full till 1911, striking extracts from it appeared as early as 1836 in W.B.C. Peabody's memoir, likely to have been read by Hawthorne. Dimmesdale's library was "rich with parchment-bound folios of the Fathers and the lore of the Rabbis and monkish erudition ..."; and Mather (possessor of the largest private library in New England) was, as Hawthorne could see from the *Magnalia*, deeply versed in the Fathers and the Rabbis. Those aptitudes were, among the Puritan clergy, singular only in degree. But the "fastings and vigils" of Dimmesdale were, so far as I know, paralleled only by Mather's.

To fasts and vigils Dimmesdale added flagellations, unneeded by the thrice-married Mather. Dimmesdale's sin, one of *passion* and not of *principle* or even of *purpose*—these three possible categories are Hawthorne's—had been an act committed with horrible pleasurable surprise, after which (since the sin had been of passion) the clergyman had "watched with morbid zeal and minuteness ... each breath of emotion, and his every thought."

It is by his capacity for passion—on the assumption that passionateness is a generic human category, and hence the man capable of one passion is capable of others—that Chillingworth first feels certain that he has detected Hester's lover. Having sketched a psychosomatic theory that bodily diseases may be "but a symptom of some ailment in the spiritual part," the "leech" declares that his patient is, of all men he has known, the one in whom body and spirit are the "closest conjoined"; Dimmesdale turns his eyes, "full and bright, and with a kind of fierceness," on the 'leech,' and then, with a "frantic gesture," rushes out of the room. Chillingworth comments on the betraying passion: "As with one passion, so with another! He hath done a wild thing erenow, this pious Master Dimmesdale, in the hot passion of his heart!"

If a common denominator between a burst of anger and a fit of lust is not immediately apparent, some sharedness there is: in both instances, reason and that persistence we call the self are made temporarily passive. A man's passions are—by contextual definition at least—*uncontrollable*; they 'get the better of' the habitual self. The man 'lets himself go'; is 'beside himself.' It is in this breakdown of habitual control that Chillingworth finds corroboration of what he suspected.

He finds more positive verification when he takes advantage of Dimmesdale's noonday nap to examine his "bosom," there finding, or thinking he finds, the *stigma* of the scarlet letter branded on the priestly flesh. In view of Hawthorne's emphasis—or, more strictly, Chillingworth's—on the close connection between soul and body in Dimmesdale, this *stigma* appears to be like (even though in reverse) the *stigmata* of Christ's wounds which some Catholic mystics are said to have manifested.

Hawthorne turns now to other aspects of Dimmesdale's 'case.' Consciousness of concealed sin may, like physical deformities, make one feel that everyone is watching him. And inability to give public confession to one's sin, the fact that (through cowardice or whatever) one cannot trust his secret to anyone, may make one equally suspicious of everyone—thus deranging one's proper reliance on some gradated series of trusts and confidences.

"Have a real reserve with almost everybody and have a seeming reserve with almost nobody; for it is very disagreeable to seem reserved, and very dangerous not to be so" is counsel bitter, but not unsage, of Lord Chesterfield. Dimmesdale has a real reserve with everyone and a seeming one, too, save when his passion briefly breaks down his habitual caution. But his cautious guard, his ever vigilant consciousness of what he conceals; has made him incapable of distinguishing between friend and foe, has broken down any confidence in what he might otherwise properly have relied upon, his intuitions. Dimly perceiving that some evil influence is in range of him, and feeling doubt, fear, sometimes horror and hatred at the sight of the old leech, he yet, knowing no rational reason for such feelings, distrusts the warnings of his deep antipathy.

Doubtless what most engaged Hawthorne's creative concern for Dimmesdale was the feature of ambivalence in his situation. Dimmesdale's sin and suffering had, in their way, educated the pastor and the preacher. Without his sin of passion and his sin of concealment, Dimmesdale would have been a man learned in books and theological abstractions but ignorant of 'life,' naive, unself-knowing. It was the self-education forced upon him by his sin which made him the pastor, the 'confessor,' the powerful preacher he is plausibly represented as becoming.

At the end of his seven years, Dimmesdale is a great—or as the American vulgate would have it, "an eminently successful"—pastor and preacher. By way of comparison, Hawthorne characterizes the categories into which his fellow-clergymen could be put—all types illustrated by Mather in the 'saints' lives' of the *Magnalia*. Some were greater scholars; some were "of a sturdier texture of mind than his, and endowed with a far greater share of shrewd, hard, iron, or granite understanding" (the preceding epithets show the noun to be used in the Coleridgean, or disparaging, sense); others, really saintly, lacked the Pentecostal gift of speaking "the heart's native language," of expressing "the highest truths through the medium of familiar words and images."

To the last of these categories Dimmesdale might, save for his "crime of anguish," have belonged. This burden kept him "on a level with the lowest," gave him his sympathy with the sinful—and his sad eloquence, sometimes terrifying, but oftenest persuasive and tender. These sermons made him loved and venerated; but their preacher knew well what made them powerful, and he was confronted with the old dilemma of means and ends.

In the pulpits Dimmesdale repeatedly intends to make a confession, and repeatedly he does; but it is a vague, a ritual confession—like that of the General Confession at Anglican Matins, except that the "miserable sinner" in whom there is no health is violently intensified by a consistently Calvinist doctrine of total depravity. No difference: Calvinist and Wesleyan and revivalist accusations against the total self can, with equal case, become ritual. Dimmesdale never confesses to adultery or any other specific sin—only to total depravity: "subtle, but remorseful hypocrite," he knows how the congregation will take his rhetorical self-flagellation: as but the greater evidence of his sanctity; for the more saintly a man, the more conscious he is of even the most venial sins.

So the clergyman was fixed in his plight. At home, in his study, he practiced not only his physical act of penance, his self-scourging; but he practiced also a "constant introspection" which tortured without purifying. To what profit this penance unpreceded by penitence, this torturing introspection which led to no resolution, no action?

As he later told Lowell, Hawthorne had thought of having Dimmesdale confess to a Catholic priest (presumably some wandering French Jesuit) as he did, indeed, have Hilda confess to a priest in St. Peter's, not her sin (for she was 'sinless') but her complicity by witness to a sin and a crime. Such an idea might have crossed the mind of a Protestant "priest" of

Dimmesdale's monkish erudition and practices. But, had he acted upon the impulse, and had the Jesuit been willing to hear the confession, there could have been no absolution, either sacramental or moral. Quite apart from having to change his religion, Dimmesdale would have had to do real penance, make real amends, and, had public confession been enjoined, not of his general sinfulness but of his specific sin, confess to the committing of adultery, and of that deeper, more spiritual, sin in which he had persisted for years, that of concealing the truth.

What has kept Dimmesdale from confession? Hester has herself been partly at fault, has made a serious error in judgment. At the beginning of the novel, Dimmesdale, her pastor, has, publicly in his professional capacity, enjoined her to speak. His injunction that she name her child's father reads ironically when one reverts to it after the chronicle of the "seven years" which ensue. "Be not silent from any mistaken pity and tenderness for him; for, believe me, Hester, though he were to step down from a high place, and stand there beside thee, on thy pedestal of shame, yet better were it so, than to hide a guilty heart through life. What can the silence do for him, except it tempt him—yea, compel him, as it were—to add hypocrisy to sin?.... Take heed how thou deniest to him—who, perchance, hath not the courage to grasp it for himself—the bitter, but wholesome, cup that is now presented to thy lips!"

Already Dimmesdale had, perhaps, begun to master the art he showed in his sermons—that of speaking the truth about himself to others (Hester excluded) in seeming to utter a salutary generalization. Arthur Dimmesdale is, "perchance," a coward, weak beside Hester, whose feeling toward him, never contemptuous, partakes certainly of the maternal. Would, she says, "that I might endure his agony as well as mine."

With all men, surely, the longer confession is delayed the more difficult it becomes. The procrastination is 'rationalized'—even though the 'rationalization' never really satisfies the 'rationalizer.'

Dimmesdale, as we see him seven years after, appears to offer his basic rationalization in his speech to Chillingworth—expressed (like his injunction to Hester in the third chapter) in generalized, in hypothetical, terms: there are guilty men who, "retaining, nevertheless, a zeal for God's glory and man's welfare, ... shrink from displaying themselves black and filthy in the view of men; because, thenceforward, no good can be achieved by them; no evil of the past be redeemed by better services."

There is some truth in what he says. And the Catholic Church, which consistently holds that the unworthiness of a priest does not invalidate the sacrament he administers, which conducts its confessionals not in the presence of a congregation, sees the degree of truth in Dimmesdale's position.

But, for all his Puritan priestliness, Dimmesdale is a Protestant; and the Catholic half-truth is not for him to appropriate. It is given to Chillingworth to utter the 'Protestant' truth. If men of secret sin "seek to glory God, let them not lift heavenward their unclean hands! If they would serve their fellow-men, let them do it by constraining them to penitential self-abasement!"

After her interview with her pastor on the midnight scaffold, Hester is shocked to reflect upon his state. "His nerve seemed absolutely destroyed. His moral force was abased into more than childish weakness." She reflects on her responsibility. Whether Hester's or Hawthorne's—two of her reflections appear to be intended as those of both, the commentator phrasing what Hester feels—the sentences read: "Here was the iron link of mutual crime, which neither he nor she could break. Like all other ties, it brought along with it its obligations." She must disclose to him Chillingworth's identity; must shield her lover.

So Hester assumes her maternal responsibility to her pastor and lover. In "The Pastor and his Parishioner" the titular roles are ironically reversed. The two meet in the "dim wood," "each a ghost, and awe-stricken at the other ghost." One chill hand touches another almost as chill; yet the grasp of the chill and the chill took away the penultimate chill of isolation which had separated them from all mankind. Their conversation "went onward, not boldly, but step by step...." They "needed something slight and casual to run before and throw open the doors of intercourse, so that their real thoughts might be led across the threshold."

Their first "real thoughts" to find expression are the mutual questions—"Hast thou found peace?" Neither has. Hester tries to reassure Dimmesdale by taking the line, the pragmatic line, which the pastor has already used, in rationalized self-defense, to Chillingworth. He is not comforted. "Of penance I have had enough. Of penitence there has been none!"

Hester sees him, whom she "still so passionately loves," as on the verge of madness. She sees her worse-than-error—originally disguised from her, as an impulse generous and protective—in not letting her lover know that his fellow lodger, physician, and torturer was her husband; she confesses it. Dimmesdale is at first violent against her for her long silence, violent with all that "violence of passion" which first gave Chillingworth the notion that the pastor had, despite his purity, inherited "a strong animal nature from his father or his mother." Then he relents: "I freely forgive you now. May God forgive us both!" But he goes on to extenuate this sin by comparison with Chillingworth's: "We are not, Hester, the worst sinners in the world. There is one worse than even the polluted priest! That old man's revenge has been blacker than my sin. He has violated in cold blood the sanctity of a human heart. Thou and I, Hester, never did so!"

Then follow the famous words of Hester. The lovers, like Dante's yet more illustrious couple, had acted in hot blood, not in cold. And—"What we did had a consecration of its own. We felt it so! We said so to each other! Hast thou forgotten it?"

Dimmesdale replies, "Hush, Hester!... No; I have not forgotten!" That Hester had said so is credible. It is difficult to credit the 'priest's' ever having used, even in the heat of romance, any such sacred word as "consecration," though Hester remembers the word as used by both; but Dimmesdale, though his "Hush" presumably implies that he in some way now thinks it wrong, does not contradict her recollection.

Then he appeals to Hester to rid him of Chillingworth and what Hester calls the "evil eye": "Think for me, Hester! Thou art strong. Resolve for me!" "Advise me what to do." And Hester accepts the responsibility. She fixes "her deep eyes" on her lover, "instinctively exercising a magnetic power" over his spirit, now "so shattered and subdued...."

Dismissing Dimmesdale's talk about the Judgment of God, Hester immediately—like a sensible nineteenth-century physician or practical nurse—recommends a change of scene, an escape from an oppressive situation, and begins to outline alternatives. At first she speaks as though her lover (or former lover—one does not know which to call him) might escape alone: into the Forest to become, like the Apostle Eliot, his recent host, a preacher to the Redmen; or across the sea—to England, Germany, France, or Italy. How, exactly, a Calvinist clergyman, is to earn his living in Catholic France and Italy is not clear; but Hester seems to have unbounded faith in her lover's intellectual abilities and personal power, once he has shrugged off New England; she seems to think of his creed—and even of his profession—as historical accidents. These Calvinists, these "iron men, and their opinions" seem to her emancipated mind to have kept Arthur's "better part in bondage too long already!" He is to change his name, and, once in Europe, become "a scholar and a sage among the wisest and the most renowned of the cultivated world." He is bidden, "Preach! Write! Act! Do anything save to lie down and die!"

In all this appeal, Hester seems to project her own energy into Dimmesdale and, what is more, seems to show little understanding of her lover's nature: could he, eight years ago, have been a man to whom changing your name, your creed, your profession could have been thus lightly considered? Can Dimmesdale ever have been a man of action in the more or less opportunist sense of which Hester sees him capable? If so, as an Oxford man (Hawthorne should have made him, as a Puritan, a Cantabrigian), he could have submitted to Archbishop Laud instead of coming to New England. What positive action do we know him to have committed in 'cold blood'? He committed a sin in hot blood once—it is tempting to say 'once,' and I have sometimes thought (unfairly perhaps) that Hester may have been the seducer. Otherwise his sins have been negative and passive—cowardice and hypocrisy.

False in its reading of his character and rashly oversanguine of programs as Hester's exhortation may be, Dimmesdale is temporarily aroused by her strength, by her belief that a man can forget his past, dismiss its 'mistakes' and 'debts,' and start again as though nothing had happened, as though he had neither memory nor conscience. For a moment indeed he believes he can start all over again, if only, invalid that he is, he has not to start alone. But Hester tells him that he will not go alone: her boldness speaks out "what he vaguely hinted at but dared not speak."

Hester and Arthur part, but not before she has made plans for passage on a vessel about to sail for Bristol. When the minister learns that it will probably be on the fourth day from the present, he notes but to himself, not to Hester, on the fortunate timing.

It is "fortunate" because three days hence Dimmesdale is to preach the Election Sermon, the highest civic honor a Bay Colony clergyman could receive. That Dimmesdale should still be pleased, should still look to this ending of his career as a dramatic close, that he should still think of his public duty more than of his private morality shocks Hawthorne as, of all Dimmesdale's doings and not-doings the most "pitably weak." What is it, finally, but professional vanity? "No man, for any considerable period can wear one face to himself, and another to the multitude, without finally getting bewildered as to which may be the true."

The minister walks home from the Forest "in a maze," confused, amazed. Hester's bold suggestions have temporarily released him from that iron framework which both confines and supports him. His habitual distinctions between right and wrong have broken down; and all that survives is his sense of decorum.

"At every step he was incited to do some strange, wild, wicked thing or other, with a sense that it would be at once involuntary and intentional; in spite of himself, yet growing out of a profounder self than that which opposed the impulse"—'profounder' in a sense Hawthorne does not define. It may be a man's subconscious or his "total depravity" left to himself—the Dark Forest in man, the Satanic.

All of his impulses are rebellions against his habitual mode of life and even, one would say, of thought and feeling. Meeting with one of his elderly deacons, he has the impulse to utter "certain blasphemous suggestions that rose in his mind respecting the communion supper." And, encountering the oldest woman of his church, pious and deaf and mostly concerned with recollecting her 'dear departed,' he can think of no comforting text from Scripture but only what then seemed to him an "unanswerable argument against the immortality of the soul" which, happily, she is too deaf to hear. To a pious young girl, he is tempted to give "a wicked look" and say one evil word, and averts the temptation only by rudeness; and to some children, just begun to talk, he wants to teach "some very wicked words." Lastly, meeting a drunken seaman from the ship upon which he plans to sail, he longs to share with the abandoned wretch the pleasure of "a few improper jests" and a volley of good round oaths; and it is not his virtue but his "natural good taste" and still more his "habit of clerical decorum" which dissuade him.

These temptations exhibit a Dimmesdale I should not have guessed to exist even in unvoiced capacity—and for which Hawthorne has given no preparation: indeed, we are never given any account of the pastor's English prehistory at all comparable to that which is furnished for Hester. "The Minister in a Maze" is, indeed, something of a brilliant sketch, a 'set piece'—something which occurred to Hawthorne as he was writing his novel, yet does not wholly fit it. Can the pastor once have been a young rake?

It is unlikely. To be sure, some of the Puritans, including the Puritan clergy, were converted not only from their ancestral Anglicanism but from worldliness if not anything more precisely sinful. And at Oxford and elsewhere Dimmesdale may have heard oaths and smutty stories, even though his principles and taste have forbidden him to use them. Likely Hawthorne meant us to see in this amazing scene a brief resurgence of that inherited "strong animal nature" which had for a lifetime, but for a lapse of act and another of feeling, been so rigorously repressed.

This brilliant chapter, if defended, will have to be defended on psychological considerations more general than specifically relevant to Hawthorne's clergyman. In the benign phenomenon called 'conversion'—the selves of a divided self reorder themselves: the self which was dominant is exorcised, or at any event decisively subordinated; the self which existed as subordinate—the 'good self'—becomes supreme, or nearly supreme. And there is a corresponding shift of positions which we may call perversion. Both of these changes with certain types of men, can occur—or show themselves—suddenly, in a moment. Some of these reorganizations persist; some are brief, impelled as they oftenest appear to be, by the 'magnetism' of an emotionally powerful propagandist—such an one as Hester.

In yielding to Hester's proposals of escape, Dimmesdale, says Hawthorne, had, in effect, made such a bargain with Satan as the witch-lady, Mistress Hibbins, suspected him of. "Tempted by a dream of happiness, he had yielded himself with deliberate choice, as he had never done before, to what he knew was deadly sin." This he now has done. Hester, out of one generous impulse, spared identifying Chillingworth to her lover and *concealed* her lover's name from Chillingworth, and now out of another 'generous' impulse she had bade her lover to escape his concealed sin not by revealing it but by abandoning his adopted country, his profession, even his name. And what have been the results of these 'generous' impulses—not wholly disinterested, perhaps, since she thinks of being reunited to her lover? What have been the results of these attempts modern Americans understand so well—attempts to help, by sparing, those we love, or think we love?

Dimmesdale returns to his study, conscious that his old self has gone. The man who returned from the Forest is wiser—wiser about himself, than the man who entered it. But—like Donatello's—what a "bitter kind of knowledge." He throws the already written pages of his sermon into the fire, and, after having eaten "ravenously," works all night on another.

What, the attentive reader speculates, is the difference between the unfinished sermon written before the Forest and the finished one of the night that followed? That difference, like the nature of the sermon delivered, seems curiously irrelevant to Hawthorne. We are told that the new discourse was written "with such an impulsive flow of thought and emotion" that its writer "fancied himself inspired." Which is the word to be stressed: *fancied* or *inspired?* We are told that he wrote with "earnest haste and ecstasy": which of the three words are we to stress? Had he something to say in the sermon which was the result of his intention (premeditated at some time before he delivered the sermon) or there after taking his stand beside Hester on the scaffold? Did the sermon have some new tone in it, some tragic or bitter wisdom wrested from that gross lapse into illusion which so bemused and amazed him as he returned from the Forest?

Melville once wrote a masterly and prophetic sermon for Father Mapple. Hawthorne writes none for Dimmesdale. During the delivery of the sermon, we readers, with Hester, are outside the meeting house. We but hear the preacher's voice, are told of its great range of pitch, power, and mood. Yet, says Hawthorne, if an auditor listened "intently, and for the purpose," he would always have heard throughout the "cry of pain," the cry of a human heart "telling its secret, whether of guilt or sorrow...." Yet in this respect, surely, the present sermon was not unique; for it had always been "this profound and continual undercurrent that gave the clergyman his most appropriate power."

When, after the sermon, we learn dimly from the admiring congregation its burden, we discover, strange to say, that it had ended with a prophetic strain. It had not been a Jeremiad—a denunciation of the Chosen people, but a foresight of New England's "high and glorious destiny." This is puzzling to interpret. That the preacher, about to declare himself an avowed sinner, cannot (like Cotton Mather) denounce his New England's sins, I can see; but why need he celebrate its high destiny? Is it that Hawthorne, to whom the 'subject matter' of the sermon does not seem to matter, has inserted and asserted, his own strong regional loyalties?

What ought to matter to the constructor of so closely constructed a novel seems not to have mattered to Hawthorne. What matters to him, and evokes his harsh rebuke, is that, seeing the error of escape, Dimmesdale has planned first to give the sermon, thus triumphantly ending his professional career, and then to make his public confession. The giving of the sermon as such, and the content of the sermon, do not really concern him—unless the giving of the sermon contributes the publicity and the drama of the scaffold confession requisite to counterpart the publicity and the drama of that first scaffold on which Hester stood—save for her baby on her arm—alone.

Implied is some final clash of wills and 'philosophies' between Hester and Arthur. Dimmesdale bids Pearl and Hester toward the scaffold. Pearl, birdlike, flies and puts her arms around his knees; but Hester comes slowly, "as if impelled by fate and against her strongest will," and pauses before she reaches him. Only when Chillingworth attempts to stop the pastor's public confession and the pastor again appeals does Hester come. But Dimmesdale has assumed the man's role at last—or a man's role: he asks Hester for her physical strength to help him onto the scaffold, but in asking her strength enjoins, "let it be guided by the will which God hath granted me." When they stand together, he murmurs to Hester, "Is not this better than what we dreamed of in the Forest?" Hester cannot assent. She palliates with "I know not"; then adds what seems to mean 'better, perhaps, if we two and little Pearl can die together.' But that, though human, is melodramatic. Hester must see that her lover is dying and that there is no way save a supernatural intervention—an 'act of God,' as insurance companies put it—which can kill her and the child concurrently with him.

After his confession to his parish and the revelation of his *stigma*, he says farewell to Hester. She speaks of their having "ransomed one another" by their consequent miseries, speaks of spending their "immortal life" together. He replies, as he did to her words in the Forest about the private "consecration" of their adulterous union. "Hush, Hester.... The law we broke!—the sin here so awfully revealed.—let these alone be in thy thoughts! I fear! I fear!" What he fears is not for his own salvation—assured, to his perception, apparently, by this, his deathbed repentance and confession—but for any reunion of the lovers after death.

V

It seems, to so close a reading as I have given to Dimmesdale, a pity that Hawthorne's "deeper psychology," and his own commentary, stop at this point. What is one to think of deathbed repentances, and of repentance so dramatic as this? And was not the repentance, if repentance there was and not yet another form of proud illusion, finally produced not by Chillingworth's malign sleuthing but by Hester's 'generous' and—in view of her lover's theology and character, if not indeed judged by any kind of absolute ethic— immoral advice that he escape from the consequences of his deed?

These are questions partly casuistical, partly universal, all of which one would expect to have interested Hawthorne. That they are not 'worked' out is partly, perhaps, Hawthorne's judgment that from earlier comments might be inferred the comments here relevant; partly, I think, a felt conflict between aesthetic and ethico-psychological considerations: aesthetically, he wants a firm, dramatic finale—something at all times difficult for him to manage, and here one which must be reconciled as best he can with his ethically psychological concerns, his probings and questionings.

Lastly, his 'conclusion' must give the modes of interpretation which the community apply to the phenomenon of the *stigma* which "most," though not all, of the spectators testified to having seen when the dying 'priest' bared his breast. In *The Scarlet Letter*, even more than in his later romances, Hawthorne sees life from inside the consciousness of a few persons—those of an introspective and meditative turn; but these persons, however insulated, are not solipsists: they believe, as Hawthorne believes, in a world they have not created by their own consciousness but merely interpreted.

The community forms, in terms of literary tradition, a Greek chorus, to the happenings in his protagonists' inner lives. Like the utterances in the choruses of Sophocles, it doesn't provide what a novice enamored of classical antiquity expects—the voice of true wisdom, the sure guide by which to interpret the too intense, and hence probably aberrative, views of the protagonists. When such a novice reads Arnold's famous praise of Sophocles that he "saw life steadily and saw it whole," the novice looks to the chorus to give that steady and whole interpretation. But the expectation is vain: the chorus partly comments, half empathetically, on what goes forward at the center of the stage, partly utters traditional maxims and apothegms.

In Hawthorne's choruses the same is true. In *The Scarlet Letter*, there are many auctorial comments on the community—comments frequently not limited to that seventeenth-century Puritan community in which Arthur and Hester lived. It is impossible to reduce them to any unitary and propositional form. Hawthorne is no Utopian, whether of the Brook Farm or any other variety; he is equally free from any extravagant individualism, even of the Emersonian variety: I say 'Emersonian' because Emerson himself was no such individualist as the half-gifted, half-eccentric people who appealed to his cars and sheltered themselves under his name.

Hawthorne's 'community'—or 'society'—is now kind, now persecuting; now foolish, now wise. Perhaps his most characteristic view of it is that, given time enough, 'the people' will show wisdom and do justice. *Given time enough*, it will forget initial suspicions and hostilities—do justice to the relatively heretic individualists—Edwards, Emerson, Thoreau, Garrison, Anne Hutchinson. What if it has not time?

The relation between individual truth (that of existential insight) and the community's slowly shifting 'wisdom' can never be either perfectly or permanently adjusted. Seneca wrote, "As often as I have been among men, I returned home less a man than I was before." But Aristotle opens his *Politics* with the maxim that "A man who can live alone must be either a god or a beast." *Society and Solitude* (the title of Emerson's last collection of essays) names two resorts, the two forces which must ever be 'checking' and 'balancing' each other.

Hawthorne's 'absolute truth' and 'ultimate reality' are not to be identified with any of their adumbrations. They are not imparted in their wholeness to Dimmesdale, or Hester, or to the chorus of the community, nor to Hawthorne as commentator on his own myth, nor to the author of this essay. We all know but in part, and prophesy but in part. Generalizations without case histories are commonplaces; case histories without the attempt at formulating 'first principles' are but (in the pejorative sense) casuistries.

This dialectical nature of truth-finding and truth-reporting Hawthorne was too honest to evade; it is to his literary as well as his 'philosophical' credit.

The Scarlet Letter

This essay has a history which I wish to give. Neither an American literature man, nor a Hawthorne specialist, I was early concerned with the history and literature of my own region, New England, and especially drawn to Hawthorne. When, in 1933, Harry Hayden Clark, editor of the projected 'American Writers Series,' invited me to prepare the Hawthorne volume (selections from the Tales, with Notes and Introduction), I responded eagerly and had my edition ready for publication the following year. And when Rinehart projected its series of paperbacks for college use, I wrote the introduction for their first issue, *The Scarlet Letter* (1947).

My but half-conscious intent in writing the present essay was to discuss Hawthorne's masterpiece as a novel rather than a 'romance' and to ignore the 'symbolism.' The symbolism and the chiaroscuro of multiple interpretations in which Hawthorne delighted are certainly more appropriate—and less fanciful and mannered—in *The Scarlet Letter* than elsewhere in his work, yet even here I could at least half wish them away; and I saw, or seemed to see, that the short, intense novel could well stand simply as a narrative concerned with the "deeper psychology" which James attributes to Hawthorne.

It was an engaging project to sit down to write on a minor masterpiece almost entirely on the basis of rereading, attentively and meditatively, the book itself. A scholar-critic, in his professional modesty, does not presume, like Lawrence, in his *Studies in Classic American Literature*, a preparation so pure, but, before and after reading on his own, corrects and multiplies his vision by the use of biographies and commentaries, the books about books and authors. My case this time was too special to generalize upon, for I had done the scholar's part of my 'homework' long enough ago so that it had receded to being what might be postulated as the right distance for 'background' to take; but it was an enjoyable and enviable experience.

Books about Hawthorne's books proceed apace; and, as Hawthorne is a literary man's novelist, critical insights continue to accumulate. The likely danger is that what was written on his work before the New Criticism and the New Scholarship shall be assumed to be superseded. But literary criticism (like theology and philosophy) is not a 'science' or even, primarily, a technology. It is a collaboration between types of readers and generations of readers; the total meaning of the literary work of art emerges from this collaboration; it accrues.

Accordingly, the older studies of Hawthorne should not be neglected—especially, I think, those written by other writers: I think immediately of Henry James's *Hawthorne* in the 'English Men of Letters' series (1879) and of the very fine early essay on Hawthorne and James by T. S. Eliot (first published as "Henry James: The Hawthorne Aspect" in 1918 and reprinted in Edmund Wilson's valuable anthology *The Shock of Recognition*). Of older essays on Hawthorne I would also especially mention Leslie Stephen's (in *Hours in a Library*, First series, 1874), Paul Elmer More's two (reprinted in Daniel Aaron's *More's Shelburne Essays on American Literature*, 1963), and W. C. Brownell's critically severe chapter in *American Prose Masters* (1909), a neglected but distinguished book. A convenient repertory of selected earlier criticism will be found in Bernard Cohen's *The Recognition of Nathaniel Hawthorne* ... (1969).

WALTER SHEAR

Characterization in The Scarlet Letter

The more we reread our classic books and discuss them in the classroom, the more we become aware of that complex interrelationship between past and present which acts to illuminate our literary experience. Our primary instinct is to explore what we feel is the importance of the work. And too often we catch ourselves hastening through (dismissing?) its conventions solely as historical fact on our way to a vital encounter with the characters as people and with the drama as a legitimate claim on our emotions. But even more frequently after filing these historical or other apparently irrelevant kinds of focus in that corner of our minds reserved for test materials and lectures, we inevitably begin to structure—for they must be ordered in some way—the significance of the literary experience in categories which even we may sense to be restrictive or confining. Our besetting errors in literary interpretation thus arise from a concern with significance that is both understandable and proper and it leads us to put an emphasis where it does not belong, to distort relationships among elements, and to work back beyond form instead of working through it.

The problem is then that literary history doesn't often seem to take us in the direction we want to go. Not many people simply want to walk into an era where the conventions are iron-clad, dead, forgotten, even obscurely vague; and those whose lives were tied mysteriously to these forms have

From *The Midwest Quarterly* 12, no. 4 (July 1971). © 1971 by *The Midwest Quarterly*.

disappeared or have been fortunately altered. The old art objects only seem to quicken in proportion to our sense of their link with us, a sense of the universal or something continuing, unresolved. Thus the past changes with us as we change, and yet it continues to cling to itself; as Robert Frost says, "there's something the dead are keeping back."

So we search for more valuable contexts (in terms of both history and relevance) for the old works in order to shield ourselves from the kind of familiarity that breeds contempt and boredom, and to describe more accurately what they seem to mean at the present moment. In doing so we see romanticism in our realists, realism in those writers we had classified as romantic. *The Scarlet Letter* is a case in point. In his book on Hawthorne, Hyatt Waggoner has claimed, "The usual contrast between 'realistic' and 'romantic' fiction, in which Hawthorne is assigned a place at the far end of the romantic side of the spectrum, is less useful for an attempt to understand Hawthorne's fiction than has been supposed." In a recent article ("'Character,' 'Nature,' and 'Allegory' in *The Scarlet Letter*," *Nineteenth-Century Fiction*, XXIII, (1968), 3–18) Seymour Katz demonstrates how Hawthorne's conception of character is one source of the novel's fascination for later eras by exploring "the underlying realism of the characters and action." Katz examines in some detail the interaction between character and society, pointing out how Hawthorne sees human nature as something related to its circumstances. In doing so Katz does a good deal toward taming the more recalcitrant—because unbelievable—romantic elements, which one suspects most readers had simply borne as the unavoidable conventions of the period, some of the curses of literary history. Though his intention to provide a useful corrective to allegorical readings of the characters succeeds admirably, his case seems so strong as to nearly persuade us that the character problems make their most effective appeal in a basically realistic context. And to see the characterizations strictly confined to this perspective is to do the characters and the novel—and probably Katz also—an injustice.

I believe (without, I hope, being unnecessarily obvious) that the broader implications of the characterizations in *The Scarlet Letter* can be best understood not merely in relationship to the extremely romantic but to the more popular literature of Hawthorne's day. I would like to suggest that one vital reason for the contemporary interest in the book—the continuing tendency to read, teach, write about it, be concerned with it—is precisely its romantic difficulties—more specifically, the way in which Hawthorne uses sentimental and melodramatic characterizations to sketch out and speculate upon those perverse and universal mysteries in human behavior which are manifested whenever man's humanity seems dependent on his emotional nature and thereby to call into question some of the basic sentimental assumptions about human nature and the way the universe works. More subtly but with the same impulse as the characters in sentimental fiction, Hawthorne's people suffer from an acute consciousness of their moral roles. Because of its intentionally close rhetorical relationship to its reader, the sentimental book features characters speaking beyond their ostensible auditors to their real audience, just as all the correspondents in an epistolary novel really address their letters to the reader, persistently wishing to be overheard, as it were. Being consistently in the process of relating to the audience, the characters' remarks tend toward the poles of justification and confession. (This movement is not uncommon in much pre-realistic fiction, but it lies at the heart of the sentimental novel.) Not surprisingly, therefore, in *The Scarlet Letter* it is in the characterizations closest to the sentimental movement that the conflict between self-preservation and self-expression is projected and weighed for its moral definition, that the drives to reveal and conceal the great personal secrets of ultimate moral identity are danced most earnestly. This conflict is, of course, an obvious forerunner to later Freudian theories and in this respect a prime example of a somewhat unusual but particularly modern link.

Otis B. Wheeler, in "Hawthorne and the Fiction of Sensibility" (Nineteenth-Century Fiction, XIX (1964), 159–70), has outlined with a few examples the relationship of popular sensibility ideas and conventions to Hawthorne's fiction in general, indicating that Hawthorne's use of conventions is, consciously or unconsciously, quite selective and varies considerably in different periods. I am convinced that Hawthorne was well aware of his relationship to the sentimental tradition. It was all around him in the periodicals he had written for and we have his statement on the band of "scribbling women" who he felt were his competitors. The letters to Ticknor in which he mentions *The Lamplighter* and *Ruth Hall* indicate a critical familiarity with these kinds of books and point toward a peculiarly hearty ferocity in his reaction to them. In *The Scarlet Letter* Hawthorne pushes sentimental conventions very deliberately to their ultimate extremes in order to question the basis of the sentimental assumptions, stopping short, however, of a mere mockery of their capacity for hope.

In a purely mechanical sense *The Scarlet Letter* shares with three representative sentimental novels—*Power of Sympathy*, *The Coquette*, and *Charlotte Temple*—a plot which draws its dramatic rhythm from a universe-shattering act of seduction (In *SL*, of course, the plot trots after the fact) and all these novels use some variation of the triangle relationship. Apparently some contemporary readers took such signals as clear indications of the kind of book Hawthorne was writing: one review of *Twice-Told Tales* mentions readers "who were charmed by his picture of the sorrows and sufferings of

Hester Prynne and Arthur Dimmesdale." Presumably there were others who saw or sensed that Hawthorne was defining a relationship to this tradition, whether or not they sensed his skepticism. But Hawthorne's use of the conventions should have indicated his obvious questioning of this tradition. The sentimental novel went out of its way to try to involve readers emotionally in the sufferings of its characters and after the emotional binges of its treatments provided its own kind of relief by directing characters' and readers' attention to another world of healing, where the sufferings of this world might be soothed for eternity. In a chapter entitled "Stepping Heavenward" in *The Sentimental Novel in America* Herbert Ross Brown claims, "A glimpse of glory was denied to few of the souls whose deaths were related in [sentimental] religious fiction." In this context we must see Hester's request to the dying Dimmesdale to "tell me what thou seest" as a deliberate use of convention in order to somberly question a sentimental certainty without ridiculing its hope. Though Dimmesdale's reply does mention God's mercy, he explains, "He [God] hath proved his mercy, most of all, in my afflictions. By giving me this burning torture to bear upon my breast!" and he intones, "The law we broke!—the sin here so awfully revealed!—let these alone be in thy thoughts!" Contrast this with Eliza Wharton's (*The Coquette*) thoughts on God's response to her as sinner: "Trusting in the mercy of God, through the mediation of his son; I think I could meet my heavenly father with more composure and confidence, than my earthly parent!"

Hawthorne seems to follow many of the sentimental conventions so closely it is not always easy to distinguish his own particular treatment. The motif of the beneficent influence of the little child, for example, becomes in Hawthorne's book so strongly thematic as to seem almost an undramatized idea: he seems almost to assume that the presence of Pearl will save Hester from the spiritual sterility of isolation without bothering to show this being done. This seems quite in the sentimental tradition, as does his conception of Pearl as a pre-sentimental being who is only made completely human when she begins to shed tears. The latter point, however, exactly defines his quarrel with this tradition: Pearl is not simply an object to gush about and be deeply touched by, she is for almost the whole book the young animal-spirit whose wildness and unnatural emotional richness puts her closer to paganism than to Christianity. The sentimentalists see the spiritual value of children, but read too much of the effect into the cause and thus do not see that children are not fully human. In some cases Hawthorne seems to use sentimental conventions to create his own ironic effects. The characterization of Dimmesdale, for instance, is in one sense an astounding deployment of what Walter Wright in his *Sensibility in English Prose Fiction*,

1760–1814 calls "feelings ... too tender to be suffered by the world." Since such an idea forms the basis for Dimmesdale's hypocrisy (he is in one sense a sentimentalist about his own feelings), he would seem to be a prime candidate for satiric treatment (and he does get a bit of this). But Hawthorne was evidently sensitive enough to his own feelings in this matter to see that this is where he had to take the sentimentalists seriously. The result is a surprising combination of judgment and sympathy in his treatment of the character. Finally, Hawthorne's use of such conventions gives rise to the strange flavor of skepticism one finds in this book—strange because in many respects it is quite religiously orthodox. The best example is the use of apparent coincidence in the night scene where Dimmesdale is going through the motions of revealing his guilt; the A which suddenly appears in the sky could refer to Dimmesdale (the adulterer) or to the dead Winthrop, could be a sign of hope or despair. Instead of confirming a virtually inevitable moral order as sentimental fiction tends to do, the coincidence here raises questions about the human ability to apprehend that order, questions which are not only central in the liteary technique of the book but which strike at the core of the sentimentalists' easy theology.

But to examine the characterization more closely. Almost every critic of the fiction seems to assume, allegory or no, that Hawthorne does work with character types, often recurrent types. The question then remains whether it is in fact these outmoded types from an unsatisfactory tradition that can, or do, involve us in this novel. Certainly Chillingworth—as a prime illustration of an unsuccessful type—would seem to be the natural argument for the contrary view. Though Katz is able in his essay to present a case for a change in Chillingworth's character and Hawthorne himself states that he was "a striking evidence of man's faculty of *transforming* [my italics] himself into a devil," most readers will smell him out as a villain from his first appearance: "A writhing horror twisted itself across his features, like a snake gliding swiftly over them, and making one little pause, with all its wreathed intervolutions in open sight. His face darkened with some powerful emotion...." Add to this his physical deformity and, for those who have read elsewhere in Hawthorne, his overdeveloped intellect—the conclusions can only be that this is one of those men who will eventually do evil. The sinister foreboding is an almost constant intrusion. Even though in the interview scene Chillingworth seems surprisingly understanding in his attitude toward Hester, the "smile of dark and self-relying intelligence," Hester's association of him and "the Black Man," and his own promise of vengeance are all the sort of hints that produce certainty in the reader's mind. We are even told that at one time a former citizen of London claims to have seen him in the company of "Doctor Forman, who was implicated in the affair of Overbury" thirty years ago. The latter statement, of course, suggests that Chillingworth has been a villain or on the verge of being one all his life.

As a villain, Chillingworth acts with appropriate cunning—burning only coolly with an intense flame—and exerts an incredible control over people and events by doing and saying very little. He will not allow the situation to lapse back into an inert moral stagnation but will have a narrative, quest plot and moral example. Hester, who seems to be so isolated at one time as to form a narrative of her own, is, through the pressure of Chillingworth on Dimmesdale, abruptly brought back, involved with the other major characters. It is Chillingworth who forces the former lovers to confront not only each other, but themselves. And it is Chillingworth who prods Dimmesdale along the anxious road to public confession.

This sort of instigation, all conducted for the most sacred cause of ferreting out moral truth, shows us the villain as a potential counter-author. In his role as a counter-orderer, of course, the villain very frequently serves this purely esthetic function. In the context of *The Scarlet Letter*, however, Chillingworth seems to offer—villain though he be—the only morally acceptable order, the only solution to a romantically clouded, indecisive vision. On the one hand, this raises the question of agency and the problem of good coming out of evil (obviously one of Hawthorne's favorite kind of mysteries). But it also presents the temptation to confine his villainy to his motives and give an unquestioned, almost inevitable approval to his version of the way this world ought to be. The characterization that emerges out of this situation—his image of himself as a man who must disguise himself, wait for more favorable circumstances (or more evidence) to expose the hypocrite (the secret sinner)—would undoubtedly argue the justice of his justice were it not buried by rhetorical counter-signs. In a very general sense he is the immoral agent of morality much as a sentimental villain might be (though more directly), but Hawthorne's uneasy detachment makes his immorality consistent with playing the moral rhetorician, eager not so much for denouement as to hear the sounds of men suffering for their sins. Like the sentimentalists, his morality has sprung loose from the theological rock of Puritanism and, like theirs, his moral pleasure moves steadily toward sadistic enjoyment.

Most readers seem to find Hester Prynne the truly fascinating character in the book, probably because the ambiguity involved in placing her leads to basic issues, not merely for the novel, but for romanticism as well. Undoubtedly there are different ways of regarding her—sinner, ideal woman, feminist, a character who dares to trust herself, tragic protagonist, etc.—but one of the most profitable views seems to me to be as the product of a weird doubling of the characterization. She is, more clearly than

Chillingworth, really two character types; in her case, however, the types are not only more nearly equal in literary emphasis, but at virtually opposite poles. In other words I think we (Hawthorne too?) respond to her differently by seeing her in different kinds of relationships.

The first scenes of the book obviously have the sort of dramatic effect Malcolm Cowley speaks of as a basic structural method in the work, one which through the implication of the individual-society opposition casts Hester as, potentially at least, the romantic rebel. The comments by the members of this society show how harshly, for the most part, they see her and it is this harshness we respond to. Most of the early description—"Her attire ... seemed to express the desperate recklessness of her mood, by its wild and picturesque peculiarity" (53)—strikes a rebellious note, and the not surrendering the name of her lover has the admirable quality of a refusal to knuckle under to the pressures of a society that we have already seen is less than perfect. Though Hawthorne also tells us in this scene "that the world was only the darker for this woman's beauty, and the more lost for the infant she had borne" (56), the rebel in her continues to reappear in the characterization throughout the book, probably reaching its height in her declaration in the forest scene, "What we did had a consecration of its own" (195).

In this role Hester seems inevitably destined to take part in sensational actions later on, since the defiance she displays at the beginning could at any time be converted into overt action which would set off the explosive emotions that her very presence evokes. Instead of presenting these dramatic fireworks, however, Hawthorne shifts his focus to the path of the penitential journey, and we have Hester as the lost soul seeking repentance. The narrative in this section would lead us to believe that some stage of forgiveness, with many tears, is the eventual destination. Outwardly, her mode of life, her humble station and service, her treatment (and Pearl's) by the community, her whole situation seems to fit in this mold. However, the hints (and sometimes definite indications) of the presence of the other, earlier Hester function as a pervading question as to how much of this is mere appearance. And if this is appearance, why is it taken to such lengths? Why such an ill-proportioned tracking of actions which are fraudulent? Why does not the author, certainly not hesitant in these matters, call our attention to the hypocrisy or self-deception? Or are we to conceive of Hester as a character with strong, passionate rebellious impulses which the Puritan society, for the most part, succeeds in subduing? If she cannot be measured by an absolute moral scale, couldn't we at least see her at the end of the novel looking back on the events with an idea or two about her own role in what one recent critic has called a tragedy?

I would argue that not only are there two characterizations at work here, they are never organically, logically, or esthetically related. The clearest relationship seems to be a rather abstract parallel on the thematic level: the rebel illustrating the results of isolation upon the intellect, the penitent the results of isolation upon the heart (and this may well be a too mechanical division, not really supported by the dramatic events). The rhetorical lines of the characterization, which function much like the modern use of multiple points of view, intersect but never join. There is in effect a blank, a void in the middle of the character, and being outside society, she has not the floor of a solid substructure of manners to contain her at a level of moral indifference. Thus while the wholeness we sense in the characterization, largely a matter of statements that seem indicative of the ambivalence in Hawthorne's attitudes, might be seen as the intersection of descriptions, more often it presents itself as a series of movements in opposite directions.

One gets a hint that the source of this peculiar kind of doubleness lies in the moral ambiguity of the early view of Hester: sinner or victim.

> Had there been a Papist among the crowd of Puritans, he might have seen in this beautiful woman, so picturesque in her attire and mien, and with the infant at her bosom, an object to remind him of the image of Divine Maternity, which so many illustrious painters have vied with one another to represent; something which should remind him, indeed, but only by contrast, of that sacred image of sinless motherhood, whose infant was to redeem the world. Here, there was the taint of deepest sin in the most sacred quality of human life, working such effect, that the world was only the darker for this woman's beauty, and the more lost for the infant she had borne. (56)

While one can argue that the more positive elements in the first half of the paragraph are merely an ironic preparation for the overwhelming condemnation in the last statement, the strange extension of its development, the almost inserted quality of "but only by contrast" effectively serve to twist the juxtaposition into an archetypal echo. Further, the final statement, the most definite of the paragraph, is completely belied by what happens in the rest of the novel.

The chapter "Another View of Hester" displays the same sort of split. The first half tells us of the transforming power of love and "the blameless purity of her life during all these years," climaxing in a new interpretation of the scarlet letter: Able. The second half questions her womanhood and tells us that the "world's law was no law for her mind," that "the scarlet letter had not done its office." By the end of the chapter she is weighed against her earlier state and found to have "climbed her way, since then, to a higher point." However, this is followed by a comparison with Chillingworth and we are told that they are nearly on the same level. The bridge between the two Hesters in this chapter also grows, appropriately, out of the dialectical complexity of the "letter" (of the sin):

> Meeting them in the street, she never raised her head to receive their greeting. If they were resolute to accost her, she laid her finger on the scarlet letter, and passed on. This might be pride, but was so like humility, that it produced all the softening influence of the latter quality on the public mind. (162)

It is the distance between the alternatives of "pride" and "humility" that not only measures the gap between two views of Hester, but also illustrates the distracting moral ambiguity invested in the simplest actions of the novel. Hester's serving contains similarly opposed possibilities:

> It is probable that there was an idea of penance in this mode of occupation, and that she offered up a real sacrifice of enjoyment, in devoting so many hours to such rude handiwork. She had in her nature a rich, voluptuous Oriental characteristic—a taste for the gorgeously beautiful, which, save in the exquisite productions of her needle, found nothing else, in all the possibilities of her life, to exercise itself upon. (83)

At the end of the novel the penitent in Hester eclipses the rebel rather thoroughly—and yet even here Hawthorne has Hester prophesying, which disclaiming the mantle of the prophetess. She senses a new relationship between man and woman, a vision which perhaps might have been more detailed to a purer soul (on the level of inner structure, one might say this makes the claim that Hester in the role of rebel is not so unfeminine as she may have seemed).

What Hawthorne has done is to present a combination of romantic and sentimental attitudes toward such a woman; either explanation could be "true" and the ambiguity may well be due to Hawthorne's speculative technique rather than to a failed fusion of views.

Oddly enough the two characterizations of Hester cause little blurring of her image as a single individual—rather there seems to be an almost continuous sense of two possibilities, either one of which could be a definite answer to the questions of what effect this kind of harsh, overt, unrelenting punishment might have on an individual and of what such an effect might indicate about the nature of the individual. It may also be a sign that she, not being an absolutist, is able to exhibit contradictory beliefs when exposed to the light and shadow of romantic love.

The questions connected with Dimmesdale's character are basic ones for the novel, dealing as they do with the problem of suffering, the kinds of suffering concomitant with sin, and the mixed blessing of a sensitive soul. Dimmesdale is at once pathetic victim and cunning hypocrite, seducer and seduced. Though identified as the other man rather early in the novel, he is, as Wheeler has pointed out, in effect violated by Chillingworth in a spiritual sense. What plot line exists in the book traces, for the most part, the attempts to conceal the terrible, vital secret, with all the psychological desperation such suspense unveils. What becomes very evident (sinful secret) to the reader and to Chillingworth—and by the conclusion, to any one who can stand to face the fact—is covered with such egotistical concern that one is convinced that the final revelation is both at last a natural act and a necessary one.

Dimmesdale's confession, of course, works itself out of the dialectic of his split being rather than any split in characterization: He wants to tell and he doesn't want to tell. But the cunning and to-be-despised hypocrite works so automatically in Dimmesdale's social role that Hawthorne seems at times to be juggling two villains, embodiments, as it were, of individual and corporate human weakness. We are told, for example, of the impulse to confess to his congregation:

> More than once, Mr. Dimmesdale had gone into the pulpit with a purpose never to come down its steps, until he should have spoken words like the above.

But then:

> He had told his hearers that he was altogether vile, a viler companion of the vilest, the worst of sinners ... They heard it all, and did but reverence him the more ... The minister well knew—subtle, but remorseful hypocrite that he was!—the light in which his vague confession would be viewed. (143, 144)

While a good many would cite this early chapter of the difficulty of telling the truth in America as an indication that his hypocrisy was merely a matter of weak character, I have heard several contemporary readers—impatient with weakness in any form—argue that this makes him doubly damned: If Dimmesdale suffers internally, it is his own fault. If he were moral at all, he would confess and take his punishment with Hester. And to some extent this kind of argument would seem supported by Hawthorne's conclusion. It would appear that Dimmesdale must confront society; he must purge himself of his hypocritical self, his most dangerous enemy.

The conversations between Chillingworth and Dimmesdale on the efficacy of confession present a more complicated version of resistance to public unburdening of the soul. Here Dimmesdale's fear of exposure shines flittingly through the idealist he would still be: "There can be, if I forbode a right, no power, short of the Divine mercy, to disclose, whether by uttered words, or by type of emblem, the secrets that may be buried with a human heart" (131). (And the more bare-faced rationalizations—"... they shrink from displaying themselves black and filthy in the view of men; because, thenceforward, no good can be achieved by them; no evil of the past be redeemed by better service" (132)—serve to convince us of the human weakness in the potential villain.) Not a vain plea, but its own crooked truth; Dimmesdale's kind of hypocrisy cannot be exposed from the outside without sacrificing the sanctity of the individual it so exasively belies.

Once Dimmesdale's problem takes these dimensions for a reader the confession becomes a way of obviating, not recognizing society. The status of social truth, as illustrated in the conflicting reactions to the mark on Dimmesdale's chest, is as problematic as it seemed definite at the beginning. The tone of this detachment grows so strong in the book that one could say its hidden motto is: society is hard to be overcome, but it must be overcome.

Though the novel uses the sentimental tradition in a sporadic and generally harsh manner, one could not simply characterize it as anti-sentimental. For in spite of the sharp strokes of its skepticism, it does reflect a concern with an idealism which has some kinship with sentimentalism. Its prayerful hope for the individual's power to alter fundamental directions, build his own identity, and square his conscience with his actions is both a stubborn and insistent effort to preserve that rapidly fading moral scaffold against the steady eraser of social opinion. At this point Hawthorne himself can become sentimental about the fate of individual morality (without, of course, failing to point out the dangers in the moral process with the characterizations, especially those of Chillingworth and Dimmesdale).

In Katz's view of the novel, the "realistic characters and action" establish one level of meaning, a dimension which is supplemented by Hawthorne's use of an unreliable narrator to suggest "the possibility of a supernatural moral order realizing its aims on earth in and through the natural means of the natures and characters of men." For many, however, these dimensions function mainly to cast doubt on each other. What one senses in the combination of the romantic and sentimental elements in the characterizations is rather the study of organic growth, the festering possibilities for character movement. Growing evenly out of the encounter with evil, the stems of the ego and its impulse toward the selfless twist separately about the pole of good and evil. So fascinating are the labyrinthian patterns formed that one can almost admire their search for a true light to replace the artificial light of society.

It is undoubtedly true that despite the physical presence of a strong woman and a fiendish and a weak man, Hawthorne's book seems to have only a remote relationship to the more radiantly sentimental—and especially to books by those whom Herbert Ross Brown characterizes as "sentimental novelists who proclaimed the excellence of human nature and gloried in the perfectability of man." But if Hawthorne's twisted forms of human nature gain anything from their piety, it is the impetus to pass through the temptations of self-righteousness and respectability to that state where the self might in the proper light confront and hopefully respect itself.

Like many sentimental characters, Hawthorne's characters aspire to feelings of justification (even the villain looks for reasons for his behavior). The narration, however (seemingly more perverse than unreliable), is always postponing final judgment—thus only outlining a sentimental moral drama (whose characters in this case are social beings as well as emotive types) on a stage as deep as eternity. Eschewing the make-believe drama of the sentimental and the outrageous spiritual righteousness it vaunted, *The Scarlet Letter* also obstinately refuses to be as anti-Puritanical in its treatment of the characters as it potentially could be. Such restrain is at the center of its art. For the book to succeed as novel, the characters must step as emotive individuals out of history without denying it.

In keeping the sentimental conventions under sharp psychological surveillance and typing the sentimental impulse so rigidly to this earth and a single social environment, Hawthorne achieves—perhaps unintentionally— a stranger artistic effect, a kind of supernatural ambiguity arising out man's misapprehension about the closeness of his mind to a Divine mind, his heart to a heart Divine. While the sources for the value the characters place on themselves exist outside the self, Hawthorne through the use of sentimental types shows that the self discovers its value in the value it sees in others. Since Richardson and Sterne, the sentimental tradition, through the use of tears for another's plight and negatively through the willful callousness of seduction, implied that such sympathies would be essential characteristics for citizens in the new Christian democracy. Presumably the fineness of such feelings reflected the concern of the Creator for all His children and, more practically, would act through a nice consideration to hold in check the base elements of the self—desire, pride, will, etc. In *The Scarlet Letter*, however, one senses that such self-sacrifice is not enough, that this may even be an inadequate basis for Christian love—that betrayal is the permanent temptation to be faced, since it is not merely an aristocratic sin (putting oneself above common humanity) but the surest way for the self to become lost in society. Hawthorne demonstrates that once society is introduced— and history gives him not only an example, but *the* example—the touchstone of sensibility too often finds its issues already defined: one is for or against the social rule. Whatever sentiments cannot be reduced to these alternatives may well, by their isolation, give rise to speculations about a moral vacuum. In such a context the impulse toward a moral absolute, especially toward a final moral realm (beyond social dictims) that has some affinity with individual feeling, would find itself on the same course as the impulse toward moral nihilism. Such is the unhappy drama of *The Scarlet Letter*.

BIBLIOGRAPHICAL NOTE

Page references in parentheses are to the Ohio State University Press Centenary edition of *The Scarlet Letter*. The nineteenth century review cited appeared anonymously in *The Carpet Bag*, I, no. 1 (March 29, 1851), p. 6.

PRESTON M. BROWNING, JR.

Hester Prynne as Secular Saint

W hile the centrality of *The Scarlet Letter* as a literary fact of our national history is a matter beyond dispute, its significance for our *religious* history has not received, I feel, the attention which it deserves. Of course, every reader of Hawthorne's tale knows that in one sense or another his subject is Puritanism, and while critics may disagree as to the precise nature of Hawthorne's relation to his Puritan heritage, no one today seriously challenges its importance to him. The significance that I have in mind refers, however, not so much to Puritanism itself—an image of Hawthorne's past— as to an alternative to Puritanism (Hawthorne's "projection" into the future) which the novel adumbrates. It is the remarkable contemporaneity of this alternative that is its most striking feature. Lionel Trilling, in an essay entitled "Our Hawthorne," attempts to establish, on grounds different from my own, a case for Hawthorne's contemporary relevance; yet he severely qualifies toward the end of his essay all that he has previously claimed. My intention, on the contrary, is to propose unequivocally that Hawthorne, at least in this one novel and especially in one of its characters, is "Our Hawthorne" indeed.

Briefly, my thesis is this: that in the figures of Hester Prynne and Arthur Dimmesdale, Hawthorne portrays two radically different ways of interpreting human existence, two divergent modes of response to life and

From *The Midwest Quarterly* 13, no. 4 (July 1972). © 1972 by *The Midwest Quarterly*.

perhaps even two distinct understandings of Christian faith. Further it is my conviction that while a number of modern readers may react to the Puritan Dimmesdale with an appreciation born of a lively historical sensibility, it is Hester, the apparent skeptic, who is likely to evoke our profoundest existentialist response. By this I in no way mean to imply that Dimmesdale is not a deeply moving literary creation. He is. His plight is tragic, his struggles are humanly credible, and his final triumph is in some sense heroic. Yet, with all this granted, it still appears that it is not Dimmesdale but Hester who touches most compellingly the jagged nerve ends of our deeper psychic life, suggesting in her lonely, alienated existence something of the quality of our own twentieth-century sense of cosmic homelessness and insecurity. More than this is involved, however, for Hester's response to her experience approximates our own more nearly than does Dimmesdale's; her "answer" is strangely like our own, or, if not our own, like that of the literary heroes who command our keenest respect and affection.

Although the concept of salvation may, on first sight, appear somewhat inappropriate for a discussion of Hester Prynne, I would suggest that one of the qualities which makes Hester so central a figure in American literature is the modernity of her vision of redemption. And her vision of redemption, in turn, consists of certain attitudes and "beliefs" which correspond quite closely to the life style and view of reality which today is frequently given the designation "secular sainthood."

That there is something saint-like about Hester Prynne most of her Puritan contemporaries are eventually forced to admit. And Hawthorne, through the reiteration of such words as "halo," "sacred," and "martyr" to describe his heroine, clearly wishes to reinforce this effect. But what is peculiarly significant about Hester's saintliness, as this is viewed from the vantage point of the second half of the twentieth century, is its fundamentally secular character. For, in twentieth century literature at least, the only kind of saint which is likely to awaken an appreciative response in sensitive readers (with a few exceptions, Eliot's Becket being an instance) is a saint whose holiness is of a radically secular nature. So much so is this the case that, thanks to R. W. B. Lewis, our critical vocabulary has been enriched with the expression "picaresque saint," a term used to characterize those representative protagonists of contemporary fiction who, in their "participation in the sufferings of mankind" and in their full sharing in human weakness and sin, image for us what many writers apparently consider the only convincing mode of sainthood in the modern world. "Dedicated," Lewis declares, "not so much, or not immediately, to a supernatural god as to what yet remains of the sacred in the ravaged human community," and sharing in human misery "as a way of touching and submitting to what is most *real* in the world today," these outcasts and rogues embody in their very lack of purity

> that trust in life and the companionship that the contemporary novel so emphasizes. They are outsiders who share; they are outcasts who enter in. It is just by taking on some of the wretchedness of the sinful, the persecuted and the dispossessed, that they experience what Henry James once called a "tragic fellowship" with suffering humanity. (*The Picaresque Saint*, 32, 33)

Lewis has in mind, of course, such writers as Silone, Camus and Faulkner, but does not his depiction of the secular saint suggest the possibility that Hawthorne's heroine prefigures what has since become a familiar mode of fictional characterization? The numerous similarities can scarcely be denied. For Hester, "participation in the sufferings of mankind" provides a means of escape from a dehumanizing world of spectral abstractions and a way of entering the more *real* world of deeply-experienced human relations. She, too, is an outcast "who enter[s] in," a sufferer who bears some of the "wretchedness" of the guilty, a sinmarked Isolato who establishes a "tragic fellowship" with those who are spiritually, if not economically and politically, dispossessed. Moreover, her saintliness is in some manner dependent upon her status as a "criminal," and, like many of the outsiders in the fiction of our own day, she can find a basis for solidarity with her human fellows "only by saying 'no!' to the official pieties" of her age. (Lewis, 101)

The last phrase is Lewis's and is an allusion to Camus; and it is from Lewis's discussion of *The Plague* that I believe the fullest and, for my purposes here, the most relevant definition of the secular saint emerges. It will be recalled that in *The Plague* both Tarrou (from whose notebooks the narrative is supposedly largely reconstructed) and Dr. Rieux (whom we discover at the novel's end to have been its narrator) dedicate themselves to combating the plague. Their motives, however, are quite dissimilar. Tarrou, who at an early age concluded that human existence is based on the death sentence, desires to free himself of complicity in human guilt; and, while he joins Rieux in fighting the disease, his principal concern is neither to be infected nor to infect others—in short, to maintain his individual purity. Thus his interest in "learning how to become a saint" and his preoccupation with the question of whether "one [can] be a saint without God." (*The Plague*, 230) Rieux, on the other hand, is striving to become not a saint but a man. "I feel," he declares to Tarrou, "more fellowship with the defeated than with the saints.... what interests me is being a man." (Camus, 231) Commenting on this exchange, Lewis points out that, while "a distinction is drawn between the ideal of sainthood and the ideal of compassion ('solidarity with the vanquished'), ... there is a clear implication that the ideal of compassion and the ambition to be a man *are* the ingredients of the one really authentic mode of sainthood in the contemporary world." (Lewis, 101) Rieux, then, while not consciously striving for sanctity, approaches the condition of sainthood because he casts his lot with those who suffer and dedicates his life to alleviating the misery which afflicts his brothers. Having risked the meaning of his personal existence on the possibility and necessity of human solidarity, Rieux seems to discover through a compassionate participation in the sufferings of others that true manhood which he seeks. And it is with Rieux, the "true healer," that Camus find himself allied. (Lewis, 100)

Using Lewis's delineation of the contemporary saint as suggested by Camus' Dr. Rieux, let us turn once more to Hawthorne's heroine. Although it should be pointed out that early in the novel Hester had consciously sought sainthood (*The Scarlet Letter*, 62), I think there is indisputable evidence that, following Dimmesdale's death (as well as for some time before it), she is motivated in her role as Angel of Mercy by an earnest desire to minister to those in need of healing. She had, Hawthorne says, "no selfish ends, nor lived in any measure for her own profit." (250) Nevertheless, it should be emphasized that Hester's return to New England and her assumption of the status of lay confessor to those of her neighbors who are tormented by loneliness, disappointment, or guilt demonstrate her conviction that her life's center and meaning (its "unity") is to be found only in a community of shared suffering. Just as Rieux wishes simply to be a man, so Hester seeks in a "sympathetic community of natural man" (Charles Feidelson, Jr., "The Scarlet Letter," *Hawthorne Centenary Essays*, 63) a ground for authentic selfhood. But, as the dynamics of some of our finest contemporary novels imply, the attainment of full humanity in the modern world is itself a feat requiring an immense amount of courage and an almost superhuman dedication and concentration of spirit. Hence, in those instances when it is accomplished, we may well feel obliged to grace this phenomenon with some phrase evocative of a holiness no longer supernatural but nevertheless so transcendent of our normal human experience as to warrant the epithet "saintly." It is to this paradox—that out of the natural and seemingly profane, adumbrations of the sacred emerge—that I take it Amos Wilder is pointing when he speaks of the "lay mystery." (Amos Wilder, "Art and Theological Meaning," *The New Orpheus*). While Hester's dedication has as its object not a supernatural god but rather what might be interpreted as the remnant of "the sacred in the ravaged human community," that dedication inspires a reverence and awe, indeed a sense of mystery, traditionally associated with the supernatural.

It would be inaccurate, therefore, to describe Hester as denying the reality of God. The most that can be said is that she appears to share with the secular saints of our day an intuition of "the division, even the incompatibility, between the religious impulse and human sympathy." (Lewis, 101) For to the extent that those adherents of the "iron framework of reasoning," the Puritan civil and ecclesiastical authorities, are the spokesmen for a supernatural deity and the most advanced exemplars their age can offer of "the religious impulse"—to this extent must *their* god and *their* piety appear alien in Hester's eyes, since it is in the name of this god and this piety that they negate the human affection, natural sympathy, and spontaneous impulse toward shared suffering which underlie her own vision of redemption.

As a careful reading of the novel reveals, the mode of existence which in Hester's view constitutes the redeemed state is entirely free of that preoccupation with one's soul and the concomitant anxiety over the possibility of damnation so distinctive of Dimmesdale. True, Hester is portrayed early in the novel as remaining in Boston through a half-conscious desire to be near him with whom she expected to share, after death, "a joint futurity of endless retribution." (75) But this, as Charles Feidelson persuasively argues, is merely one element in Hester's creative transformation of Puritan values: she is tormented by the Puritan view of her love for Dimmesdale as "wholly evil," yet she makes this "evil" the basis for communion—to her an infinitely precious good. (Feidelson, 56-58) The communion is one of the damned, but, as the context shows, it is the communion, and not the damnation, which ultimately interests her. So too, when at the moment of Dimmesdale's death Hester inquires concerning the soul's destiny, her concentration is fixed upon the possibility of a shared eternity: "Shall we not meet again?" "Shall we not spend our immortal life together?" (244)

This extreme disjunction between Hester's understanding of salavation and Dimmesdale's is suggestive of a development in contemporary Christian thought closely paralleling the emphasis on secular sanctity in recent imaginative literature. This is the movement, deriving principally from the work of Dietrich Bonhoeffer, usually referred to as "religionless Christianity." In his *Letters and Papers from Prison*, Bonhoeffer speaks of the modern epoch as a time when "men ... simply cannot be religious any more" and goes on to ask, "Is there any concern in the Old Testament about saving one's soul at all?" (*Letters and Papers from Prison*, 91, 94) Throughout these letters Bonhoeffer inveighs against what he calls "an individualistic doctrine of salvation" which he believes to have distracted the Christian man from his proper concern with "this world as created and preserved and set subject to laws and atoned for and made new." (Bonhoeffer, 94–94) In short, it is historical salvation and not an otherworldly and supernaturalist salavation— offered in compensation for ills suffered in this life—that Bonhoeffer holds to be the true proclamation of the Christian Gospel.

Now it seems to me that in her most typical attitudes and actions, Hester Prynne demonstrates an extraordinary conformity to Christian faith as interpreted by Bonhoeffer. There is, most notably, her this-wordly orientation and her affirmation of the natural and the human. Also, her conviction that "at some brighter period ... a new truth would be revealed, in order to establish the whole relation between man and woman on a surer ground of mutual happiness," (251) is a patently historical hope; and, given the centrality of a communion of affection and sympathy in Hester's scheme of redemption, it seems hardly an exaggeration to say that the realization of this hope would constitute a form of salvation. Moreover, while Hester's expectation of a permanent change in human relations is projected into the temporal future, her immediate gaze is focused upon "this world as created"; for, once Dimmesdale is dead, she is apparently never distracted from her mission of "healer" in *this* world by speculation concerning his fate (or her own) in some other. Nor is there any sign in Hester of that "religiosity" which causes men, as Bonhoeffer maintains, to turn God into a *deus ex machina*.

Bonhoeffer's thought in the *Letters and Papers* is notoriously fragmentary and enigmatic, and perhaps none of his cryptic comments has proved more resistant to precise exegesis that the one about the weak God who is "powerless in the world" and who can help us only in his weakness. It is in a world without god (that is, the stopgap god, the *deus ex machina*), Bonhoeffer appears to say, that the true God, the suffering God, manifests himself. Therefore man must "plunge himself into the life of a godless world, without attempting to gloss over its ungodliness with a veneer of religion...." "To be a Christion," Bonhoeffer continues, "does not mean to be religious in a particular way ... *but to be a man*. It is not some religious act which makes a Christian what he is, but participation in the sufferings of God *in the life of the world*." (Bonhoeffer, 122, 123)

It is noteworthy that here Bonhoeffer seems to claim that the only God modern man can know anything about is a suffering God and that the one theater of God's self-disclosure is "the life of the world." That is, in the suffering of the world is to be seen the suffering of God himself, and it is for this reason that men are called to plunge into this "godless world," for only in so doing will they know and serve the God who is truly God. Bonhoeffer's wording clearly excludes from Christian faith any anxious seeking after a God found somewhere other than in the world, just as it excluded substitution of religious practice for trust in life. ("Jesus does not call men to a new religion, but to life.") (Bonhoeffer, 123–134) Christianity, Bonhoeffer believes, addresses itself to those who ask the most basic of human questions, how to be a man; and its answer is that true fulfillment lies in voluntary participation in the suffering of the world ("of God in the life of the world")—for which Jesus Christ is the ultimate paradigm.

As the motif of sharing in the world's sufferings and the question of authentic manhood converge in Bonhoeffer's thought, our attention is inevitably forced back to Lewis's definition of the secular saint and thence to Hester Prynne. The secular saint, as we saw, is really a saint only in the sense that he images a manhood so vibrant with "trust in life and ... [dedication to] companionship" and compassion that he incarnates a kind of this-worldly transcendence. (Bonhoeffer, we should recall, defines "the experience of transcendence" as the "concern of Jesus for others.") (Bonhoeffer, 165) Yet the secular saint's commitment to "what ... remains of the sacred" in a "ravaged" humanity is markedly similar to the commitment to a suffering God found in the midst of the world which Bonhoeffer interprets as the essence of Christianity. And in both cases, it seems to me, what is truly problematic is not God but man. By this I mean that both the secular saint and Bonhoeffer's Christian seek a strategy or a stance on the basis of which human existence may be validated and authenticated. But to find such a stance is to do more than merely discover "an image of meaningful human existence"; for man's self-understanding and his apprehension of God are so intimately bound together that when he no longer possesses a vision of what it means to be a man, God also dies. Thus interpreted, the struggle to become a man is, whether acknowledged or not, a struggle to establish contact with that depth and ground of human existence with which many persons today, following Paul Tillich, are accustomed to associate the word "God."

It is not surprising, therefore, that in the name of God Bonhoeffer should repudiate the supernatural god who has dominated a good deal of Christian history and should reject the "religious impulse" associated with him. For much Christian supernaturalism, especially perhaps in its extreme Protestant forms, has tended to be little more that a negation of man and of human existence itself. It is such a supernaturalism that we encounter in the Puritanism of *The Scarlet Letter*, though it might more accurately be called a form of antinaturalism predicated on belief in the "utter and total unlikeness of the creature and the Creator." (Eugene Fairweather, "Christianity and the Supernatural," *New Theology No. 1*, 241) Here grace is no longer that which completes and fulfills nature but that which denies and negates it. Accordingly, both nature and human existence are placed under a ban, and the possibility of God's manifesting his love by way of these is precluded. The relationship of God and man becomes a negative one, defined almost exclusively in terms of the distance which separates them. Salvation, in such a scheme, represents not the transformation of the life of the self in this world, but the most abject renunciation of the self through "blind submission of the human will to the inscrutable divine will." (Fairweather, 241) And Christian faith under such a dispensation comes perilously close to simply life-denial. Only in what appears to be unfaith—*i.e.*, in Hester's unblessed communion of the natural human heart—do we discern intimations of a vision of life sufficiently transparent to the depths of the authentically human to be at the same time a reflection of the truly divine.

In the world of *The Scarlet Letter*, where the harsh abstractions of Puritanism tend to bind selfhood and redemption to an external code of laws imposed by a supernatural, "wholly other" God, Dimmesdale is forced, as it were, to choose between this supernatural God and life, and he chooses—as he must—that God. Faced with the same choice, Hester chooses life. And while Dimmesdale is faithful to his God, it is at least arguable that Hester is no less so to hers. For to deny human existence is to deny that (Biblical) God who is the God of the living. Put another way, to affirm the world and human existence with all its evil, sin and suffering is at the same time to affirm God; "for trust in God, at its deepest level, means trust in existence." (Maurice Friedman, *Problematic Rebel*, 17) It is this kind of trust in existence which Hester achieves through her suffering, shame and despair.

While *The Scarlet Letter* is far too complex a novel to permit an unqualified claim for this response to life as Hawthorne's final vision, it would yet seem that a balanced reading of the story requires acknowledgment of the essential validity of such a view in the work's total meaning. Probably, as has frequently been suggested, Hawthorne's sympathies are divided; certainly, as a character, Dimmesdale is much more attractive than the "iron framework of reasoning" out of which grows his almost pathological guilt and anxiety and to which he finally submits. Yet the question of Hawthorne's deepest metaphysical perceptions involves a good deal more than merely Hester and Dimmesdale as characters; an author may, and often does, feel great sympathy for a character while remaining skeptical of his choice among alternative modes of interpretation of reality and human existence. Given the bent of his mind, I think it likely that Hawthorne maintained his skepticism to the end: skepticism of both Hester's and Dimmesdale's vision of redemption. And yet I am left with a nagging conviction that, whether he so intended or not, in his portrayal of that image of redemption which comes to be the distinguishing feature of Hester's life, Hawthorne too has said "yes" to existence.

BIBLIOGRAPHY

Bonhoeffer, Dietrich. *Letters and Papers from Prison*, ed. Eberhard Bethge. London: Fontana Books, 1960.

Camus, Albert. *The Plague*, trans. Stuart Gilbert. New York: Modern Library, 1948.

Fairweather, Eugene. "Christianity and the Supernatural," in *New Theology No. 1*, eds. Martin E. Marty and Dean G. Peerman. New York, 1964.

Feidelson, Charles Jr. "The Scarlet Letter," in *Hawthorne Centenary Essays*, Ed. Roy Harvey Pearce. Columbus, Ohio: Ohio State Univ. Press, 1964.

Friedman, Maurice. *Problematic Rebel: An Image of Modern Man*. New York: Random House, 1963.

Hawthorne, Nathaniel. *The Scarlet Letter*. New York: Holt, Rhinehart and Winston, 1961.

Lewis, R. W. B. *The Picaresque Saint*. Philadelphia, 1959.

Wilder, Amos. "Art and Theological Meaning," in *The New Orpheus*, ed. Nathan A. Scott, Jr. New York, 1964.

MICHAEL J. COLACURCIO

Footsteps of Ann Hutchinson:
The Context of The Scarlet Letter

I

In the first brief chapter of *The Scarlet Letter*, the narrator pays almost as much attention to a rose bush as he does to the appearance and moral significance of Puritan America's first prison. That "wild rose-bush, covered, in this month of June, with its delicate gems," contrasts with the "burdock, pig-weed, apple-peru" and other "unsightly vegetation"; yet all flourish together in the same "congenial" soil which has so early brought forth "the black flower of civilized society, a prison" (48).[1] And thus early are we introduced to the book's extremely complicated view of the natural and the social. Moreover, as the rose bush seems to offer Nature's sympathy to society's criminal, it becomes essentially associated with Hester Prynne, almost as *her* symbol. Accordingly, criticism has been lavish in its own attention to that rose bush: it has, out of perfect soundness of instinct, been made the starting point of more than one excellent reading of *The Scarlet Letter*; indeed the explication of this image and symbol is one of the triumphs of the "new" Hawthorne criticism.[2]

But if the "natural" and internal associations of this rose bush have been successfully elaborated, its external and "historic" implications have been largely ignored. And yet not for any fault of the narrator. This rose bush "has been kept alive in history," he assures us; and it may even be, as "there

From *ELH* 39, no. 3 (September 1972). © 1972 by The Johns Hopkins University Press.

is fair authority for believing," that "it had sprung up under the footsteps of the sainted Ann Hutchinson, as she entered the prison-door."

We are, I suppose, free to ignore this critical invitation if we choose. Obviously we are being offered a saint's legend in which Hawthorne expects no reader literally to believe. Perhaps it is there only for the irony of "sainted"—a trap for D.H. Lawrence or other romantic (later, feminist) readers; for Hawthorne will have nearly as many reservations about Hester's sainthood as John Winthrop had about Mrs. Hutchinson's. Certainly the natural language of flowers is a more available and universal sort of literary knowledge than that overdetermined system of historical fixities and definites which laborers in the field of American studies call "Antinomianism." And is not Hawthorne himself responsible for the idea that he was not all *that* serious about those old books he borrowed from the Salem Athenaeum or went up to Boston to buy?

Still, a conscious decision *not* to look for and press a Hester Prynne-Ann Hutchinson analogy might be risky, the result of a critical bias. We should not, it seems to me, want to believe Hawthorne a casual name dropper unless he prove himself one. We should prefer a more rather than a less precise use of literary allusion, not only in this opening reference but also in a later one which suggests that, except for the existence of Pearl, Hester "might have come down to us in history, hand in hand with Ann Hutchinson, as the foundress of a religious sect" (165). The references are, after all, pretty precise: Hester walks in the footsteps of (but not quite hand-in-hand with) Ann Hutchinson. And before we invest too heavily in Hawthorne's well known demurrer to Longfellow, we might remind ourselves that Hawthorne did write—near the outset of his career, in clear and close dependence on "a good many books"[3]—a well informed sketch called "Mrs. Hutchinson." He mentions her again, prominently, in those reviews of New England history entitled *Grandfather's Chair* and "Main Street." Now he seems to be apprising us of a relationship between Hester Prynne and that famous lady heretic. The man who created the one and memorialized the other ought to be in a position to know.

Clearly the relationship is not one of "identity": tempting as the view can be made to appear, *The Scarlet Letter* is probably not intended as an allegory of New England's Antinomian Crisis. Hawthorne's historical tales never work quite that simply: "The Gentle Boy," "Young Goodman Brown," and "The Minister's Black Veil" all have something quite precise and fundamental to say about the Puritan mind but, in spite of the precision with which they are set or "dated," they are not primarily "about" (respectively) the Quaker problem, the witchcraft delusion, or the great awakening.[4] Their history is not quite that literalistic. And here, of course, the setting is "literally" Boston, 1642 to 1649—not 1636 and 1637.[5] More importantly, but equally obviously, the career of Hawthorne's fictional Hester Prynne is far from identical with that of the historical Mrs. Hutchinson. However "antinomian" Hester becomes, it would be positively ludicrous to forget that her philosophical career is inseparable from adultery and illegitimate childbirth, events which have no very real counterpart in the life of that enthusiastic prophetess Hawthorne calls her prototype.

But as important as are the simple differences, and as dangerous as it must always seem to turn away from the richness and particularity of Hester's own love story, Hawthorne himself seems to have invited us temporarily to do so. And if we follow his suggestion, a number of similarities come teasingly to mind.

Like Ann Hutchinson, Hester Prynne is an extraordinary woman who falls afoul of a theocratic and male-dominated society; and the problems which cause them to be singled out for exemplary punishment both begin in a special sort of relationship with a pastor who is one of the acknowledged intellectual and spiritual leaders of that society. No overt sexual irregularity seems to have been associated with Mrs. Hutchinson's denial that converted saints were under the moral law, but (as we shall see later) no one could read what seventeenth-century Puritan observers said about the "seductiveness" of her doctrines without sensing sexual implications everywhere. Evidently such implications were not lost on Hawthorne. Further, though with increasing complications, both of these remarkable and troublesome women have careers as nurses and counsellors to other women: Ann Hutchinson begins her prophetic career this way, whereas Hester Prynne moves in this direction as a result of her punishment. And most significantly—if most problematically—both make positive pronouncements about the inapplicability of what the majority of their contemporaries take to be inviolable moral law.[6]

To be sure, it takes Hester Prynne some time to catch up with Ann Hutchinson; but when Hawthorne says of Hester, in the full tide of her later speculative freedom, that "the world's law was no law to her mind" (164), we may well suspect that he intends some conscious pun on the literal meaning of "antinomianism." If Hester's problems begin with sex more literally than do Ann Hutchinson's, her thinking eventually ranges far outward from that domestic subject. In some way, and for complicated reasons that need to be examined, Hester Prynne and sex are associated in Hawthorne's mind with Ann Hutchinson and spiritual freedom.

So teasing do Hawthorne's connections and analogies come to seem, that we are eventually led to wonder whether *The Scarlet Letter* shows only this one set of historical footprints. If Hester Prynne bears relation to Ann

Hutchinson, would it be too outrageous to look for similarities between Arthur Dimmesdale and John Cotton, that high Calvinist who was variously asserted and denied to be the partner in heresy? And—granting that what is involved is neither allegory nor *roman à clef*—might there not be some fundamental relation between the deepest philosophical and theological "issues" raised by the Antinomian Controversy and the "themes" of Hawthorne's romance?

To the first of these questions, a certain kind of answer comes readily enough. Although the portrait of Dimmesdale is physically unlike the one Hawthorne gives of Cotton in his early sketch of "Mrs. Hutchinson," their positions are disturbingly similar: both are singled out from among distinguished colleagues as models of learning and piety; and both relate very ambiguously to a wayward woman on trial. It is impossible not to feel that John Cotton's drastic change of relation to Ann Hutchinson—a phenomenon as fascinating to scholars now as it was momentous to Puritans then—lies somewhere behind Dimmesdale's movement from partner in to judge of Hester's adultery. Both men sit in public judgment of an outrage against public order in which there is reason to believe they bear equal responsibility with the criminal.

Although his sketch of "Mrs. Hutchinson" suggests in one place that her enthusiasm had earlier been restrained from public manifestation by the influence of her favorite pastor, Hawthorne actually takes a rather harsh view of Cotton's role in her trial: "Mr. Cotton began to have that light in regard to her errors, which will sometimes break in upon the wisest and most pious men, when their opinions are unhappily discordant with those of the powers that be" (XII, 222).[7] That is to say: Cotton and his female parishioner have been what their society calls "antinomians" together, both "deceived by the fire" (221): but the respected minister saves himself. Not all modern commentators would agree that Cotton's behavior is to be judged this harshly, but that is not the issue here. At some point Cotton did clearly reverse his relationship to Ann Hutchinson, reproving doctrines she thought were his own offspring; and clearly Hawthorne's view of Cotton has influenced his treatment of Dimmesdale.[8] Except for the rather too delicate question of who first lit the strange fires, both Mrs. Hutchinson's treatment by Cotton and Hester's by Dimmesdale might almost be subtitled "Seduced and Abandoned in Old Boston."

Although the significance is completely ironic in *The Scarlet Letter*, both pastors are reminded by their colleagues that "the responsibility of [the] woman's soul" is largely within their sphere; Wilson's urging Dimmesdale to press repentence and confession upon Hester sounds a good deal like an ironic version of the ministerial pleas which Cotton, because of his doctrinal affinities with Ann Hutchinson, so long refused to heed. And to the end, both men are spared from denunciation by their partners. Although Puritan defenders of Cotton's doctrinal reputation (like Cotton Mather) insisted he had been slandered by even being named in the same breath with the seductive Mrs. Hutchinson, there is no evidence to suggest that the "abandoned" one ever pointed a finger of public accusation at Cotton, or reproached him for infidelity to what she continued to believe were their shared experiences and beliefs. Cotton alone, Hawthorne reports, is excepted from her final denunciations. And in spite of Dimmesdale's false and unfaithful position on the balcony overlooking her scaffold, of his own part in her troubles, Hester "will not speak."

The Cotton-Dimmesdale analogy may seem treacherous on these internal grounds alone. After all, Cotton is not named by Hawthorne and Mrs. Hutchinson is. But there are also arguments which "implicate" Cotton in Dimmesdale—external reasons for believing that John Cotton could not be far from Hawthorne's mind when he wrote of the Reverend Mr. Dimmesdale. And in the light of these, the very omission of the name of Cotton seems glaringly to call attention to itself. The historically alert reader of *The Scarlet Letter* comes to sense the presence of Cotton's absence on almost every page.

First of all, in the public judgment of Hester, Dimmesdale stands as the partner of John Wilson, at the head of the Boston church of which Hester is a member: Wilson is the fervent, Dimmesdale the reluctant enforcer of discipline. Now it seems to me inconceivable that the man who wrote about the Hutchinson situation explicitly three separate times, using highly detailed contemporary sources as well as later histories (and who built into *The Scarlet Letter* certain colonial details so minutely accurate as to convince one recent critic that he wrote the romance with a number of books open before him) would not know that the famous partnership at Boston throughout the 1630's and 1640's was Wilson and Cotton.[9] It might be too much to suggest that Dimmesdale is conceived and dramatized as a younger version of Cotton, one whose pastoral involvement with Hester Prynne amounted to a less metaphorical seduction than Cotton's relationship with Ann Hutchinson; but it is hard to believe Hawthorne could pair Wilson with *Dimmesdale* without thinking *Cotton*.

Several other, more curious "displacements" also implicate Cotton. Hawthorne had certainly read in Mather's *Magnalia* of a case in which John Wilson and John Cotton joined together publicly to urge public repentance upon a woman who had killed an illegitimate child; Mather's account surely lies somewhere behind Hawthorne's first scaffold scene. Also he could scarcely have *not* known that it was with Cotton's death in 1652 that the fiery signs in the sky were associated—not with Winthrop's in 1649. One could argue, of course, that this points *away* from Cotton; but just as cogently one can say that Hawthorne cannot *make* the transference without having Cotton in mind; and that the reader who knows the facts will make the application, especially when, standing on his midnight scaffold, Dimmesdale applies "Cotton's" sign to himself. And finally, it was not exactly a secret (despite Mather's silence) that Cotton's son, John Cotton, *Junior*, was deprived of his pastorship and excommunicated from church membership at Plymouth for adultery. Perhaps Dimmesdale is to be thought of—metaphorically, and with a certain irony—as a sort of offspring of Cotton's principles.[10]

Now all of this may not add up to a completely rational calculus of "influence," but it does suggest that, at some level, *The Scarlet Letter* reflects a complicated response to more in the historic Puritan world than Ann Hutchinson alone. To this point, however, we still know very little about the importance of historical context to the realized intentions of Hawthorne's first long romance—as opposed, that is, to some complex, Road-to-Xanadu association that lies somewhere behind it, perhaps even close to its source. The rest of this essay is conceived as a cautious and tentative answer to the less positivistic, more pragmatic question of what *The Scarlet Letter* may mean if it does indeed call up a fairly extensive set of associations from Puritanism's most crucial theological controversy.[11]

II

The place to begin an exploration of the inner similarities between Hester Prynne and Ann Hutchinson is with a closer look at Hawthorne's early sketch. In many ways a puzzling piece of historical fiction, the sketch does clear up one fundamental point immediately: Hester's sexual problems can be related to those of Mrs. Hutchinson because the latter are, in Hawthorne's view, themselves flagrantly sexual.

The sketch introduces itself, too heavily, as a lesson in that forlorn subject we used to call the nature and place of women. Mrs. Hutchinson is first presented as "the female"; she is offered as a forerunner of certain nameless public ladies of 1830, and the line from Hawthorne's remark here about "how much of the texture and body of cisatlantic literature is the work of those slender fingers" (XII, 217) to the more famous but equally sexist one later about "the damned mob of scribbling women" seems to run direct. The revelation is damaging enough, but fairly simple: Hawthorne enjoyed competing with women for the readership of magazines and gift books at the outset of his career as little as he did for the "gentle reader" of romances later.[12]

But if Hawthorne's own sexual politics are easy and largely irrelevant to the present question, certain subtler forms of the feminist problem treated in "Mrs. Hutchinson" throw an important light on Hester Prynne (as well as on a significant woman-problem in Hawthorne's larger career). Once we read on and apprehend Hawthorne's dominant image of Ann Hutchinson— formerly a spiritual counsellor to Puritan women, interpreting to them the best of the male theological mind; now a prophet in her own right, giving voice to a new spirit of freedom and embodying within herself a new awareness of female intelligence and social power—we immediately grasp the significant context of Hawthorne's views of the later Hester Prynne.

In the epilogue which Hawthorne calls a "Conclusion," Hester has returned to Boston to wear her scarlet letter "of her own free will," with something like an internalized acceptance of its appropriateness. She now accepts as reasonable what in the forest she tried to deny and many years earlier she could, in very much the same words, only rationalize: "Here had been her sin; here, her sorrow; and here was yet to be her penitence" (263).[13] But this is not the whole story. Whether to affirm a yet undestroyed inner-direction and unreconstructed self-reliance, or else to assert once again the mortal irreparability of ruined walls, the narrator informs us that Hester is still a visionary and has become a counsellor to women. Earlier—even in her most antinomian moments—she had stopped short of that critical move from undisciplined private speculation to unsanctioned public prophecy; providentially she had been prevented from joining hands (metaphorically) with her sister Hutchinson because "in the education of the child, the mother's enthusiasm of thought had something to weak itself upon" (165). Now, although Hester has apparently picked up and pieced together again "the fragments of [the] broken chain" formerly cast away; although "the world's law" is now apparently *some* law to her mind; and although she would not now presumably claim for her adultery a totally sufficient "consecration" in feeling, she has now found a way to make public her ideas about sexual justice.

Earlier she had pondered the "dark question" of the "whole race of womanhood": could its lot ever be a happy one without a tearing down of "the whole system of society" and an essential modification of "the very nature of the opposite sex" (165)? Now—with important modifications of tone and in separation from all traces of antinomian self-justification—her ideas are expressed to other women, especially those whose lives have been made miserable through excess or absence of passion.

Hester comforted and counseled them, as best she might. She assured them, too, of her firm belief, that, at some brighter period, when the world should have grown ripe for it, in Heaven's own time, a new truth would be revealed, in order to establish the whole relation between man and woman on a surer ground of mutual happiness. (263)

What Hester's experience comes to finally—in an epilogue, and after a painful and complicated development forced upon her by others—is some insight about the double standard, or perhaps about the new morality.

Thus, if we can bear the temporary critical reduction, it is easy to see that Hester passes through a phase of antinomianism comparable to (though not identical with) that of the historical Ann Hutchinson, only to emerge as a version of the sexual reformer already "typed out" in Hawthorne's "figure" of Mrs. Hutchinson as independent and reforming "female." And though the equation might need to be clarified by an examination of the precise quality of Hester's anti-legal phase, we can already calculate that her final position is, in Hawthorne's mental universe, just about half way between Ann Hutchinson and Margaret Fuller; and we can sense that when Hawthorne describes her later career as counsellor to troubled and searching women, he has certain seventeenth-century, Sunday-evening doctrinal meetings and certain nineteenth-century "Conversations" just about equally in mind. (What this clearly suggests, in consequence, is that interpreters of the problem of women in Hawthorne can make a less autonomous use of Margaret Fuller than they have often supposed.)[14]

To this point, as I have indicated, Hawthorne seems open to the charge of a fairly radical sort of reductivism: he seems to have presented an historical woman whose heretical ideas once caused a profound religious and social crisis as a simple case of uneasy or misplaced sexuality; and the opportunity to reduce Hester Prynne to a woman whose sexuality got quite literally out of control and never did entirely recover itself is therefore ready to hand. Such a reduction is, presumably, as distasteful to old male literary critics as it is to new women.

The way to stop being reductive and offensive about Hawthorne's use of the "female" Mrs. Hutchinson as a type of Hester Prynne is not, therefore, to appeal to the masterful modern psycho-historical interpretation of Mrs. Hutchinson's career. It is probably of some value to notice that its author (Emery Battis) devotes almost as many pages to the complicated female problems of her relation to her strong father, her weak husband, and her beloved pastor as he does to her ideas; that he convincingly urges a relation between menstrual cycle, pregnancy, menopause and the more public aspects of her career; and that he introduces his treatment of the character of this unusual woman with the astonishingly Hawthornean speculation that "had she been born into a later age, Mrs. Hutchinson might have crusaded for women's rights."[15] It is perhaps more than a nice polemical point to observe that Hawthorne is not alone in reading sexual implications in Mrs. Hutchinson's theologic and prophetic career, but the observation leaves out all the subtle considerations. They concern not only the ways in which Ann Hutchinson and Hester Prynne are related in a very serious approach to the "theological" meaning of sexuality, but also the historical reasons Hawthorne had for linking enthusiasm, individualism, and femaleness.

If we glance again at the early sketch, we can notice that, embattled and argumentative as it is, it is yet about sex in some more elemental way than our discussion about "feminism" has so far indicated. With structural intention (and not, clearly, by obsession), the sketch tries hard to focus on several scenes in which Mrs. Hutchinson is the center of all male attention, prophesying doctrines that astound the male intellect. Most of the "historical" facts are there, but only a fairly well informed reader can feel assured of this; and except for an initial, one-paragraph reminder, the facts seem to fall out incidentally, so as not to distract from the dramatic confrontation. The implications, in turn, are not in the ordinary sense "theological": there is no mention of the famous eighty-two errors Mrs. Hutchinson is said to have spawned—as there is, self-consciously, in *Grandfather's Chair*; we are, historically and psychologically, beyond that sort of consideration. The issue is not sanctification as an evidence of justification, but the woman's own prophetic abilities. Having formerly cast aspersions on legal doctrines of salvation, the enthusiast now claims the spiritual "power of distinguishing between the chosen of man and the sealed of heaven" (XII, 224). What further need of witnesses? Clearly the progress of the strange fire of her enthusiasm is far advanced.

Nor is there any significant ambiguity about the source and significance of that fire: Mrs. Hutchinson's spiritual openings and leadings are inseparable from her female sexuality. Although her "dark enthusiasm" has deceived the impetuous Vane and the learned but mildly illuministic Cotton, it is clearly her own "strange fire now laid upon the altar" (XII, 221). The men, variously affected, must make of it whatever they can. Hawthorne does not quite identify enthusiasm with "the female," but we do not distort his intentions if—supplying our own italics—we take as the very heart of the sketch the following sentence: "In the midst, and in the center of all eyes, we see *the woman*" (XII, 224).

This may still be sexist, but it is no longer petty or carping. Mrs. Hutchinson's influence is indeed profound. Even the male chauvinist is compelled to admit it. The impulse to challenge the Puritan theocracy's dominant (and socially conservative) assumptions about "visible sanctity" evidently comes from a fairly deep and powerful source. It seems to be coming from—"the woman."

Evidently, in Hawthorne's view, fully awakened women accept the inevitability of a given legal order far less easily than their male counterparts. And clearly this is the central issue. What caused a state of near civil war in Boston and what creates the crackling tension in Hawthorne's sketch is Mrs. Hutchinson's proclamation—variously worded at various times, but always as far beyond the reach of the "trained and sharpened intellects" of the most scholastic Puritan controversialists as are Hester Prynne's sexual secrets— that "the chosen of man" are not necessarily "the sealed of heaven." Here, in her last, most devastating, and for Hawthorne most insupportable formulation, Mrs. Hutchinson is claiming that sort of direct inspiration and divine guidance necessary to distinguish between true and false, spiritual and legal teachers. But she has been forced to this last claim by the pressure of investigation and over-response; this, presumably, is what you are made bold to say when facing the legalistic integrity of John Winthrop—not to mention the holy wath of Hugh Peters, the satiric antifeminism of Nathaniel Ward, and the sheer adamant intolerance of John Endicott. Behind her last claim— as Hawthorne well knows—lies a series of far less drastic attempts to affirm that the Spirit does not always obey the laws of ordinary moral appearance. And even though she has moved from the dangerous to the intolerable, the weight of Hawthorne's subtlest moral judgment falls no more heavily on her head than on those of her judges.

In simple ironic fact, she is their natural opposite—induced into individualistic heresy by their organized, legalistic intolerance in much the same way as Hester's later denials are induced by the violence of the community's over-response. Beginning, apparently, with only a purer sort of Calvinism than was customarily preached in New England, Mrs. Hutchinson's ultimate claim to a totally self-sufficient private illumination seems the inevitable response to an emerging Puritan orthodoxy which, in its undeniable tendency to conflate the visible with the invisible church, was really claiming that for nearly all valid human purposes the "chosen of men" *were* the "sealed of heaven."[16] If the community overextends and mystifies its authority, the individual will trust the deepest passional self to nullify it all. Or at least "the woman" will.

What Hawthorne's figure of Mrs. Hutchinson suggests is that "the woman" is not by essence the safe and conserving social force the seventeenth and the nineteenth century (and much Hawthorne criticism) decreed her to be.[17] On the contrary female sexuality seems, in its concentration and power, both a source for and a type of individualistic nullification of social restraint. Obviously Hawthorne's feelings about this are not without ambivalence. Personally, of course, he would always prefer some less powerful, more submissive "Phoebe"; and in one way or another he would continue to protest that "Woman's intellect should never give the tone to that of man," that her "morality is not exactly the material for masculine virtue" (XII, 217–18). But his clear recognition of the antisocial meaning of self-conscious female sexuality, first formulated in the theological context of Puritan heresy, goes a long way toward explaining the power and the pathos of Hester Prynne.

Hawthorne reformulates his insight in "The Gentle Boy." Despite the complexities introduced by a "calm" male enthusiast and by the presence of the "rational piety" of that unreconstructed lover of home and children named Dorothy Pearson, we can hardly miss the elemental clash between "the female," Quaker Catherine, and the entire legalistic, repressive Puritan establishment. Against that male system of enforced rationlistic uniformity, she extravagantly testifies to the reality of an inspired and pluralistic freedom. Her response is, of course, extreme; Hawthorne is no more than faithful to history in judging it so (even though he does not have her walk naked through the streets of the Puritan capital). But, in a terrifying and elemental way, her response is effective. Tobias Pearson can only puzzle over and feel guilty about his drift toward the sect whose doctrines he thinks quite irresponsible; but this "muffled female" *must* stand up in the midst of a Puritan congregation (authoritatively and symbolically divided, by a wide aisle, into male and female) and denounce the minister's cruel and sterile formulation of the Puritan way.

The relevance of Quaker Catherine for Hester Prynne is simple and evident: here is the woman who has *not* been prevented from joining hands with Ann Hutchinson; her enthusiasm (and her sufferings) are such that not even little Ilbrahim can hold her back from a career of public testimony to the autonomous authority of conscience itself. Quaker Catherine does "come down to us *in history*, hand in hand with Ann Hutchinson." No doubt several historical women lie behind Hawthorne's figural portrait of Quaker Catherine, but surely none more powerfully than Mary Dyer, Ann Hutchinson's strongest female ally—who literally took her hand and accompanied her out of Cotton's church after her excommunication, went with her into exile, and (years after Mrs. Hutchinson had been providentially slaughtered by the Indians) went on to become notorious in the Quaker invasion of Massachusetts.[18]

Accordingly, another level of history is also involved: virtually all commentators have recognized that in New England, in dialectic with the Puritan Way, Ann Hutchinson and the Quakers go together; that the latter represent, chiefly a more organized and self-consciously sectarian espousal of the values of individualistic (or "spiritual") freedom which is the essence of Ann Hutchinson's doctrine. If one is committed and hostile, the cry against both is simply devilish and seductive enthusiasm, unregenerate impulse breaking all bonds of restraint and decorum. If one is committed and sympathetic, the cry is just as simple: the martyrdom of human dignity and divine freedom by aggressive repression. If one is a cautious modern commentator, one can only pity the victims and worry that both the Hutchinsonian and the (seventeenth-century) Quaker doctrines do rather tend to elevate the "individual conscience above all authority"; that both promote a "monistic egotism" which tends to dissolve "all those psychological distinctions man had invented to 'check, circumscribe, and surpass himself.'"[19]

None of these formulations would have been unfamiliar to Hawthorne. And neither would his knowledge or speculation be significantly advanced by the modern historian who, after discussing the Ann Hutchinson question as a "Pre-Quaker Movement," begins his chapters on Quakerism proper with the observation that as in London and at the great Universities of England, "so too, the first Quakers to reach the American hemisphere were women."[20] In every way it comes to seem the reverse of surprising that radical freedom and awakened female sexuality are inextricably linked in Hawthorne's most obviously historical romance. History itself had forged the link.

What is perhaps surprising is that Hawthorne is as sympathetic to a sex-related understanding of freedom as he is. His "Mrs. Hutchinson" is a profoundly troubled and dangerous woman; his Quaker Catherine becomes, in her "unbridled fanaticism," guilty of violating her most sacred duties (even if Ilbrahim is *not* a Christ-figure); even his Hester Prynne is far from the "Saint" she has occasionally been made out to be. But Hawthorne sympathizes with the problems as deeply as he fears the dangers; his compulsion to record warnings is no stronger than his desire to discover the laws by which powerful half truths generate their opposites or to feel the pain of those being destroyed by that implacable dialectic. The context of the sex-freedom link in *The Scarlet Letter* is not adequately sensed, therefore, until we are in a position to measure Hawthorne's emotional distance from his seventeenth-century sources who first raised the issue of sex in connection with Ann Hutchinson's law-denying theology.

The measurement is swiftly made. It begins with Cotton Mather and runs backward directly to John Winthrop and Edward Johnson.[21] All three are, through the typology of Ann Hutchinson, important sources for *The Scarlet Letter*. And except that they are all highly scornful in tone, it might almost be said that these Puritan historians began the transformation of Ann Hutchinson into Hester Prynne. Certainly they reduced Ann Hutchinson to a sexual phenomenon far more egregiously than did Hawthorne.

The emphasis of Cotton Mather's treatment of the Hutchinson

controversy is double—but not very complex of subtle. On the one hand he utterly rejects the charge that his grandfather John Cotton was hypocritical in declining to espouse Ann Hutchinson as his partner in heresy: it is not, he pedantically insists, a case of a Montanus refusing to stand by the side of his Maxilla; rather, obviously, of a notorious woman whom an infamous calumny connected with the name of an Athanasius. (One thinks, perhaps, of certain obdurate refusals to believe Dimmesdale's final confession.) On the other hand, more expansively and with more literary flair, he is determined to treat the sectaries themselves in a frankly sexual way.

The following reflection—from a special sub-section titled "Dux Faemina Facta"—may stand for Mather's theological antifeminism:

> It is the *mark of seducers* that *they lead captive silly women;* but what will you say, when you hear *subtil women* becoming the most *remarkable* of the *seducers?* ... Arius promoted his blasphemies by first proselyting seven hundred *virgins* thereunto. Indeed, a *poyson* does never insinuate so quickly, nor operate so strongly, as when *women's milk* is the *vehicle* wherein 'tis given. Whereas the prime seducer of the whole faction which now began to threaten the country with something like a Munster tragedy, was a woman, a gentlewoman, of "an haughty carriage, busie spirit, competent wit, and a voluble tongue."[22]

The quotation marks around the final descriptive phrase point back, of course, to a contemporary phase of anti-feminist response to Ann Hutchinson. As usual Mather is only elaborating what has come down to him.

But equally important in the "Wonderbook" which so pervasively influenced Hawthorne is the primary sexual language which informs Mather's account. Far more memorable than any formulation concerning the self-evidence of justification is a bastardy metaphor which helped to shape *The Scarlet Letter*: the doctrines of the Antinomians are "brats" whose "true parents" are to be discovered by the guardians of orthodoxy. And related to this basic concept is the whole grotesque business of the "very surprising *prodigies*" which were looked upon as testimonies from heaven against the ways of the arch-heretic: "The erroneous gentlewoman herself, convicted of holding about *thirty* monstrous opinions, growing big with child ... was delivered of about *thirty* monstrous births at once." Or—behold the Puritan wit—perhaps "these were no more *monstrous births* than what is frequent for women, laboring with *false conceptions*, to produce."

Again, none of this is strictly original with Cotton Mather: the heretical-idea-as-illegitimate-child conceit is in the windy pages of Edward Johnson, and Winthrop himself labors the ugly details of monstrous births—which are at least the providential consequence of her criminal heresies. But the full "literary" elaboration of this sort of talk is Mather's, and his account seems most to have influenced Hawthorne.[23]

The influence is very curious. On the one hand, Hawthorne specifically declines to repeat the story of monstrous births in his "Mrs. Hutchinson"; such details are fitter for the "old and homely narrative than for modern repetition" (XII, 225). And the sketch makes no use of any bastardy metaphor. On the other hand, however, in a rather startling display of creative process, it all comes back in the story of Ann Hutchinson's typic sister, Hester Prynne. Not only does Hester conceive a very real, natural child to accompany (and in some measure embody) her quasi-Hutchinsonian conception of spiritual freedom; but she finds it almost impossible to convince herself that Pearl is not in some sense a monstrous birth. Along with many other characters in *The Scarlet Letter* (and not a few critics) Hester daily stares at the child, waiting "to detect some dark and wild peculiarity" (90), unable to believe that a sinful conception can come to any valid issue. This *might* be no more than the too-simply Puritan inability ever to separate the moral order from the physical (like looking for "A's" in the midnight sky), but with Mather's elaboration of Johnson and Winthrop behind it, it is evidently a bit more. As almost everywhere, Hawthorne seems to be making Hester Prynne literally what orthodox Puritan metaphor said Ann Hutchinson was "really" or spiritually.

One more telling detail from Mather—to which we can only imagine Hawthorne's convoluted reaction. Not quite faithful to the wording of Winthrop, Mather has John Cotton express the opinion that Mrs. Hutchinson ought "to be cast out with them that 'love and make a lie.'"[24]

Except for this peculiar formulation—which is not really related to Mather's basic set of sexual equivalences, but which just happens to read like an epitome of Dimmesdale's career—nearly all of Mather's basic vocabulary is second-hand. Mather's own debts are tedious to detail, and clearly Hawthorne could have got all he needed from the *Magnalia* (though it is certain he read most of Mather's sources independently). The basic antifeminist construction seems to originate with Winthrop—not only with his specific characterization of Mrs. Hutchinson as "a woman of a haughty and fierce carriage, of a nimble wit and active spirit, and a very voluble tongue" but also with the clear implication in his whole account that one very deep issue is Mrs. Hutchinson's female invasion of male "literary" prerogative. Mrs. Hutchinson insists, out of *Titus*, that "elder women should instruct the younger"; Winthrop might admit, under exegetical duress, that "elder women must instruct the younger about their business, and to love their husbands and not to make them to clash," but his deeper feeling is rationalized in *Timothy*: "I permit not a woman to teach."[25]

This last makes the sexual politics of Hawthorne's remark about women's intellect not giving the tone to men's seem liberal. It also enables us to imagine, by simple contraries, what new and surer "relation between man and woman" Hester is teaching at the end of *The Scarlet Letter*. But, again, this is too easy.

If there is one formulation behind those of Cotton Mather worth savoring on its own, it is something from Edward Johnson. His impassioned account of the seductive appeal of Mrs. Hutchinson's doctrines gives us the clearest sense that Puritans themselves feared sexual implications more profound than those involving ordinary decorum. Upon Johnson's return to New England, he was alarmed to discover that a "Masterpiece of Woman's wit" had been set up by her own sex as a "Priest"; and Johnson was invited to join the cult:

> There was a little nimble tongued Woman among them, who said she could bring me acquainted with one of her own Sex that would shew me a way, if I could attaine it, even Revelations, full of such ravishing joy that I should never have cause to be sorry for sinne, so long as I live.

Here, as clearly as we need, is the simply hostile version of Hawthorne's suggestion that "woman's morality it not quite the standard for masculine virtue"—as well as the perception, registered in anger and in fear, that antinomian doctrine is not separable from the tone and from the unsettling consequences of awakened female sexuality.[26]

To write *The Scarlet Letter* out of Hutchinsonian materials Hawthorne would have to feel that tone, but he would have to feel others as well. Fear "the woman" as he might, he would yet feel the justice of setting her—in reality, and as a symbol of radical and self-contained moral freedom—against the omnivorous legalism of the Puritan establishment. If he would reduce Ann Hutchinson to a female "case," his reduction would be less drastic than that of his ancestors. And he would preserve, amplify, and revalue certain deeper hints. *The Scarlet Leter* might not be "about" Ann Hutchinson, but it would be, consciously and emphatically, about antinomianism and "the woman."

III

We are now, finally, in a position to "begin"—to look directly at Hester walking in the footsteps of Ann Hutchinson, and to approach *The Scarlet Letter* itself in the one historical context Hawthorne seems most urgently to suggest. Legitimately, that task would require twice as many pages and distinctions as we have already set down. But perhaps the sympathetic reader will waive his right to charge reductive or text-ignoring historicism against a necessarily schematic suggestion about Hawthorne's romance in the Antinomian context.

The Scarlet Letter is, as I have suggested, not *roman à clef*: we are not to look for secret informations about literal, existent singulars in the seventeenth-century world. Neither is it quite an "allegory" of the real significance of a theological controversy: the Antinomian Crisis has historical ramifications which defy critical ingenuity to discover in *The Scarlet Letter*. And yet, to repeat, it is about antinomianism and "the woman."

It is, as in one recent formulation, about "passion and authority," but it is not about those timeless human realities *as such*. The experiences of Hester and Dimmesdale are subject to an exquisite (and painful) historical conditioning. Their Puritan world may be, as in another formulation, some version of the "modern" world, but this is far too imprecise to account for the historical specificity of Hawthorne's intention and achievement. To be sure, *The Scarlet Letter* details the items of Hester's beliefs even less than the early sketch specifies those of Mrs. Hutchinson; and yet the romance undoubtedly is, as one very excellent reading describes it, a "literary exercise in moral theology."[27]

That theology is, so far as the *characters* are concerned, "Puritan." So profoundly Puritan are the historically conditioned experiences of Hester and Dimmesdale, in fact, that *The Scarlet Letter* must be seen as Hawthorne's way of testing the limits of Puritan theology as a way of making sense out of the deepest and most passionate human experience. The limits of that theology are understood by Hawthorne to be—what I take it in fact they are—antinomian; and those antinomian limits of Puritan theology are associated by Hawthorne—as they were by his orthodox predecessors—with "the woman." When the limits are reached, as historically they were and as philosophically they must be, the theology fails what a twentieth-century critic of Puritanism has called "the pragmatic test." And as the theology fails, *The Scarlet Letter* becomes (in the context of the Ann Hutchinson problem, at least) a powerful contribution to what a nineteenth-century critic called "the moral argument against Calvinism."[28]

The Scarlet Letter is about the reasons why "the woman" Hester Prynne reaches certain antinomian conclusions not unlike those of Ann Hutchinson; and why, though her progress seems somehow necessary, and though personally she enlists our deepest sympathies, both the tale and the teller force her to abandon those conclusions. More elliptically, it is also about Dimmesdale's lesser portion of the "strange fire"; about the failure of his

Cottonesque, semi-antinomian theology; and, in the end, about his much-misunderstood "neonomian" emphasis on "the law" and "the sin." If we understand Hawthorne's relation to Mather, Johnson, and Winthrop properly, we can profitably view *The Scarlet Letter* as Hawthorne's own *Short Story of the Rise, Reign and Ruine of the Antinomians, Familists, and Libertines*.

In these terms, Hester's career is fairly easy to plot. At the outset she is not unambiguously antinomian. But she is conceived, like Hawthorne's Ann Hutchinson, as a woman who bears "trouble in her own bosom" (XII, 219); and her "desperate recklessness" on the scaffold, symbolized by the flagrancy of her embroidered "A," and issuing in "a haughty smile, and a glance that would not be abashed" (52), seems deliberately to recall Mrs. Hutchinson's courtroom defiance:

> She stands loftily before her judges with a determined brow; and, unknown to herself, there is a flash of carnal pride half hidden in her eye, as she surveys the many learned and famous men whom her doctrines have put in fear. (XII, 224)

That might describe Hester easily enough. She begins, let us say, in a not very repentant spirit. Strong hints of her later denials and unorthodox affirmations are already there.

To be sure, Hester feels a deep sense of shame, and we scarcely need the still, small quasi-authorial voice of a young-woman spectator to tell us so; the "reduction" of Ann Hutchinson's doctrinal bastard to a living illegitimate child must, in a Puritan community, at least, count for something. And yet even here Hester feels little enough of what we should call "guilt." [29] Just after the trauma of public exposure, she does confess a real wrong done to Chillingworth; but defiance of hopelessly unqualified and painfully uncomprehending male judges seems clearly the dominant element in her early characterization. It is probably true to say that (ignoring the "epilogue") Hester is nearer to "repentance" at the very opening of *The Scarlet Letter* than she ever is again. But she is not very near it. And by the time she finds herself in the forest with Dimmesdale, she has evidently found that she "should never have cause to be sorry for sinne" again.

For that antinomian moment, the narrator severely instructs us, Hesters "whole seven years of outlaw and ignominy had been little other than a preparation" (200). The moment includes not only the decision to cast by all outward pretence of living by the Puritan "world's law" and run away with Dimmesdale but also, and even more radically, her attempt to convince that unreconstructed Puritan theologian that what they earlier did "had a consecration of its own"—they having felt it so and said so to each other. The painfulness of Hester's development toward this moment in no way lessens our sense of its inevitability. From the first she has seemed perilously close to defying her judges with the affirmation that her spirit posits and obeys its own law.

The narrator seems convinced that Hester has indeed sinned—deeply, and "in the most sacred quality of human life" (56); at one level of our response, the seventh commandment remains real enough. But what he urges far more strongly is the outrage to both human privacy and human conscience perpetrated by the "unpardonable" Puritan practice of exposure and enforced confession.[30] And he also feels—with Hester—that her adultery was, in quality, not entirely evil: the sacred is present along with the sinful; or, less paradoxically, that Hester has fulfilled her passionate self for the first time in her life.

But of course there are no Puritan categories for this ambiguity. There is no way for Hester to say to herself that her action had been naturally perfect and yet had introduced an element of profound social disharmony. And no way for the Puritan mind to treat her evident unwillingness *fully* to disown and un-will the affections and natural motions which caused the disorder as anything but evidence of unregenerated natural depravity. She evidently loves her sin, and theocrats in the business of inferring the ultimate moral quality of the self from the prevailing outward signs can reach only one conclusion. And, thus, when the Puritan establishment moves from the *fact* that Hester *has sinned* to the *conclusion* that she is essence *is sinful*, her rich and ambiguous personality has no life-saving resource but to begin a career of antinomian speculation, of internal resistance to all Puritan categories.

If Society must treat the negative implications of one mixed act as the symbol of the natural depravity of the Self, that Self is likely to respond with a simple affirmation of all its own profound impulses. If the Puritans begin by turning Hester into a sermon, a type, and an allegory of "Sin," she will end by nullifying their entire world of external law and interference with her own pure freedom. Ideally we might wish for Hester to cease feeling shame and to discover the real though limited extent of her guilt. But this, in the Puritan mental and social world seems impossible. Extremes of public legalism seem to breed their antinomian opposite by natural law.[31] At any rate, Hester finds no way to affirm the legitimacy of her powerful sexual nature without also affirming total, anarchic spiritual freedom.

Of course she begins in outward conformity, playing the game of "sanctification"—the single rule of which is that the true Self is the sum of all its outward works; indeed, by the time we see her in the chapter called "Another View of Hester," she has learned the game so well as to have covered her undestroyed inner pride with an external appearance "so like humility, that it produced all the softening influence of that latter quality on the public mind" (162). But all the while she is "preparing," moving toward the moment when she announces a doctrine of personal freedom which every orthodox Puritan sensed would lead directly to passionate license and judged a more serious threat to public order than adultery itself.

Her own version of the antinomian heresy does not, obviously, express itself in theological jargon; for the most part Hawthorne eschewed it even in treating Mrs. Hutchinson. No dogmatist, Hawthorne is looking for difference that *make* a difference; and the antinomian difference is identically expressed in Mrs. Hutchinson and Hester Prynne, in association with but not quite reduced to a discovery and affirmation of the legitimacy of their female sexuality. Call it Spirit with the seventeenth, or Passional Self with a later century, one's affirmation is not very different: the significance of a life is *not* the sum of its legally regulated outward works; or, more radically, what one does has a consecration of its own provided the quality of deep inner feeling is right—i.e., authentic.

Now plainly this is all too partial a truth for Hawthorne; we are not wrong in hearing his own advice when Dimmesdale twice bids Hester's revolutionary voice to "Hush." And yet he understands how it all comes about. He even presents it as necessary for Hester to reach this stage of self-affirmation and release from shame before she can settle into anything approaching final peace.

While she cannot affirm her adultery, she cannot truly accept Pearl as a valid human person. It is probably too much to ask her to accept a good-out-of-evil doctrine all at once. Certainly it is better to affirm the natural order than to treat Pearl chiefly as a living sermon; clearly nothing good can happen as long as the mother is allegorizing the child even as the community has allegorized the mother; and surely a parent who is watching for a child to become a moral monster will not be disappointed.

And then there is the simple matter of Hester's integrity. Speculating so boldly and conforming so relentlessly, she has become—no less than Dimmesdale himself—two people. At one primal level, the whole antinomian controversy is about the inner and the outer, the private and the public person: what do our outward works, positive and negative, really reveal about our salvation status, or, in naturalized form, about our selves? Hawthorne's romance is, of course, busy denying total autonomous validity to the private or "spiritual" self; and the explicit "moral" about freely "showing forth" some inferential "token" clearly embodies the authorial realization that inner and outer can never be completely congruent. Hawthorne has not written "Young Goodman Brown" and "The Minister's Black Veil" for nothing. And yet Hester must stop living a life so completely double. Quite like Dimmesdale, she must heal the wide and deep, "hypocritical" split between her outer and inner self. She may never realize as clearly as Dimmersdale finally does the extent to which (or the profound reasons why) the Self must accept the demystified implications of the visible, and dwell—though not as the great body of Puritans do—among moral surfaces.[32] But in the terms of her own developing theory of spiritual self-reliance, she must be, as fully as possible, whatever she truly is.

And we sense her self-acceptance and self-affirmation coming. She may seem to wander in confusion—thinking the sun of universal benevolence shines only to illuminate her scarlet letter, and deceiving herself about why she remains in New England; but from time to time, when a human eye (presumably Dimmesdale's) falls upon her "ignominious brand," she wills her old passion anew. She may worry about the condition and quality of Pearl's right to existence; but when the watchful theocratic government considers removing her natural child to some more socialized context of Christian nurture, Hester is simply defiant: "I will not lose the child!" (113). She may argue from Pearl's moral use, but she is also affirming the validity of her sexual nature.

We can say—if we wish to maintain a *modern only* reading of *The Scarlet Letter*—that this is *all* Hester is affirming when she argues, finally, that her adultery had "a consecration of its own"; that Hawthorne has engaged Hester *entirely* in an *overt* struggle with the unruly and unsatisfied sexual emotions which the Puritans obscurely felt to lie unsublimated behind Mrs. Hutchinson's public career, and which they clearly felt would be unleashed upon their community by a public acceptance of her doctrine. (Male self-control being difficult enough when all women are passive or frigid.) But if our conclusions concern only Hester's movement from sexual shame to sexual affirmation, then Hawthorne has wasted a good deal of historic understanding and surmise as mere costume and color. It seems far more adequate to say—as we have already said—that Hawthorne regards awakened and not conventionally invested female sexual power as a source and type of individualistic nullification of social restraint.

Waiving the problem of vehicle and tenor, we may validly conclude that in *The Scarlet Letter* "the woman's" discovery of an authentic, valid, and not shameful sexual nature is not unlike the Self's discovery of its own interior, "spiritual" sanction. The *donnée* of Hawthorne's romance is such that Hester discovers both together, and each reinforces the other.

And further, by way of completing our contextual approach to *The Scarlet Letter*, it seems appropriate to suggest that Hawthorne's treatment of Dimmesdale, the less clearly antinomian partner, provides cogent reasons for not divorcing the theology from, or reducing it too simply to, the sexuality.

For Dimmesdale's predicament is not to be understood without some fairly explicit reference to the most theological of the antinomian questions—certainly not without a sense of the peculiar moral shapes one can be molded into only by a fairly high Calvinism. Indeed there is, as I have already suggested, strong evidence that Hawthorne thought of Dimmesdale as some intellectual and literary relative of John Cotton.

IV

In a number of related senses, Dimmesdale's problem is "hypocrisy." Most simply, he is not what he outwardly appears; he may or may not be "vile," but he is not the apotheosis of saintly purity the Puritan community takes him for. More technically, he is an enforcing agent of public discipline who has himself sinned against a clear and serious public law whose absolute validity he (unlike Hester) never questions for a moment; and who refuses to confess and submit to the discipline he has sworn by covenant to uphold and enforce. In so refusing, he may very well be avoiding the question of whether he is really sorry for his sin, or whether in fact be loves his own satisfactions more than he loves God; if so, if Dimmesdale's adultery is really "idolatry," as in the common religious equivalence, then of course he is a "hypocrite" in the very most technical Puritan sense of all: he is an unconverted man who has found his way not only *in to* but to the very *apex* of the purest church the world has ever known. This is clearly what he fears: that the minister, whose election is sure if anyone's is, whose conversion is the norm for the members' admission, and who—at this level, incidentally—is universally revered as a miracle of preternatural holiness and supernatural humility, is really an unregenerate sinner simply.

He fears, but he is not certain. He also hopes. In such tension Dimmesdale is a classic Puritan case of conscience—an advanced and exacerbated form of the too-common problem of lingering sinfulness and naturally attendant doubt which seems to have followed most honest Puritans into full communion with New England's congregations of "visible saints." What, after all, could the unreconstructed Arminianism of natural conscience make of the fact that after one professed to have received saving grace by the direct operation of the spirit (and had that profession accepted by all other spiritual men) one continued to be roughly the same sort of moral person one was before?[33]

The *simple* answer is antinomianism: "works" argue nothing. The sons of God being under no law, it is as fatal a confusion to argue from the presence of sin to the absence of grace as it is to infer justification of the person from sanctification of the life. Grace is a spiritual indwelling, and whatever the Spirit is, is right. Just ask Hester.

Dimmesdale, of course, can accept this limit-interpretation of Pauline and Protestant theology as little as Cotton could. And yet Dimmesdale seems caught in a trap set for him by certain of the spiritual principles Cotton laid down carefully to distinguish himself from both the covenant legalists on the one side and the "antinomians, familists, and libertines" on the other. Everyone wanted to admit that the forensic transaction of justification did not imply or create immediate and perfect operational sanctity, but Cotton's critics wanted him to narrow the gap as much as Protestant loyalty could possibly admit. They put it to him: when you say "A Christian may have assurance of his good estate maintained to him when the frame of his Spirit and course is grown much degenerate, we want much satisfaction." Your doctrine is very dangerous, they instructed him; there ought to be more "symmetry and proportion" in this matter of "faith and holiness" or you "open a wide door of temptation, as into Sin with less fear, so into a bold continuance and slight healing of sin, and breaches hereby."[34]

As always, the legalists have conceived the problem rather too crudely: Dimmesdale's "continuance," for example, is far from "bold," and his physical and moral self-flagellations amount at some level to more than a "slight healing of sin." And yet there is sense in their position. A man who *fears* he may be a hypocrite and yet has good theological reasons to *hope* that even gross sins do not necessarily prove the case either way is likely to clutch at every available theological straw. And indeed Cotton's answer to the legalists offers far more than a straw. It is worth quoting at some length for it marvellously illuminates Dimmesdale's predicament. If a man

> know the riches of Gods grace in Christ, he ordinarily both may, and (by ordinary rule) ought to believe that his justified estate doth still remain unshaken, not withstanding his grievous sin. For as Justification and the faith of it doth not stand upon his good works, so neither doth it fall or fail upon his evil work.[35]

Cotton's difference from the antinomians is, evidently, a fairly subtle one— and not of primary interest to us here. Of significance is the fact that the strictest Calvinist of New England's first generation provides Dimmesdale with a perfectly plausible way to avoid the obvious, most "natural" conclusion about his technical hypocrisy.

And Cotton brings the case even closer to our own:

> Because men of great measure of holiness be apt to live besides their faith, in the strength of their own gifts and not

in the strength of Christ, it pleaseth the Lord sometimes to leave them to greater falls, than other weaker Christians, who being of weaker gifts do find more need to live by faith in Christ than upon the strength of their gifts.

It seems to me entirely likely that some conception such as this—a highly religious man being tested by a great fall—lies very close to Hawthorne's idea of Dimmesdale.[36] And that Hawthorne is testing this Cottonesque way of conceptualizing the problem of sin and sainthood as he watches Dimmesdale fail to work out his salvation in these terms.

For the terms do fail him, even more plainly than, in the epilogue, Hester's appear to have failed her. The psychological dynamic of their failure is delicately wrought, but it is "there," in the romance. To see it requires only to look at Dimmesdale's few key speeches very closely.

We do not begin to get inside Dimmesdale until Chapter X, where "The Leech" is working on "His Patient." With the worst imaginable motives, Chillingworth is trying to get Dimmesdale to do what the structure and basic conception of the romance clearly indicates he must if he is to save his soul, in any imaginable sense—clearly and openly admit his guilt, whatever the consequences. Dimmesdale offers several "good" reasons why some men find it impossible to confess before the Last Day, or to any but the Searcher of Hearts. His reasons are all, we easily sense, speculative or notional, unreal; the two men are talking "objectively" about "some men." And yet before Dimmesdale waives the whole subject as if "irrelevant or unreasonable," he is betrayed into a modestly revealing hint. The best of his rationalizations is that "some men" do not confess because in spite of their sin they yet retain "a zeal for God's glory and man's welfare"; they realize that once exposed "no good can be achieved by them; no evil of the past be redeemed by better service" (132). Hypocrisy, Dimmesdale seems to argue, is not without an important social, even spiritual use.

Chillingworth, however, that perfect devil's advocate, recognizes the desperate character of this logic at once. Hypocrisy for the sake of the kingdom is the worst hypocrisy of all. Would Dimmesdale have us believe "that a false show can be better—can be more for God's glory, or man's welfare—than God's own truth" (133)?

The irony here is very keen. It seems impossible to escape the sense that Hawthorne is deliberately playing with one of the most famous arguments in a massive Puritan literature of propagandistic self-defense—the idea of "the usefulness of hypocrites." Attacked by English Presbyterians for a wildly utopian collapse of the invisible church into the visible, defenders of the New England Way loudly protested that they fully *expected* to receive hypocrites into their churches, despite the revolutionary tests for saving grace; that they indeed could rest easy in this practical knowledge, despite their purist theoretic aims, because in outward practice the hypocrite was very often more zealous, set a more striking public example than the true saint. The most authoritative spokesman for this Puritan "foreign policy" was—of course—John Cotton.[37]

The irony is only slightly less telling when we remember that neither Dimmesdale nor Hawthorne really sees the case in these terms. Hawthorne could very *easily* accept hypocrites into his church, since it is universal and consists *only* of hypocrites who never *can* fully "show forth" what they ultimately are. Limited to his historic world, however, Dimmesdale is obviously far from this insight. Indeed he is even farther away from it than his use-of-hypocrites rationalization would indicate.

Where he is, morally and theologically speaking, becomes perfectly clear only in the forest with Hester—though anyone versed in the literary cure of Puritan souls senses it long before. The meaning of his entire predicament is encapsulated into two sentences, and logically enough he speaks them in direct reply to Hester's antinomian plan for adulterous escape:

> "If, in all these past seven years," thought he, "I could recall one instant of peace or hope, I would yet endure, for the sake of that earnest of Heaven's mercy. But now,—since I am irrevocably doomed,—wherefore should I not snatch the solace allowed to the condemned culprit before his execution?" (201)

Again the irony is fairly complex. First of all we recognize in Dimmesdale's decision to "seize the day" the crassest sort of antinomian response possible for a Calvinist to make: since I am predestined to hell anyway, I might as well.... But this is the least of it.

More crucially, Dimmesdale reveals that he has to this point been looking at his life in a way that is very "properly" Calvinist: he has been regarding his acts, good and evil, and his spiritual states, hopeful and discouraging, not as sequential parts of a moral life that he is *building*, bit by bit, but rather as *evidences* of his status relative to divine decree. The difference may often seem subtle in practice, but it is absolutely profound; and the meaning is to be read in any Puritan diary. One does not repent sin in order to undo it and atone for it and get back into divine favor; only Catholics and other Arminians think this. Rather one examines sins along with every other significant fact about the moral life in order to detect, if one possibly can, whether or not an eternal decree of salvation has made itself temporally manifest as a spiritual experience of justification, usually issuing more or less "proportionally and symmetrically" in sanctification.

For *most* Puritans sins are, therefore, an essential sign; for all, repentance is an absolutely necessary one. Even for Cotton. The great man may have great sins and not lose heart and hope; but even the great man must find that he truly *can* repent. Gross outward lapses may be at best a crude indicator of the spiritual estate, but enduring love of sin is not.

"Of penance," Dimmesdale admits—of that melodramatic outward punishment and gothic inward torture—there has been a surfeit; "Of penitence," however—of that true spiritual rejection of the soul's rejection of God—"there has been none!" (192). And now, he concludes, things look very bad indeed. He may as well admit he has been, all along, the hypocrite he feared he might be and yet hoped (in spite of his rationalization to Chillingworth) he might not be. In the forest then, finally, after seven years of self-torturing hope against hope, Dimmesdale gives over the attempt to see himself as the man whose justification does not, in Cotton's words, "Fall or fail upon his evil works." Semi-antinomian to this point, he now concludes that his hope has all been in vain—that he has not repented his sin, that he has been granted no further spiritual assurances, and that his crime of adultery is precisely what all vulgar Puritanism would take it to be, "visible" (if only to himself) evidence of manifest unregeneracy.

Spiritually, then, Dimmesdale is further from Hester Prynne during their sexual reunion in the forest than he has ever been before—as far away, in fact, as it is possible to be within a Puritan world. Their decision to escape, though they may "say it" to each other, means two dramatically opposed things. To Hester it is that triumphant escape into the higher antinomian freedom of spiritual self-reliance; to Dimmesdale it is a pitiful retreat from the hope-against-hope to that miserable alternative of sinful freedom left to the despairing reprobate. One may wish their original adulterous meeting involved more of real mutuality.

Thus Hawthorne's subtlest view of Dimmesdale is as a man who is so ineffectual an antinomian as not to be able to overcome the conscientious suspicion that, his serious sin proves him a hypocrite; not even with the subtle categories of John Cotton. Hawthorne's men, as we know, are weaker than his women. Or perhaps it is simply that "woman's morality is not quite the standard for masculine virtue." Or perhaps he is simply honest. In any event, neither his sexuality nor his doctrine can justify the life he has been leading or, now, sanctify the new freedom he has been seduced into accepting. He will run away, in a sense, to settle his doubts, once and for all, into a certainty of reprobation.

If we are sufficiently aware of the positivistic pitfalls, it becomes useful to speculate about Dimmesdale's fictional relation to John Cotton. Should we say he is some curious version of Cotton's son, who did commit adultery and suffer ignominious excommunication? Or might we see him as a provisional John Cotton who by Providential mischance happened to seduce (or be seduced by) Ann Hutchinson? What if, Hawthorne might have brooded, what if Ann Hutchinson had literally been what Puritan metaphor implied she was? And what if Cotton were implicated, literally, to the very extent his English detractors said he metaphorically was? What, in short, would a "high" but not antinomian Calvinist do if he *had* played the part of a sexual Montanus to some sexual Maxilla? What would a real sin, all passionate and ambiguous, do to the delicate balances of personality required to maintain that exquisite "Doctrine of the Saints' Infirmities"? What sense might a younger, less robust, less settled version (or disciple) or Cotton be able to make out of a passionate adultery?

In this light, it is just possible that Dimmesdale owes something to the writings (*not* to the *life*) of John Preston, Cotton's most famous orthodox convert and disciple. Mather's *Magnalia* calls Cotton the "spiritual father" of Preston, and his most famous work (*The Doctrine of the Saints' Infirmities*, 1638) owes a profound debt to Cotton's ideas about assurance in spite of sin. Like Cotton, Preston is at great pains to prove that the Puritan saint "may have many infirmities, and the covenant remain unbroken." But there is one peculiar and illuminating hesitation in Preston that is entirely lacking in Cotton's answers to the American legalists of the 1630's. Unlike Cotton, Preston is anxious about an exception—or at least a possible misunderstanding. Not *all* sins can be written off as mere "infirmities"; "some sins" are so radically idolatrous that they must be taken to mean that a person has not *been* in the covenant—that he has been a hypocrite all along. Preston does not specify; but his one hint is telling indeed: the exceptions are sins which "untye the marriage knot" as, in human marriage, "Adultery."[38] That revelation would seem to explain Dimmesdale's career pretty well: the reason he *cannot* repent is that he *is not* a saint; *probably* Preston's emphasis is sounder than Cotton's. And so he gives over the desperate seven-year effort to believe himself not a hypocrite in the worst sense. His peculiar "infirmity" is too real, too true a sign of unregenerate infidelity. Justification and sanctification are not to be conflated, but "some sins" are unsupportable. And thus, until Dimmesdale's very last moment, Puritan doctrines with sexual implications and overtones seem to be damning him as surely as they seem to be saving Hester.

At the last moment, of course, a major reversal occurs. Ceasing to "live in the strength of [his] own gifts"—even though he has just exercised them magnificently in a bad-faith election sermon—Dimmesdale asks for Hester's strength and God's grace to help him up the scaffold. Once there, his words indicate that somehow he has freed himself from his old Calvinist entrapment. If he has not entirely detheologized himself, at least he has got his doctrine down to certain saving essentials. Hester calls on his far-seeing vision to predict their final destiny. But Dimmesdale, who has been reading evidences of *faits accompli* for too long, rightly refuses to predict: "Hush, Hester, hush!" What has often been called his final "gloom" is no more than elemental moral and theological honesty. "The law we broke!—the sin here so awfully revealed!" Stern instructions to an Antinomian. Yet these alone must be in them thoughts, their only proper concern. For the rest, "God knows; and He is merciful!" (256).

Law, Sin, Mercy—these are now the only terms in Dimmesdale's new moral scheme. We know there are laws to restrict our Selves in the name of our communities which, well or ill, sustain our common life; we know we break these laws; the rest is up to God. This may or may not conceal Arminian heresy, but "neonomian" Hawthorne has clearly designed it to be. I think we may grant the writer of "Young Goodman Brown" and "The Minister's Black Veil," and the creator of Dimmesdale's problems of ever "outering" what he truly is inside, the right to affirm the operational primacy of "the public."

It takes Hester longer, and it requires a years-later epilogue, but she too relents from her doctrine of the autonomous private—she repents, turns her game of "penance" into authentic "penitence." She still holds out for a feminist reformer, but she can now separate the valid sexual expectations of her sisterhood from the supposed spiritual freedom of the Self from the world's law.

The final ironies of Hawthorne's use of Hutchinsonian motifs and antinomian ideas are striking indeed. If his early sketch seems to reduce a dangerous female heretic to a sexual case, his effort can be regarded as a commentary on a Puritan response as validly as it can be taken for his own; and, he puts *all* the subtlety back into *The Scarlet Letter*. He maintains, even literalizes, all the sexual suggestions in his creation of Hester Prynne, but he leaves them in tension with some very profound (if, for him, dangerous) religious ideas. With Dimmesdale he allows the full theological complexity to operate, though we never forget that Dimmesdale is related to Hester in the sexual problems which form the context of their spiritual struggles. The perfect context, we feel, given Puritan problems with "privacy" of all sorts. And in the end, after he has fully explored the antinomian and Cottonesque ramifications of his imaginative vision of a Puritan heresy, in doctrine and in metaphoric implication, Hawthorne brings both his principal characters back to something like his own "neonomian" norm. The ending is by no means "happy"—any more than Hawthorne's "Antinomians" and "Libertines" are in any sense that would satisfy Winthrop or Mather "Ruined." But their "Short Story" does end in an important doctrinal transformation.

The Self is not to be regularly inferred from its Works; it is quite naive to think so. But human sin, guilt, and sorrow are not to be transcended or "spiritually" suspended in this life. The Self is spiritually more free than any human establishment, theocratic or otherwise, can recognize or "tolerate." But the world's law validly exists to restrain our disruptive social excesses, however powerful and authentic we feel or "say" their private consecration to be. That, or something like it, equally simple, was the usable historical truth to be discovered from a tracing of Ann Hutchinson's footsteps.

NOTES

1. All quotations from *The Scarlet Letter*, identified by page numbers in the text, refer to the Centenary Edition, Vol. 1 (Columbus, Ohio, 1962).

2. See, particularly, Hyatt H. Waggoner's *Hawthorne* (Cambridge, Mass., 1955, 1963) and Roy R. Male's "From the Innermost Germ," *ELH*, 20 (1953).

3. The critic must always be alert for tones of mock self-condescension in Hawthorne. In the famous letter to Longfellow (4 June 1837) Hawthorne calls his "studious life" at Salem a "desultory" one; but when he complains that his reading has not brought him "the fruits of study," he may well be remembering that it is *Longfellow* who went on from Bowdoin to become Professor of Modern Languages in Harvard University, rather than "the obscurest man of letters in America."

4. I have explored these relationships, among others, in a book-length manuscript on the "history" in Hawthorne's early stories, which I hope to publish within the next year. The clue to the "unobvious" relation here—that between *MBV* and the Awakening—comes from the similarity of some of Hooper's concerns with those expressed in various election sermons preached "during Governor Belcher's administration" (I, 65).

5. For the "dates" of *The Scarlet Letter*, see Charles Ryskamp, "The New England Sources of *The Scarlet Letter*," *AL*, 31 (1959); and for a speculation about the "libertarian" meaning of those dates, see H. Bruce Franklin's "Introduction" to *The Scarlet Letter and Related Writings* (Philadelphia and New York, 1967).

6. I have assumed a basic familiarity with the career and heresies, spoken and alleged, of Ann Hutchinson. A full study of her "influence," at least indirect, leads virtually everywhere in the seventeenth century. The following items seem most relevant: for primary sources beyond those *demonstrably* read by Hawthorne (Winthrop's *Journal*, Edward Johnson's *Wonder-Working Providence of Sion's Savior*, Cotton Mather's *Magnalia*, and Thomas Hutchinson's *History of Massachusetts Bay*). consult Charles Francis Adams' collection of material on *Antinomianism in the Colony of Massachusetts Bay*, 1636-1638, published as Volume 21 of the *Publications of the Prince Society* (Boston, 1894) and David D. Hall's *The Antinomian Controversy: A Documentary History* (Middletown, Conn., 1968). This last contains some sources which Hawthorne probably could not have seen; but both contain the crucial transcripts of her two "trials" as well as Winthrop's *Short Story of the Rise, Reign, and Ruine of the Antinomians, Familists, and Libertines* (1644). For modern commentary on the meaning of Mrs. Hutchinson's ideas and career, two works seem

indispensable: Emery Battis, *Saints and Sectaries* (Chapel Hill, N. C., 1962) and Larzer Ziff. *John Cotton* (Princeton. N. J., 1962). Also useful is Part Two of C. F. Adams' *Three Episodes in Massachusetts History*, 2 vols. (Boston, 1893).

7. "Mrs. Hutchinson" first appeared in the *Salem Gazette* for 7 December 1830. Quotations in this essay are from the "Riverside Edition" of *Hawthorne's Works*, Vol. 12 (Boston, 1882–83).

8. The harshest modern judgment is that of Perry Miller: "Cotton tried hard to adhere to the Protestant line until his colleagues forced him to recognize that he, for all his great position, would be sacrificed along with Mistress Hutchinson unless be yielded. As many another man in a similar predicament, Cotton bent" (*The New England Mind: From Colony to Province* [Cambridge, Mass., 1953], pp. 59–60). For a view which emphasizes Cotton's "idealistic" naivete see Ziff, *Cotton*, pp. 106–48.

9. For an account of the un-desultory scholarship behind *The Scarlet Letter*, see Ryskamp, "New England Sources."

10. The facts in this paragraph have been noticed by other Hawthorne critics, but they have not pressed the Cotton-Dimmesdale implication. Besides Ryskamp, see Austin Warren's "Introduction" to the Rinehart Edition of *The Scarlet Letter* (New York, 1947).

11. In "spirit" this essay derives from a suggestion by Roy Harvey Pearce that Hawthorne criticism has "tended to rush on, identifying and collocating his symbols and their forms, and then pursuing them out of time—out of space, too often beyond the consciousness of those whose life in art they make possible" ("Romance and the Study of History," in *Hawthorne Centenary Essays*, Columbus, Ohio, 1964). My general view of Hawthone is also congruent with that elaborated by Q. D. Leavis in "Hawthorne as Poet," *Sewance Review*, 59 (1951). I have not tried to reread all *Scarlet Letter* criticism in preparing this essay, nor to cite specific debts at every point. I should, however, acknowledge the special influence of Austin Warren, "*The Scarlet Letter*: A Literary Exercise in Moral Theology," *Southern Review*, 1 (1965); and E. W. Baughman, "Public Confessions and *The Scarlet Letter*," *NEQ*, 40 (1967).

12. After lecturing on Hawthorne to a course on "Women in Literature," my Cornell colleague Dan McCall reported to me that, in such a context, Hawthorne is a "sitting duck." He also suggested, quite cogently, that Hawthorne's later statements about women writers being interesting only when they expose their "natal mind" and come before the public as it were "naked" are not to be separated from the sexual overtones of the early sketch of Ann Hutchinson; perhaps not even from his historical memory of certain Quaker women whipped half-naked through the streets of New England by his ancestor.

13. The earlier form is in Chapter V: "Here, she said to herself, had been the scene of her guilt, and here should be the scene of her earthly punishment." The change from "punishment" to "penitence" is obviously significant. Also notice that the earlier paragraph in question begins by suggesting that "doubtless" she has a "secret" reason for remaining (80).

14. Even as the abundant and familiar discussion of Margaret Fuller and Zenobia reaches the point of diminishing returns, criticism is proposing "Margaret Fuller as a Model for Hester Prynne"; see the article by Francis E. Kearns in *Jahrbuch Für Amerikastudien*, 10 (1965).

15. *Saints and Sectaries*, p. 6.

16. For an authoritative discussion of the way Puritan theory made the visible church *nearly* identical with the *invisible* (i.e., mystified the prime agent of "discipline") see Edmund Morgan, *Visible Saints* (New York, 1963). Some strong sense of the process seems implied everywhere in Hawthorne's writings about the Puritans; and, indeed, one could scarcely read Mather's *Magnalia* without grasping that it was with the Ann Hutchinson affair that the mystified public achieved precedence, in the Puritan world, over the mystical private.

17. This point is made very effectively in a recent article by Nina Baym, in spite of an ill-informed and logically inconclusive "negative" argument about the lack of meaningful Puritan categories in *The Scarlet Letter*. See "Passion and Authority in *The Scarlet Letter*," *NEQ*, 43 (1970).

18. There is no satisfactory reading of "The Gentle Boy" in print. The basic, old-fashioned "source" study—which includes some relevant material on Mary Dyer—is G. H. Orians, "Sources and Themes of "The Gentle Boy,'" *NEQ*, 14 (1941).

19. The larger quotation is from Battis (p. 287); he, in turn, is quoting from Gertrude Huehns' *Antinomianism in English History* (London, 1951). The same sentiments can be found in many modern treatments of any of the more individualistic or "spiritual" forms of religious experience in the seventeenth century.

20. Rufus Jones. *The Quakers in the American Colonies* (London, 1911), p. 26. See also Geoffrey Nuttall, *The Holy Spirit in Puritan Experience* (London, 1946). Nuttall treats early Quakerism as a "limit" of one sort of Puritan logic and experience; though he does not argue the case, one cannot help being struck by the prominence of women in his accounts of early Quaker prophecy.

21. Thomas Hutchinson's masterful, three-volume *History of Massachusetts Bay* probably provided Hawthorne with his most judicious account of the Hutchinson affair; certainly it was useful in providing the transcript of Mrs. Hutchinson before the General Court at Newtown in November, 1637—where she gave a far better account of herself than would appear from Winthrop's *Short Story*. But the account given by *this* Hutchinson contains no hint of sexual language. For Hawthorne's reading of Hutchinson, Mather, Johnson, and Winthrop, see Marion L. Kesselring, *Hawthorne's Reading* (New York, 1949).

22. Of necessity I quote from a nineteenth-century edition: *Magnalia Christi Americana* (Hartford, Conn., 1855), II, 516.

23. The heresy-bastard conceit is also in Thomas Weld's "Preface" to Winthrop's *Short Story* (reprinted in Adams and Hall; see note 6); the *Short Story* is, in turn the main source of Mather's account. It is not certain, but it seems likely, that Hawthorne saw Winthrop's book independently.

24. *Magnalia*, II, 518. Probably this is only Mather's pedantry at work—re-translating from Revelations. In Winthrop's *Short Story* Cotton says "make and maintaine a lye" (see Hall, *Antinomian Controversy*, p. 307).

25. Quoted from Hall, *Antinomian Controversy*, pp. 315–316 and p. 267. Hawthorne would have found all he needed in the "Appendix" to Thomas Hutchinson's second volume; see his *History* (Cambridge, Mass., 1936), II, 366–91, esp. 368–69.

26. *Wonder-Working Providence of Sion's Saviour*, ed. by Franklin L. Jameson (New York, 1910), p. 134. Note also that Winthrop, besides his relentless pursuit of "monstrous" evidences against both Ann Hutchinson and Mary Dyer, does not overlook instances of irregular sexual practice resulting from Hutchinsonian principles; see his *Journal*, ed. by James Kendall Hosmer, 2 Vols. (New York, 1908), esp. II, 28.

27. The three formulations are, respectively, those of Nina Baym, "Passion and Authority," Charles Feidelson, Jr., "*The Scarlet Letter*," *Hawthorne Centenary Essays* (Columbus, Ohio, 1964), and Austin Warren, "*The Scarlet Letter*: A Literary Exercise in Moral Theology."

28. The "pragmatic" (or moral) argument against Calvinism runs backwards from Henry Bamford Parkes' essay "The Puritan Heresy" (in *The Pragmatic Test* [New York, 1941]) to William Ellery Channing, at least (probably to Jonathan Mayhew). Only critics who do not feel themselves challenged by Puritan beliefs fail to argue from Puritanism's seeming inability to square with natural conscience and adequately to interpret moral experience.

29. My Cornell colleague Michael Kammen first suggested to me that the modern

sociological and anthropological distinction between "guilt" and the more primitive, less rational and internalized "shame" was useful in distinguishing Dimmesdale's from Hester's response to their adultery.

30. For the Puritan doctrine and practice of confession—and for a very useful approach to *The Scarlet Letter*, which I regard as supplementary to my own—see Baughman, "Public Confession and *The Scarlet Letter*."

31. Through John Winthrop is only a background figure in *The Scarlet Letter*, his moral presence is strongly felt. It is surely the famous "little speech" on liberty of this most energetic opponent of Ann Hutchinson that Hawthorne had in mind when he wrote in "Main Street" that what the Puritans "called Liberty" was very much "like an iron cage" (III, 449). In fact, it is Winthrop's doctrine of liberty as holy obedience which sinews the clerical doctrines of visible sanctity, preparation, and sanctification, to make the Puritan world the massive and unitary legal construct Hawthorne represents it to be in the opening pages of *The Scarlet Letter*. Hawthorne gives us that world as of the 1640's: one could argue that rigidification was not complete by that point and that Hawthorne is really describing a later stage of development, when "one generation had bequeathed ... the counterfeit of its religious ardor to the next" (III, 460); for this view see E. H. Davidson, "The Question of History in *The Scarlet Letter*," *ESQ*, 25 (1951); but one can also argue that, though Hawthorne does indeed "encapsulate" a long historical sequence into the moments of its beginning, he clearly intends to point us to the banishment of Ann Hutchinson (1636–1638) as the crucial defeat of spiritual libertarianism in the Puritan world.

32. The lesson of the ultimate autonomy of the spiritual self, along with the coordinate subjection of the outward man to civil authority, is (presumably) the lesson Hawthorne learned from the career of Roger Williams—of whom Hawthorne seems a true spiritual disciple.

33. Conveniently, one might look at *The Diary of Michael Wigglesworth*, ed. by Edmund Morgan (New York, 1956) for a sense of the painful doubts experienced by the already encovenanted saints. I have studied a coordinate problem—how could the sinning and doubting Christian really see fit to *declare* himself a saint?—in an analysis of Edward Taylor: "*Gods Determinations* Touching Half-Way Membership," *AL*, 39 (1967). If Solomon Stoddard is to be believed (that Puritan theory had turned Communion Sundays into "days of torment") then *some* version of Dimmesdale's problem was widespread indeed.

34. Quoted from Hall, *Antinomian Controversy*, pp. 66–66. The document in question is "The Elders Reply"—to the answers Cotton had given to sixteen questions addressed to him by those same "Elders."

35. From "Mr. Cotton's Rejoynder," quoted in Hall, p. 88.

36. "Rejoynder," in Hall, pp. 88–89. I do not suppose that Hawthorne could have seen this then-unpublished document. I do assume, however, that Hawthorne did somewhere acquire a first-hand familiarity with some of Cotton's works, or with at least some Puritan writers who introduced the problem of justification *in spite* of a rather imperfect sanctification. It would be very naive to assume that Hawthorne's reading of Puritan writers is exhausted by the list of his borrowings from the Salem Athenaeum, when so many of them were available on the bookstands of the 1880's.

37. See Miller, *Colony to Province*, pp. 79–80.

38. *The Doctrine of the Saints' Infirmities* (London, 1638), pp. 36–38. No less a scholar than John F. H. New has interpreted the passage in question to mean, simply, that adultery is a cardinal example of a sin which disproves covenant status—whereat, according to my reading, only some analogy is intended (see *Anglican and Purity* [1964], p. 93). The critic of *The Scarlet Letter* will be rewarded by a reading of Preston's treatise, especially the first sermon. His encouragement to even a *lifelong* struggle against "infirmities" forms an

appropriate background to Dimmesdale's weakening after seven years; and, on the other side, his clear statement that "a sin committed simply with deliberation cannot be an infirmity" seems to supply the ironic context for Hawthorne's comment on Dimmesdale's state just after he has lost the *struggle*: "he has yielded himself, with deliberate choice, as he had never done before, to what he knew was deadly sin" (922). Thus, in a sense, it is only when Dimmesdale gives up the belief that his sin is an infirmity that it truly ceases to be one.

NINA BAYM

Who? The Characters

The "neutral territory" of Hawthorne's fiction serves the author's general goal of embodying his conviction that "reality," for all of us, is not a given something but is constructed by the interaction between our selective perceptions and what exists "out there." Some people are more objective than others, but nobody can attain a purely objective vision. Besides this general goal, the neutral territory provides Hawthorne with a fit habitat for a mix of characters, some fairly "realistic" in the way they are portrayed, others far more abstract or fantastic.

The cast of characters in *The Scarlet Letter* is quite small, and none of them is a wholly realistic character. The Puritans are portrayed as instances of a single type, not as individuals; Pearl and Chillingworth are developed as much for their symbolic values in relation to Hester and Dimmesdale, respectively, as they are for their own personalities; and even Dimmesale, and Hester are in part subjected to an allegorizing and typifying scheme. (Briefly, we can distinguish symbol from allegory by saying that a symbol attaches, by suggestion, a range of various abstract meanings to an object, while an allegory stands more forthrightly for a single idea. A character can be allegorical and symbolic simultaneously.) Every one of these personages would be out of place in the richly detailed and particularized world of a conventional realistic fiction. As Hawthorne himself described his practice,

From The Scarlet Letter: *A Reading.* © 1986 by G.K. Hall.

he kept the lights of his fiction dim so that these characters would seem life-like, knowing full well that in a bright glare they would fade away. Sometimes he regretted his inability to write purely realistic fiction: but he could not resist his own imaginative tendency to "embroider" a realistic scene with suggestions and implications.

HESTER

In Hester Prynne, Hawthorne created the first true heroine of American fiction, as well as one of its enduring heroes. Hester is a heroine because, she is deeply implicated in, and responsive to, the gender structure of her society, and because her story, turning on "love," is "appropriate" for a woman. She is a hero because she has qualities and actions that transcend this gender reference and lead to heroism as it can be understood for anyone.

"Such helpfulness was found in her,—so much power to do, and power to sympathize,—that many people refused to interpret the scarlet *A* by its original signification. They said that it meant Able; so strong was Hester Prynne, with a woman's strength" (161). "Neither can I any longer live without her companionship; so powerful is she to sustain,—so tender to soothe!" (201). It is impossible to miss, in these and many other passages, the stress on Hester's remarkable strength as well as the fundamentally humane uses to which she puts it. Without going beyond the license that Hawthorne allows, one might allegorize Hester as Good Power, which is, after all, precisely what, in the basic structural scheme of all narrative, one looks for in a hero. The power is remarkable in that its existence seems so improbable in an outcast woman. If the Puritan state draws its power from the consensual community and the laws that uphold it, then clearly Hester has access to a completely different source of power—or is, perhaps, herself an alternative source of power. And it is a power that even the Puritan world cannot deny, for "with her native energy of character, and rare capacity, it could not entirely cast her off" (84).

Perhaps, however, it is precisely her essential alienation from the community that explains this power. Although Hester can hardly doubt the power of the Puritan community to punish her and define the circumstances of her life, she knows—as we do—that they have this power only because she has granted it to them. She is free to leave Boston whenever she chooses. Her decision to stay entails a submission to Puritan power, but since she can withdraw her consent at any time this submission is always provisional. Her reasons for staying may be misguided, but they are her own. In schematic terms, if the Puritans symbolize the law, then Hester symbolizes the individual person—with this important proviso: she also symbolizes good. It would be easy to deduce from this polarity that Hawthorne wants us to think that law is bad and the individual good—but that would be too easy. Matters in Hawthorne are never so clear-cut. But he certainly gives us a situation wherein two kinds of power confront each other in conflict, and strongly suggests that any society that regards the power of the individual only as an adversary to be overcome, is profoundly defective and deeply inhuman.

Hester's situation, even before the commission of her "sin," is that of an outsider, She was sent to Massachusetts in advance of her husband; he had decided to emigrate, not she. The native strength of her character is certainly abetted by the fact that, as a young woman in a society dominated by aging men, she has no public importance. Even when she becomes a public figure through her punishment, her psyche is largely left alone. The magistrates condemn her to wear the letter but thereafter seem to have only a very superficial interest in her. A minister who sees her on the street may take the opportunity to preach an extempore sermon; people stare at the letter; children jeer; but none of this behavior represents an attempt to change Hester's mind. It is hoped that the external letter will work its way down into Hester's heart and cause repentance, but nobody really cares and this indifference is Hester's freedom. In fact, the effect of the letter so far as Hester's character is concerned is the opposite of what was intended: turning her into a public symbol, it conceals her individuality and thus protects it.

As the representative of individuality, Hester, rather than subjecting herself to the law, subjects it to her own scrutiny; as I have said, she takes herself as a law. She is not, by nature, rebellious; and during the seven-year period of The Scarlet Letter's action, she certainly attempts to accept the judgment implicit in the letter. If she could accept that judgment she would be able to see purpose and meaning in her suffering. But ultimately she unable to transcend her heartfelt conviction that she has not Sinned. She loves Dimmesdale with whom she sinned; she loves the child that her sin brought forth. How, then, can she agree that her deed was wrong?

She goes so far in her thinking as to attribute her own law to God, thus denying the entire rationale of the Puritan community, their certainty, that their laws conform to divine intention. "Man had marked this woman's sin by a scarlet letter, which had such potent and disastrous efficacy that no human sympathy could reach her, save it were sinful like herself. God, as a direct consequence of the sin which man thus punished, had given her a lovely child, whose place Was on that same dishonored bosom, to connect her parent for ever with the race and descent of mortals, and to be finally a blessed soul in heaven!" (89).

In fact, while the outward Hester performs deeds of mercy and kindness throughout the seven-years; the inward Hester grows ever more alienated and over time becomes—what she was not at first—a genuine revolutionary and social radical.

> The world's law was no law for her mind. It was an age in which the human intellect, newly emancipated, had taken a more active and a wider range than for many centuries before. Men of the sword had overthrown nobles and kings. Men bolder than these had overthrown and rearranged—not actually, but within the sphere of theory, which Was their most real abode—the whole system of ancient prejudice, wherewith was linked much of ancient principle. Hester prynne imbibed this spirit. She assumed a freedom of speculation, then common enough on the other side of the Atlantic, but which our forefathers, had they known of it, would have held to be a deadlier crime than that stigmatized by the scarlet letter. (164)

Had she spoken her thoughts, she probably would "have suffered death from the stern tribunals of the period, for attempting to undermine the foundations of the Puritan establishment" (165). If it were not for the existence of Pearl, for whose sake she lives quietly in Boston, she would have become, like Anne Hutchinson, a religious reformer.

But just as Hester refuses to take the road to witchcraft on account of Pearl, she rejects Hutchinson's radical path for the same reason. She feels particular obligations to human beings far more than she feels general social responsibilities. She behaves as a sister of mercy in the community because this is the way to live unmolested, not because she believes in doing good. And she want to live unmolested so that she can bring up Pearl. Staying in Boston on account of Dimmesdale, and living there as she does on account of Pearl, Hester's behavior is appropriate to her role as representative of individual and personal, rather than social, power. A reformer is dedicated to social power and has abandoned an individual center. No doubt this makes the whole issue of social reform on behalf of individualism highly problematic; so far as Hester is concerned—and this is our concern at present—the very consistency of her individualism keeps her within the sphere of the personal. At the end of the story, with her group of women clustered about her, she invokes the memory of Hutchinson only to contrast with it. The subject of talk among the women is entirely personal, centered on secular love; Hester counsels patience. Thus, the narrator's suggestion that her radicalism stems from an unquiet heart is partly validated by her behavior. If in Hawthorne's world a true radical, motivated by the impersonal, is somehow anti-individual, and if a true individual, motivated by the personal, is ultimately not radical, then our current popular understanding of these terms is quite different from Hawthorne's. His distinction is between ideologues and individuals rather than between varieties of ideology: an "individual-ist" is an ideologue. The individual as a reality rather than a concept is always extremely vulnerable.

Among Hester's key defining traits we cannot overlook her "skill at her needle." If her nature includes the characters of outcast, rebel, lover, mother, and sister of mercy, it also includes the character of artist. Her gift for needlework is the expression of an artist's nature; the embroideries that she produces arc genuine works of art.

We meet her skill first, of course, in the letter, which, "surrounded with an elaborate embroidery and fantastic flourishes of gold thread," is "so artistically done, and with so much fertility and gorgeous luxuriance of fancy, that it had all the effect of a last and fitting decoration" to her splendid apparel (53). Hester's grand costuming for the scaffold scene, far more elegant than what the dress code of the colony normally would allow her, is not seen again. She wears nothing but drab gray gowns. Her dreary dress, however, becomes a frame for the letter, and the letter remains, as it is clearly meant to be, an ornament. Beautifying the letter through art is another way in which Hester breaks the Puritan law (although the Puritan rulers—unlike the women in the crowd—are too literal-minded to notice it). The letter becomes the chief ground for the struggle between Hester and the Puritans, and it is able to play this role because of Hester's gift as an artist.

It is tempting here to associate artistic skill with social rebellion, but the equation does not hold. For Hester supports herself in Puritan Boston chiefly by making the elaborate decorative garments that the magistrates wear for public occasions and that are allowed to the better-off in the colony. "Deep ruffs, painfully wrought bands, and gorgeously embroidered gloves, were all deemed necessary to the official state of men assuming the reins of power; and were readily allowed to individuals dignified by rank or wealth" (82). Art does not have an inherently political nature, although—as the instance of the letter shows—it can become highly politicized. Rather, it is the expression of an original and creative energy, of fertility, of imagination, and of the love for the beautiful, even the gorgeous. This energy and creativity have no reference to society at all. Artists and their products can be appropriated by society or condemned by it; but society cannot make art, only individuals can. Indeed, only individuals who retain, or contain, a profound nonsocial element in their makeup (as Hester does) can make art. Although the social structure of the age denies virtually all forms of artistic expression to women, it does allow this one, and Hester makes use of it as an outlet for this side of her nature. For its part, society makes use of *her*. The

Puritans may be incapable of producing art, but they certainly want to possess, it. Therefore, despite everything, they want Hester in their community; and they want her *as she is*. But this is something they have to learn about themselves; and if they do not learn in time, there will be a society with no more Hesters.

HAWTHORNE AS PSYCHOLOGIST

An examination of characters in *The Scarlet Letter* would not be complete if it did not stress Hawthorne's contribution to psychological understanding. Even though the book often introduces allegorical or partly allegorical characters, and depends on old-fashioned personifications and other techniques to bring out inner truths, the very fact that it is concerned with *inner* truth puts it at the forefront of the development of psychological fiction. In his recognition of the hidden life and his description of mental processes Hawthorne was a psychologist ahead of his time.

Psychological speculation is as old as Aristotle, but the idea of a scientific, analytic psychology was new in the nineteenth century, and there did not yet exist the rich array of concepts, the wide vocabulary, and the accumulation of data that would later develop. This is why Hawthorne was apt to depend on outmoded literary techniques for representing some of his insights into mental states and processes. Moreover, since science in his time was intensely materialistic in its approach, he probably meant to suggest, by using old-fashioned rhetoric, that some important human truths known to earlier generations had been lost sight of in the positivist intellectual orientation of contemporary scientific thought. For such an implication, outdated language and techniques would be quite fitting.

Even so, however, certain elements of the psychological representation in *The Scarlet Letter* are strikingly innovative and advanced, and liable to be overlooked if we succumb entirely to the novel's intentional archaisms. For example, it is an advanced idea to split the inner life fundamentally from the outer, as Hawthorne does in the cases of Hester and Dimmesdale, and at the same time to place the key to identity in the thoughts, emotions, and fantasies of these characters rather than in their behavior. Today this idea is commonplace; in Hawthorne's time it was not, and the novel as a genre was taking the lead in investigating the "interior of a heart," as Hawthorne's chapter title describes it. The vast increase in awareness of, and attention to, the interior world was an offshoot of the general romantic movement with its tremendous focus on the single self. Among intellectual forms, fiction was especially well suited to treat the concept in depth and with detailed examples.

But along with a stress on the mental life of his major characters, which he shares with many other novelists of his time, Hawthorne offers us other, more personal psychological insights. He suggests the existence, not exactly of a single, unified unconscious as Freud was to hypothesize, but certainly of continual unconscious thought processes, with accompanying defenses and rationalizations on the part of the conscious mind as it seeks to contain while pretending not to know its deeper layers. The usually hidden unconscious becomes visible in periods of mental conflict, and also in states of unusual excitement. Important scenes in *The Scarlet letter* show Hester or Dimmesdale at such times.

The first episode of extreme mental stimulation occurs at the beginning of the story when Hester is exposed on the scaffold. After describing her from the outside, as she appeared to the Puritan multitude and as she might have appeared to a cultural outsider, the narrator moves into her mind and follows her own currents of thought. "Her mind, and especially her memory, was preternaturally active, and kept bringing up other scenes than this ... one picture precisely as vivid as another; as if all were of similar importance, or all alike a play. Possibly, it was an instinctive device of her spirit, to relieve itself, by the exhibition of these phantasmagoric forms, from the cruel weight and hardness of the reality" (57). Here Hester's mind seems out of control, or rather the conscious mind is simply a screen on which another, deeper mind (an "instinctive device of her spirit") is casting its images; at times of enormous stress, the controlling mind gives way to reveal the presence of layers of usually obscured or—to use a modern term—repressed mental activity.

As a character distinguished, however, by striking self-control, Hester does not often succumb to eruptions of the unconscious in this manner. Her conscious mind is occupied nonetheless with excluding unacceptable thoughts from its precincts. In devoting so much of her needlecraft to creating "coarse garments for the poor," the narrator suggests, "it is probable that there was an idea of penance," which, however, was "morbid," betokening "something doubtful, something that might be deeply wrong, beneath" (83–84). The word *beneath* here divides the mind into layers, and identifies the center of the psyche not in surface rationality but in the hidden desires beneath, thus portioning mental life into conscious and unconscious layers, as Freud was to do half a century later.

Earlier in this same chapter Hawthorne has attempted to explain why, "with the world before her," Hester chose to stay in Boston, and here he distinguishes even more carefully between surface explanation—what the mind tells itself—and "true" explanation, which, because it doesn't suit one's self-image, the mind rejects. "It might be, too-doubtless it was so, although she hid the secret from herself, and grew pale whenever it struggled out of her heart, like a serpent from its hole,—it might be that another feeling kept her.... She barely looked the idea in the face, and hastened to bar it in its dungeon. What she compelled herself to believe,—what, finally, she reasoned upon, as her motive for continuing a resident of New England,— was half a truth, and half a self-delusion" (80). What is this idea, this feeling? Simply that she continues to love Dimmesdale and to hope that somehow circumstances will bring them together. This is one of the striking early instances in literature of the depiction of the mind as a divided space, and of the processes of rationalization that impose a spurious wholeness on it.

Another occurs later on, after Hester has spoken with Chillingworth about her decision to break her vow of secrecy. Hester has previously constructed for herself a noble—which is to say, unselfish—explanation of the act she has decided to perform: "Hester could not but ask herself, whether there has not originally been a defect of truth, courage, and loyalty, on her own part, in allowing the minister to be thrown into a position where so much evil was to be foreboded. She determined to redeem her error, so far as it might yet be possible" (166–67). Nobody can disapprove, after all, of an act motivated by the desire to be true, courageous, and loyal.

But after her interview with Chillingworth, Hester finds her mind in a turmoil, and other motives come to the surface: her lively hatred of Chillingworth for having betrayed her into loveless marriage and cheated her of deserved happiness, for one; her continued love for Dimmesdale; her living desire, despite everything, for an intimacy with him. "The emotions of that brief space ... threw a dark light on Hester's state of mind, revealing much that she might not otherwise have acknowledged to herself" (177). Yet even as hidden emotions come to the attention of the conscious mind, they continue to evade its control. For the first time since putting on the letter Hester lies about it and grows harshly defensive with Pearl; and, the narrator comments, such behavior suggests that perhaps "some new evil had crept" into her heart, "or some old one had never been expelled" (181). When Hester, her patience at an end, threatens to shut Pearl in the dark closet, she is expressing in outward behavior the mental gesture of denying or suppressing the feelings that have revealed themselves to her—shutting them away with Pearl in the dark closet. The heart, as Hawthorne tells us often in his allegorical figures, is a cave or cellar where corpses have been buried, a closet where evil thoughts have been discarded. It is not only, as optimistic Americans would prefer to believe, the source of a fountain of pure feeling and innocent goodness.

With Dimmesdale, whose mind is more fragile and more badly divided than Hester's, Hawthorne can more fully elaborate this model of the inner world. Dimmesdale, it might be said, operates in a continual state of extreme excitement; this is what is killing him. His regular fasting induces hallucinatory states: "his brain often reeled, and visions seemed to flit before him"—devils, angels, the dead friends of his youth, his parents, Hester and Pearl. These visions were; the narrator remarks, "in one sense, the truest and most substantial things which the poor minister now dealt with" (145).

Yet even in his keyed-up existence there are peaks of much greater agitation—in particular, his secret penance on the scaffold (chapter 12, "The Minister's Vigil") and his return from the forest after meeting Hester (chapter 20, "The Minister in a Maze"). In both episodes the minister's conscious mind becomes a passive receiver for images and impulses projected from lower mental depths. And in both, the images express a counterforce to the minister's continual effort to be good, to be perfect, to be better than anybody else has ever been; they reveal all the contrary impulses to be what we might today call "normal." Dimmesdale interprets these impulses as evidence of evil, and we must interpret their eruption at the least as psychological breakdown.

On the scaffold (chapter 12), Dimmesdale actually delights in the possibility that he may be discovered, even while, as the narrator comments, his behavior is a mockery, "in which his soul trifled with itself" (148). As was the case with Hester on the scaffold earlier, the organizing power of the conscious mind, its ability to discriminate between inner and outer, important and trivial, disappears: watching an approaching light, Dimmesdale sees it shine on a post, a garden fence, a pump, a water trough, an oak door, an iron knocker, noticing "all these minute particulars, even while firmly convinced that the doom of his existence was stealing onward" (149–50). As the night wears on, he comes close to hallucinating, in a phantasmagoric scene wherein the whole town rises up at dawn and comes running out to see him on the scaffold: patriarchs in their nightgowns, Governor Bellingham with his ruff askew, and the young virgins of his parish who had made a shrine for Dimmesdale in their "white bosoms; which, now, by the by, in their hurry and confusion, they would scantly have given themselves time to cover with their kerchiefs" (151–52). Dimmesdale's desire to mock the decorum of the elders is expressed in his disrespectful images of their disarray; and his suppressed sexuality turns the young women of his parish into half-clothed groupies. His unconscious mind relieves itself in irreverent and disruptive jokes.

This episode comes to a climax with the appearance of a comet in the sky, whose eerie light shows "the familiar scene of the street, with the distinctness of mid-day, but also with the awfulness that is always imparted to familiar objects by an unaccustomed light" (154). Here three interpretive modes converge: a naturalistic interpretation, in which the comet simply appears when it appears for reasons having to do with the movement of heavenly bodies; a social interpretation, whereby the Puritans together find a meaning in the comet pertinent to their "infant commonwealth"; and a private interpretation, with Dimmesdale assuming that the A-shaped comet has appeared especially as a message for him. Such an interpretation, according to the narrator, could "only be the symptom of a highly disordered mental state, when a man, rendered morbidly self-contemplative by long, intense, and secret pain, had extended his egotism over the whole expanse of nature, until the firmament itself should appear no more than a fitting page for his soul's history and fate" (154–55). The narrator prefigures here the condition that we would today call paranoia, the outward projection of obsession.

The same processes are at work again in the scene of Dimmesdale's return from the forest; once more he is the passive and almost helpless spectator of his own forbidden and threatening impulses. This is a much more dramatic scene than the meditation on the scaffold, for the minister has now taken a conscious, willful step toward rebellion. He is beset by appalling temptations. "At every step he was incited to do some strange, wild, wicked thing or other, with a sense that it would be at once involuntary and intentional; in spite of himself, yet growing out of a profounder self than that which opposed the impulse" These desires, willed but resisted, recognized but denied, have an obvious aspect of disruptive humor about them, a wish to mock the puritanical code and his own submission to it. Dimmesdale wants to make blasphemous suggestions to an elderly, respectable deacon and a devout old widow; to make a lewd proposal to a young and beautiful parishioner; to teach dirty words to children; to trade obscene jokes with a sailor.

Yet if these impulses arc funny and, to a twentieth-century mind, rather pathetic than wicked, there is no doubt that their emergence is not a sign of the minister's having won his emotional and mental freedom but rather of his near approach to mental breakdown. To recognize divisions and conflicts in the mind, the presence of the repressed, the power of the unconscious, is not necessarily to become an advocate of what, in the twentieth century, we might call "sincerity" or "authenticity." Nor does the narrator suggest that the newly revealed impulses are expressions of Dimmesdale's essential and natural goodness; on the contrary, he says firmly that these impulses represent "scorn, bitterness, unprovoked malignity, gratuitous desire of ill, ridicule of whatever was good and holy" (222).

Examining Dimmesdale's hypocrisy in refusing to confess his sin,

Hawthorne relies, just as he did in showing Hester's denied yet over-whelming passion for Dimmesdale, on concepts of such mental processes as self-delusion and rationalization. Dimmesdale justifies his silence to himself chiefly on altruistic grounds: he wishes to do good for his congregation and would lose this ability were his sin known. He stands up in the pulpit and delivers sermons calling himself a great sinner, all the while knowing that these words will be interpreted figuratively by his listeners and thus that, far from revealing his sin, they will only further conceal it. Unable to "assign a reason" for his distrust and abhorrence of Chillingworth, he explains away these feelings as products of his general morbid state of mind (140). Although in Dimmesdale the self is more dangerously embroiled in civil war than it is in Hester, the dilemmas of both characters depend on concepts that, though Hawthorne lacks a modern vocabulary to label them, anticipate later psychological understanding.

Notably, too, Hawthorne make no distinction between men and women in his depiction of mental processes. At this basic level of mind there are no sexual differences. On the other hand, his representation of Hester—not so much of Dimmesdale, except by implication—seems to assume innate psychological differences between men and women. To the extent that *The Scarlet Letter* claims our attention as a work of psychological analysis, this point needs to be pursued. When Hawthorne uses the word *man* for Dimmesdale, it is generally no more than an empty identifier; not so with the term woman for Hester. In her case, the word *woman* and its cognates seem to imply a specific female essence.

Sometimes, to be sure, the word is used by characters who have their own individual or cultural ideas of sexual difference. Thus, when Hester first refuses to name her lover, Dimmesdale pays tribute to the "wondrous strength and generosity of a woman's heart" (68); later, as Hester comes into favor with the townspeople through her behavior as a "self-ordained sister of mercy," when they find her helpful, "with power to do, and power to sympathize," they praise her as strong, "with a woman's strength" (161).

But, in chapter 13, "Another View of Hester," the narrator studies her at length in light of what seems presented as an objective, trans-historical ideal of womanhood. On the one hand, she appears to be faulted for having deviated from this ideal (even if she could not help herself); on the other, her good traits appears to be compatible with it. And we cannot fail to note that the worst result of Hester's seven-year isolation, to this narrator, appears to be her loss of beauty—beauty that he describes as attractiveness to men.

"There seemed to be no longer any thing in Hester's face for Love to dwell upon; nothing in Hester's form, though majestic and statue-like, that Passion would ever dream of clasping in its embrace; nothing in Hester's bosom, to make it ever again the pillow of Affection," the narrator says, in a progression increasingly intimate—from desire, to sex, to intimate slumber. And he sums it up: "Some attribute had departed from her, the permanence of which had been essential to keep her a woman" (163). This conclusion is reached even while it has been acknowledged that in her errands around town her "nature showed itself warm and rich; a well-spring of human tenderness" (161); and even while her passionate devotion to Pearl is a constant motif in the narration. Thus, it can only be the power to inspire sexual desire in men that Hester has lost; this is what the narrator equates with her essential womanhood. And why is Hester no longer attractive to men? Almost certainly, in view of the narrator's elaboration of her freedom of thought and her independence, it is because she has become altogether self-reliant. Thus, we are faced with the irony that a woman is only herself, a woman, if she is an object of the amorous male regard. "Womanhood" and "selfhood" may be incompatible concepts.

Hawthorne develops this paradox at precisely the era in American literary and cultural history when Transcendentalists were firmly preaching self-reliance to all and sundry—but at the same time allocating to women the role of dependent helpmate, thus indicating that self-reliance was for men only. In 1844 Margaret Fuller (whom Hawthorne came to know well while he lived at the Old Manse) wrote an essay on the topic, "The Great Lawsuit," subsequently expanded into a book called *Woman in the Nineteenth Century*, which is generally considered the earliest document in the American woman's rights movement. Fuller argued passionately that until the Transcendentalists expanded their message to include both sexes, their entire program was suspect.

It is evident that Hawthorne has this and other early manifestations of feminism in mind, and that the question of a specifically female psychology was preoccupying him, as it would have to if he were seriously attempting to work with a female protagonist. The first woman's rights convention had been held in 1848, the year before he began to write *The Scarlet Letter*; his sister-in-law Elizabeth Peabody was a feminist; his wife, Sophia, was adamantly antifeminist; one of his sisters (Elizabeth) was feminist in inclination, the other (Maria Louisa) was not. Chapter 13 shows Hester's thoughts moving naturally from her own situation, to Pearl's, to the situation of "the whole race of womankind" (165). The problems—which are real— are not to be overcome "by any exercise of thought," the narrator opines; they cannot be solved; they can only disappear—if and only if the woman's "heart chance to come uppermost"

Hawthorne is not denigrating the quality of Hester's mind here, nor suggesting that women are incapable of thought and ought to leave reasoning to men. Nor is he intending to trivialize her strength, courage, and magnanimity; indeed, the story cannot work without his recognizing these virtues. Yet Hester's character is formed by elements specific to her gender— elements partly enforced on her by society, but partly innate. It is not society's fault that she loves one man and only one passionately and for life, for example; this is part of Hester's womanly nature.

Yet, while Hawthorne makes Hester a real woman in all sorts of ways, he also seems to insist that she isn't one: "Some attribute had departed from her, the permanence of which had been essential to keep her a woman. Such is *frequently* the fate, and such the stern development, of the feminine character and person, when the woman has encountered, and lived through, an experience of peculiar severity" (163, emphasis added). Womanhood, then, is an inalienable essence that is nevertheless completely vulnerable. This contradiction implies that the idea of "woman" is a social construction and, as such, an additional burden on those human beings who must conform to it. The narrator's judgments of Hester vary according to whether she is seen as a person or as a woman, and vary even when she is seen only as a woman: strong with a woman's strength, with the wonderful strength and generosity of a woman's heart, Hester has yet ceased to be a woman! These inconsistencies are perhaps inevitable reflections of the debate over female psychology that the woman's rights movement had precipitated, and that has not yet been concluded.

LOIS A. CUDDY

Mother-Daughter Identification in
The Scarlet Letter

It is a delightful irony that an author like Nathaniel Hawthorne, who has come under attack for his attitudes toward women, should have created in Hester Prynne one of the richest female characters in American fiction. It is even more remarkable (and ironic) that this author—in every way a product of his time—had the capacity for observation and intuitive insight that allowed him to create a child like Pearl and a mother-daughter relationship that remain in literature unsurpassed for their psychological validity and integrity. In fact, when viewed from a psychoanalytic and feminist perspective, *The Scarlet Letter* becomes a case study of mother-daughter identification and bonding. In that context, the character of Pearl functions not only as an illustration of mother-daughter symbiosis and of the stages in child development, but also as Hawthorne's unique strategy for clarifying the complexity of his heroine.[1]

That the *relationship* between Hester and Pearl is of primary significance in this novel is illustrated by the fact that Hester is immediately introduced with her three-month-old baby in her arms and then described as "the young woman—the mother of this child."[2] Though the narrator refers to her ironically in terms of "the image of Divine Maternity" (p. 166), Hester's role as mother is at least equal to her role as sinner in the novel. The mother and child appear together in just about every scene, especially those situations in which Hester must deal with other members of the community.

From *Mosaic* 19, no. 2 (Spring 1986). © 1986 by *Mosaic*.

151

In fact, "Never, since her release from prison, had Hester met the public gaze without her" (p. 198). Being a mother is both Hester's perceived avenue for personal redemption and also her psychological salvation as Pearl speaks for and acts out all of Hester's repressions and passions.

Because Pearl is described paradoxically, her psychological attachment and function in the novel have been generally ignored, despite critical acknowledgement of Hawthorne's psychological facility.[3] Pearl's being called an "elf," "sprite," "dryad," "a demon offspring," and so on, actually reflects the perspective of the Puritan society and its superstitions which, despite her intellectual independence, condition Hester's style of thinking, add to her sense of inadequacy and torment her conscience. The narrator, however, subtly contrasts Hester's Puritan perceptions with a more rational view when he comments on Hester's fears about her "fiend-like" child: "It was *as if* an evil spirit possessed the child, and had just then peeped forth in mockery. Many a time afterwards had Hester been tortured, though less vividly, by the same *illusion*" (p. 201; emphases mine). Through such diction Hawthorne repeatedly asks us to distinguish between the Puritan point of view—distorted by fear of the spirit world—and a more balanced "modern" perception of Pearl as a "normal" child in an "abnormal" situation. Just as the narrator uses irony when referring to the townspeople's lack of compassion and religious "purity," so also a careful examination of Pearl reveals additional ironic touches, as the myopic view of childhood in the seventeenth century is consistently juxtaposed with the image of Pearl as a "real" child. It is a matter of perspective, and we are required to contrast the darkness of the Puritan mind with Hawthorne's own lucid observations of a daughter in relation to her mother and her world.[4]

Pearl is never seen without Hester in this novel because it is not her function to stand alone. Hawthorne designed Pearl to capture all the complexity of a growing child in order to reflect the conflicting forces within the mother. In their close attachment, made even more so by their enforced isolation from society, Pearl is everything that Hester would deny about herself; and in her identification with mother—as both female and love object—Pearl expresses all of Hester's needs, desires, fears, anxiety and rage. Like any ordinary daughter, Pearl identifies with Hester's unconscious as well as conscious attitudes. And it is the unconscious part of herself that Hester sees in Pearl, cannot understand, fears, dislikes, yet finds emotionally satisfying. Thus, Pearl was created to complete her mother, for in each scene Hester behaves in one way, according to Puritan principles, but her feelings are often in conflict with her external appearance. It is Pearl, getting her unconscious cues from her mother, who acts out what Hester feels yet tries to hide from herself, her society and even her God.

Though Hawthorne would likely explain human behavior in terms of morality, heredity and the "physiological psychology" popular in his day,[5] his perceptions are accurate even from our own contemporary perspective. As Theodore Lidz has explained, even before birth there is a symbiotic relationship that develops between mother and infant that transcends physical dependence: "the mother's emotional state can influence the fetus.... Even though no direct nerve connections exist between the mother and the fetus, there is a neurochemical bond through the placental circulation.... There is evidence that the newborn of disturbed mothers may tend to be hyperactive in their responsivity to stimuli, and have more labile heart action and gastrointestinal functioning."[6]

Hawthorne also realized and makes a case for this prenatal "influence," which helps him to establish the subsequent unity and identification between mother and child: "Hester could only account for the child's character—and even then, most vaguely and imperfectly—by recalling what she herself had been, during that momentous period while Pearl was imbibing her soul from the spiritual world, and her bodily frame from its material of earth.... Above all, the warfare of Hester's spirit, at that epoch, was perpetuated in Pearl. She could recognize her wild, desperate, defiant mood, the flightiness of her temper, and even some of the very cloud-shapes of gloom and despondency that had brooded in her heart" (pp. 195–96). Hester thinks within a Puritan context in trying to understand Pearl's "wild" nature; however, Hawthorne, writing with an "enlightened" nineteenth-century view of children and insight emanating from acute observational skills and sensitivity to human emotion, is using Hester's "vaguely" defined concepts to express the psychological bond between the mother and daughter.

When we are introduced to Hester and Pearl in the first scaffold scene, they have had three months to strengthen that bond. And because Hester and Pearl have been isolated in a prison cell "or other darksome apartment of the prison" (p. 163), as they are virtually isolated from the community in the next few years, this novel becomes almost a laboratory experiment of a mother-daughter relationship uncomplicated by a father, siblings, or others present in the household. Pearl depends entirely on Hester for survival, nurturing, and for the model that defines her own sense of self. Thus, the first scene is notable for revealing the "psychic osmosis"[7] and non-verbal communication which are precursors of Pearl's eventual identification with mother and the consequent oedipal feelings for father.

According to René A. Spitz, as soon as a baby is born there is "a complementary relation" that begins to develop, a "psychological *symbiosis* with the mother" or primary nurturing person. [8] The infant responds to the mother's cues first by instinct then gradually by a "special form of interaction [which] creates for the baby a unique world of [her] own, with its own emotional climate" and which transforms every action "into meaningful signals" (pp. 42–43). In fact, an infant responds to every aspect of the mother's physical and emotional state, to the mother's "tension (muscular and otherwise), posture, temperature, skin and body contact," and so on (p. 135).

Thus, when Hester is holding Pearl on the scaffold and must hide all her anxiety, humiliation, shame and rage, the infant senses the discomfort and expresses the emotion. This is evident when Hester "felt, at moments, as if she must needs shriek out with the full power of her lungs, and cast herself from the scaffold down upon the ground, or else go mad at once" yet she stands immobile (p. 167); Pearl, on the other hand, "during the latter portion of [Hester's] ordeal, pierced the air with its wailings and screams" (pp. 176–77). The mother's "least action—be it ever so insignificant—even when it is not related to the infant, acts as a stimulus" (Spitz, p. 123). Though the community cannot discern the internal storm beneath Hester's "haughty" demeanor, then, Pearl can sense her mother's turmoil and becomes her mother's voice.

Earlier in the same scene, Pearl behaves in a way that seems more symbolic than "real" when she holds out her arms to the stranger, Reverend Dimmesdale. However, her behavior is both fictionally viable and psychologically consistent with what we know about child development. First, "to the three-month-old ... one human face is as good as another" (Spitz, p. 155), so she might well hold up her arms to the stranger whose soft voice seems to be the only soothing emotional message received in the noon sunlight. Furthermore, since a child of any age responds more readily to the mother's "unconscious attitudes" than even to her "conscious actions" (p. 124), Pearl—*for* her mother—is reaching out to the only person in the community who can understand Hester's anguish.

In our introduction to Hester, Hawthorne immediately contrasts her behavior with her interior world. In her pride she refuses to let the congregation know what she feels. With what appears to be "hardness and obstinacy," she likewise admits no weakness to the Reverend John Wilson, who speaks for the laws that would intimidate her into capitulation and confession. Her public response even to Dimmesdale's appeal to name the father of the infant is to remain silent. However, the "counterpart to the mother's capacity for empathy is the baby's perception of the mother's moods, of her conscious as well as her unconscious wishes" (Spitz, p. 127). Thus, it is at this point that Pearl first acts out the "wishes" of her anguished mother: "Even the poor baby, at Hester's bosom, was affected by the same influence; for it directed its hitherto vacant gaze towards Mr. Dimmesdale, and held up its little arms, with a half pleased, half plaintive murmur" (p. 175). Though the mother could not bring herself to name her "fellow-sinner," or reach out to him with the love and grief within her, the child does so. This is the first of numerous times that Pearl supplements the narrator's description of Hester's hidden desires and agony. Her behavior foreshadows the revelation about Dimmesdale's culpability and paternity while she also functions to express to the reader what is in Hester's heart and mind.

Each time Hester is placed under public scrutiny she controls her emotions with an iron will while Pearl reveals Hester's internal battles—with love or rage, anguish or hostility, defiance or fear. We see this again when Chillingworth enters her cell: "Hester Prynne had immediately become as still as death, although the child continued to moan" (p. 178). Pearl's expressive role in every scene is the same; only her behavior changes to mirror what Hester is feeling or thinking at the moment.

This response of an infant to the mother's emotional state is not restricted to one gender. However, Hawthorne immediately establishes the oneness of mother and child so that as Pearl grows into a little girl, she becomes the acting image of her mother's true character, the feminine and passionate impulses that the mother must repress in this Puritan world. An obvious example is when Hester and Pearl walk through town. Hester again stonily endures the cruelties of the Puritan children who also "imbibed from their parents" their attitudes and hostilities: "She was patient,—a martyr, indeed,—but she forbore to pray for her enemies; lest, in spite of her forgiving aspirations, the words of the blessing should stubbornly twist themselves into a curse." Yet, "Hester had schooled herself long and well": except by "a flush of crimson" on her cheek, she never betrays her submerged hostility and anger or her desire to "curse" them all for their lack of compassion (p. 191).

Pearl, however, responding to her mother's cues, is not so forbearing and openly vents the rage and bitterness that her mother manages to hide: "Pearl felt the [children's hostile] sentiment, and requited it with the bitterest hatred that can be supposed to rankle in a childish bosom" (p. 198). The issue here is not one of Pearl's morality or amorality, as many critics have contended. Though Hester is not aware of the "signals" she gives to Pearl, the child is acutely aware of her mother's emotions, for the ability "to 'read' mother's face" develops in the early part of the second year: "the mother's facial expressiveness ... contributes to the emotional reciprocity. The originally spontaneous facial display of affect on the part of the mother in response to her child can in time become a tool of her conscious or unconscious attempts to influence the child's behavior."[9] Pearl reads these signs well, and is therefore Hawthorne's instrument—her behavior his opportunity—to let us scrutinize Hester's emotions beneath the appearance of cold composure and acceptance of an unjust situation that would enrage any human being. Only by recognizing that Pearl is acting out her mother's, and not just her own, "bitterest hatred" can we recognize Hester for more than a stone effigy of woman and accept the depth and intensity of the anger in both of them.

Though Hester—as a mother—is required to chide Pearl for such passion, as a woman she is secretly relieved by her daughter's "outbreaks of a fierce temper ... because there was at least an intelligible earnestness in the mood, instead of the fitful caprice that so often thwarted her in the child's manifestations" (p. 198). Hester rationalizes the reasons for her own pleasure in the "value, and even comfort" of Pearl's outbursts against their torturers, but the truth is simply that Hester enjoys the vicarious pleasure in returning the attacks.

In fact, Hester again acknowledges the affinity between herself and her more honestly aggressive child: "It appalled her, nevertheless, to discern here, again, a shadowy reflection of the evil that had existed in herself. All this enmity and passion had Pearl inherited, by inalienable right, out of Hester's heart.... and in the nature of the child seemed to be perpetuated those unquiet elements that had distracted Hester Prynne before Pearl's birth, but had since begun to be soothed away by the softening influences of maternity" (pp. 198–99). Of course Hester does not understand how she directs Pearl's actions by the cues that become behavioral directives to the child. But she is also dishonest with herself. She knows that Pearl has taken on her own "evil," but in the name of maternity and the moral principles desired of mothers, she denies all present feelings of a base nature. She needs to believe that such "unquiet elements" in herself are "soothed away" by the sanctity of motherhood.

Hester's attitudes fit perfectly the psychoanalytic model for the mother's discrepant behavior: "For the mother, witnessing and condoning infantile behavior reactivates all the guilty and at the same time delectable fantasies which she has had to conquer.... she will deny, displace, turn into the opposite, scotomize, repress, and her behavior toward the baby's 'innocent' activity will vary accordingly. In the course of this process, the mother prevaricates, consciously or unconsciously; she says one thing and does the other, and ends up with the well-known injunction given to the school child: 'Don't do as I do, do as I say!'" (Spitz, p. 126). No wonder that in her constant, often unconscious, denial of the impulses which Pearl acts out for her, Hester is baffled and asks, "Art thou my child, in very truth" (p. 201). And "in very truth" Pearl has identified so completely with her mother that she is the essence and mirror image of Hester's mind and heart.

By the time we observe "Pearl's witchcraft"—according to Hester's interpretation of the child's imaginative, creative play and curiosity—Pearl has fully identified with her mother. Identification in the psychological sense "refers to modifying the subjective self or behavior, or both, in order to increase one's resemblance to an object taken as a model."[10] Moreover, "[i]n its fullest sense, the process of identifying with an object is unconscious" and may be "partial" so that only certain aspects of the model may be internalized (pp. 140, 143). This is particularly relevant to the Pearl-Hester identification. Since Hester dresses Pearl differently, in both clothing and hair style, and since Hester must manifest the Puritan restraint and composure demanded of a religious matron, Pearl is not modeling herself on the mother's external image, but rather on Hester's hidden character. Pearl has internalized those aspects of Hester that the community no longer sees but that in private moments peep through the stone wall of Puritan repression: "it was often the case that a sportive impulse came over [Hester], in the midst of her deepest suffering." Yet, Hester fears Pearl as "a demon offspring" (p. 202) for the same kind of behavior. Given Hester's conflicts, it is understandable that Pearl alternates between playful, teasing responses to her mother's frown and the emotional outbursts that both frighten and comfort the mother.

Part of Pearl's identification with her mother is as a daughter, and in that regard the novel makes clear the transition from genderless infant to female child. In the scene with the Puritan children, the evolution has already taken place from "the babe in arms, and afterwards as the little girl, small companion of her mother." Hawthorne says explicitly that "Mother and daughter stood together" (p. 198). That Pearl is no longer just an "infant" or "child," without gender or personality, is important in understanding the quality of empathy and nonverbal communication that Hawthorne seemed to recognize intuitively and deductively and that make her behavior both comprehensible and psychologically valid.

As Carol Gilligan states, "Female identity formation takes place in a context of ongoing relationship since 'mothers tend to experience their daughters as more like, and continuous with, themselves.' Correspondingly, girls, in identifying themselves as female, experience themselves as like their mothers, thus fusing the experience of attachment with the process of identity formation. ... Thus, 'girls emerge from this [early] period with a basis for "empathy" built into their primary definition of self.'"[11] Throughout the novel, no matter how rigorously Hester tries to hide emotion, as the Puritan prescription for virtue requires, Pearl's empathetic sensitivity to subtle cues from the mother effectually penetrates the wall of denial. Consequently, because mother and daughter are so attached and "continuous" with each other, Hester's sensitivity about the significance of the scarlet letter on her breast cues and thereby encourages the child, from infancy, to focus attention on the bright emblem as an object of intense curiosity as well as defiance.

Though Hester attributes Pearl's teasing about the scarlet letter to an "evil spirit [that] possessed the child," in fact Pearl's interest in the letter is quite understandable. On the visual level, the infant would naturally reach out for the richly embroidered ornament designed with the vivid color that is in stark contrast to Hester's drab clothing. And emotionally, the response that the infant elicits, the look on Hester's face or her movements, would of course reinforce Pearl's interest in the object. In the "feedback system"[12] in which a mother's conscious or unconscious response becomes the stimulus for repeated behavior by the child, Pearl senses Hester's discomfort and enjoys her sense of power and control over the adult's emotions. Yet Hester, in her guilt, perceives the child's normal interest as perversity stemming from infernal forces sent to torment the sinner further. Therefore, as the child enjoys a perceptible response from this mother who struggles to subdue all feeling in the interest of morality, Pearl repeats the action to enjoy yet another reaction.

Pearl's identification with her mother further explains her interest in the scarlet letter. Because she is dressed in the same color as the letter on Hester's bosom, she would recognize the affinity between herself and that aspect of her mother. Thus, she seems to be preoccupied with this emblem which sets both her mother and herself apart from the community. She throws flowers at it to arouse emotion in this expressionless woman and to show her rejection of and independence from the very figure with whom she is bonded. In other instances, Pearl's response to the emblem reflects her identification with her mother's creative endeavors: "She inherited her mother's gift for devising drapery and costume.... Pearl took some eelgrass, and imitated, as best she could, on her own bosom, the decoration with which she was so familiar on her mother's." Instead of walking in her mother's shoes, as little girls do, she identifies with the thing that makes her mother unique in the community and uncomfortable as a mother, "the letter A,—but freshly green, instead of scarlet!" (p. 271). Clearly Pearl's activities, which cause such discomfort to the wearer of the scarlet letter, are reinforced not by her own wickedness or demonic influences but by the reactions of her mother and by her identification with this parent who is always in attendance.

The way Hester dresses Pearl is another signal that helps the child "to form an image of herself and her relationship to the world."[13] Critics have commented generously on what the apparel says about Hester's imagination, temperament, artistic capacities, rebellion against Puritan standards of dress and comportment, and even the irony of her "subversive and cunning" behavior in "dressing Pearl to look like the letter."[14] I would like to suggest two other possibilities for Hawthorne's emphasis on the child's wardrobe: the use of clothing to mark Pearl as Hester's psychological image—that which is opposite from what the world sees—and the effect of Pearl's singular clothing on the child's self-image.

Pearl's wardrobe and appearance, as critics have noted, clearly represent the other side of Hester—the imagination, spirit, youth, gaiety and fire—which she can no longer admit or reveal openly. Her needlework is the only external evidence of her artistic and sensual temperament: "to Hester Prynne [sewing] might have been a mode of expressing, and therefore soothing, the passion of her life. Like all other joys, she rejected it as sin" (p. 190). Through Pearl's garments, however, Hester could sublimate her "sinful" Romantic tendencies in the name of maternal fondness. Thus, as the novel progresses, Hester outwardly conforms to the laws of her society; yet, Pearl's dresses reveal that Hester is not really changed in character and that she continues to be at odds with her society. Hester is in her situation precisely because she deviated from the social and ethical principles of her world, and with the scarlet dresses, Hester puts Pearl in the same role of opposition to the community. Little wonder that the "child could not be made amenable to rules," for she reflects not only the beauty and brilliance of her mother but also the "disorder" (p. 195).

With his knowledge of history, Hawthorne would have known that Puritan children were dressed exactly like miniatures of the adults.[15] Yet he makes a point of designing Pearl to be the only child in the community who does not conform either to her own mother's appearance or to social standards. That her wardrobe represents all of Hester's repressed creativity and imagination is stated explicitly, and that her clothing signifies Hester's rebellion is now accepted. But Hawthorne was also sensitive enough to realize that the disparity between Pearl's appearance and that of her mother and others would not escape the notice of this clever child and would even prompt the wayward behavior of which she is accused. Her actions reflect the nonconformity of her dress which is the hidden "passion" of her mother's temperament (p. 190).

Furthermore, that Pearl's beautiful hair is free and flowing while Hester's dark and lovely hair is now hidden within a Puritan cap not only intensifies the putative contrast between Hester's inner and outer "spheres," but also suggests the permission for freedom and "wildness" which Hester unconsciously grants to the little girl but denies to herself. The cues given by Hester are important in forming the community's image of the child as well as Pearl's own self-image of being different from the "good" Puritans who hold to the rules of behavior and dress. Such consistency of detail belies coincidence or unconscious naïveté on Hawthorne's part, for every scene in which the child appears has a psychological significance designed with equal skill.

Perhaps the most touching scenes requiring Hester's enclosure and Pearl's expressive function are those which include Arthur Dimmesdale when other people are present. The first of such impassioned scenes, as earlier noted, is on the scaffold when the infant reaches up her arms to Dimmesdale. The second time is in the Governor's Hall when Pearl is only three years old. Hester has heard rumors that "some of the leading inhabitants" of the community are planning "to deprive her of her child" (p. 203). The ensuing scene confirms Hester's fears.

While mother and child await the entrance of the Governor and the other church fathers who will pronounce on the fate of them both, Hester seems unmoved by the gravity of her errand. Only Pearl responds with appropriate expression: "in utter scorn of her mother's attempt to quiet her, [Pearl] gave an eldritch scream, and then became silent" (p. 209). Then when Mr. Wilson interrogates the child to determine Hester's "worthiness" to be guardian and teacher to this young mind, Hester is again silent while Pearl rebels. Having had enough of their questions, "the child finally announced that she had not been made at all [by a Heavenly Father], but had been plucked by her mother off the bush of wild roses, that grew by the prison-door" (p. 213). Consistent with what we know of child psychology, she says exactly the opposite of what Hester would consciously have her say.

But Pearl does not bear the burden of her mother's conscious thoughts. Rather, Pearl again projects what Hester dare not admit even to herself, for during a religious lesson, Hester had earlier prepared her daughter for such irreverence: "But [Hester] said ['Thy Heavenly Father sent thee'] with a hesitation that did not escape the acuteness of the child." Taking her cue from her mother's uncertainty, Pearl had at that time responded to what Hester did *not* say and answered, "'I have no Heavenly Father'" (p. 202). Now in the Governor's Hall, Pearl's comment reflects once again the doubts and conflicts, the intellectual inquiry and religious rebellion, within Hester's own mind.

After tense moments in which it gradually becomes clear that losing Pearl is no idle rumor, Hester becomes frantic but still cannot defend herself. She turns to Dimmesdale: "'Speak thou for me!' cried she." After Dimmesdale speaks eloquently on her behalf and softens the hearts of this informal tribunal, Pearl reveals the affection and gratitude that Hester must hide: "The young minister, on ceasing to speak, had withdrawn a few steps from the group, and stood with his face partially concealed in the heavy folds of the window-curtain.... Pearl, that wild and flighty little elf, stole softly towards him, and, taking his hand in the grasp of both her own, laid her cheek against it" (p. 216). What Hester cannot do for herself Pearl manages to express for her with a gentleness that is presumably alien to the child.

In light of Erik Erikson's observations concerning identity formation,[16] Pearl's age in this scene is significant. Hawthorne's observations are precise in dating the developmental stage at which Pearl is defined as "separate" from Hester in her dress and in her defiance of catechism and adult expectations and, at the same time, still an extension of her mother. As Hammer also points out in her volume on the psychology of mothers and daughters, "The child's sense that she possesses a separate self evolves slowly. By the age of three, however, it is thought that a child will have developed a clear sense of self and nonself, and of his or her gender. ... But there are many indications to suggest that not only is the social concept of self different for men and women, but that daughters tend to stay more closely involved with their mother's identities—that to some extent they never achieve a clear sense of a separate self at all" (pp. 15–16). Pearl's apparent independence yet close involvement with her mother's identity partly account for the daughter's behavior in the Governor's house. While Pearl separates herself from Hester's conscious statements, the girl's empathy for her mother's emotional needs is evidence that Hawthorne's observations of his own daughter's behavior and development were both perceptive and reliable.

There is another aspect of Pearl's attachment to Dimmesdale that also requires consideration. As Erikson has explained, when a daughter identifies with her mother both in gender and in relation to other people and society, she also forms an attachment—as her mother has done—with the father figure in what is termed the oedipal stage of development. In this interpersonal and psychosexual configuration, the daughter is both bonded to and in competition with the mother (p. 117). This situation has interesting consequences for Pearl's behavior in *The Scarlet Letter*. For example, when she takes Dimmesdale's hand in the Governor's hall and then kisses him at the end of the novel, these actions would ordinarily be attempts to compete with mother for father's love and attention. Though Pearl could not consciously know that Arthur is her father, she has literally reached out her hands to him since her introduction to the community, for she senses that he has a special meaning to Hester. For that reason, Pearl's affectionate behavior, which seems so at odds with her own and her mother's nature, has psychological integrity. Since Hester cannot reveal her love for the minister openly—and thereby create conflict and competition with her daughter—the child is free to express the emotions for both her mother and herself.

In the second scaffold scene, Pearl again wants father to "belong" to her and have the courage to announce his love for them in the light of day. Once more she acts out Hester's emotions, first by asking the minister to announce their communion publicly, then by laughing at Dimmesdale's cowardly refusal. As a daughter, she competes with mother for father's attention while feeling guilty over her disloyalty to mother. In this scene the loyalty wins out as she expresses the desires for revelation and revenge that undoubtedly persist in Hester's heart. Pearl, in her identification with her mother, provides the punishment to Arthur that Hester cannot exact.

In *Barriers Between Women*, Paula J. Caplan examines in detail the basis for identification between daughters and mothers. Citing Kohlberg and Zigler's theory of identification as "a kind of self-actualization," Caplan goes on to explain a "crucial" aspect of their theory: "the hypothesis that an intimate part of the identification process is the child's need to feel a sense of competence, security and certainty, and freedom from anxiety." The daughter enjoys the "pleasures and rewards inherent in the process" of being like mother—her mother's love, approval, protection, and so on—while she also "discovers that becoming more and more like her mother brings her up against the restrictions of the female role in our society." Caplan concludes that "[i]n this way, her relationship with her mother lands her in a conflict: she is torn between accepting unpleasant restrictions on her behavior in order to become 'female' and sacrificing the pleasures attendant upon becoming 'female'."[17] This is surely Hester's own conflict in *The Scarlet Letter*, and it is also Pearl's. Each time they are confronted by society, Hester becomes powerless, even being unable to speak for herself or her child. Pearl then responds to this sense of anxiety and uncertainty by rejecting her impotent mother on the one hand and, on the other hand, taking on her mother's role and speaking for her. Little wonder that Pearl alternates between being an "angel" and a "fiend" as she manifests her mother's conflicts in every situation.

In her identification with her own mother, Hester apparently assumed the same anxieties, for each generation is a repetition of the past—to Hawthorne and in the psychoanalytic theories on parental influence.[18] In the first scaffold scene, for instance, Hester remembers her mother's face, that "look of heedful and anxious love which it always wore ... and which, even since her death, had so often laid the impediment of a gentle remonstrance in her daughter's pathway" (p. 168). This behavior by the mother sets the stage for what Caplan calls "restraints on [a] daughter's freedom." Thus, Caplan's discussion applies perfectly to Hester's relationship to her own mother and then to Pearl in a cyclical recurrence of behavioral patterns: "What usually strengthens these nonverbal or, more rarely, verbal messages is the mother's own early experience of rejection when she herself behaved 'inappropriately'"—according to society's determination of appropriate behavior. Consequently, this situation "adds a kind of emotional shudder and dread to the mother's demeanor as she attempts to teach her daughter to live within the prescriptions of society" (pp. 77–78).

Thus, for Hester being a daughter means anxiety and a guilty conscience, never giving her mother satisfaction or peace; and motherhood means doing the same thing to her daughter, imposing restrictions of affection and pleasure, frowns instead of smiling approval. Hester's definition of motherhood reflects the generational repetition of dynamics and behavioral responses; for just as Hester identifies with her mother as frustrator and as superego, so also Pearl becomes both frustrator and conscience for Hester.

When Hester appears to be a controlled and morally purified "goodwoman," Pearl behaves with a deviance that seems to be explained in her community only by the touch of Satan; obversely, when Hester's passions come to the surface, Pearl becomes the conscience for both of them. Pearl alternates between acting out Hester's repressed *id* impulses and her conscience, or *superego*.

Only when Hester is alone and does not require Pearl to mediate for her in public do we see Hester's thoughts at work in an honest display of rebellion and skepticism. We observe this in the chapter, "Another View of Hester," when her ruminations reveal Romantic inclinations more than Puritan reverence, and in the scene with Chillingworth when she admits to herself after their interview, "Be it sin or no ... I hate the man!" (p. 269). Again in the forest scene when Pearl is across the brook and playing alone in the "wild" wood, Hester opens her heart to Arthur and acts out for herself the passionate and willful nature that first led to her "fall." Only when Pearl is sleeping or temporarily absent can Hester admit her real feelings, but Pearl's reappearance always functions to remind Hester of her own "sinful" nature and thereby restore her to maternal "virtue."

It is in those moments of freedom—of speculation or action—that Hester ignores the Puritan principles which define her conscience. When Hester dares to defy such moral laws, dares to hope that life may be freedom and love, truth and happiness, Hawthorne uses Pearl to provoke and draw to her consciousness the Puritan commandments for virtuous thoughts and behavior. At those times Pearl no longer expresses the hostility or passion in Hester's character but instead reflects the Puritan restraints that Hester impulsively resists.

When Hester throws away the letter and "let down her hair," she ignores and defies the moral and psychological chains that bind her irrevocably to her Puritan "fate"—her sin and its consequences. So Pearl now acts as both daughter and conscience to bring her mother back to the prison of emotional and ethical sobriety. Pearl has always acted out the tender and affectionate aspects of Hester's feelings for Dimmesdale, the Romantic part that necessarily remains hidden, like her beautiful hair, and is even repressed until these moments in the forest. Now, with Hester expressing for herself the passion and freedom, Pearl is understandably disturbed and confused. Their roles, so linked to the scarlet letter, have been immutable and consistent throughout her life, but now the letter is gone, the roles seem reversed, and Pearl must force a reconstruction of their fixed identities.

Only after Hester resumes her recognizable exterior, suppresses the passionate responses of her heart, and becomes once more the Puritan "goodwoman" does Pearl show the affection that Hester longs to reveal for herself: "In a mood of tenderness that was not usual with her, [Pearl] drew down her mother's head, and kissed her brow and both her cheeks" (p. 301). Always speaking out for the inner world that Hester tries to hide, Pearl shows that her mother's superego is alive and well. Thus, Pearl is clearly the ordering principle for her community here, but when she kisses her mother, we see more than a gesture of approval for the resumption of virtue.

Pearl's kiss in the forest reflects the oedipal conflict and the guilt she feels unconsciously as a result of her jealousy over the parents' attentions to each other. As Erikson says, "The little girl, in turn, becomes attached to her father and other important men and jealous of her mother, a development which may cause her much anxiety, for it seems to block her retreat to that self-same mother, while it makes her mother's disapproval much more magically dangerous because it is secretly 'deserved'" (p. 117). Dimmesdale is the closest thing to a father that the child has known, and indeed she attaches all filial feeling to the minister. Suddenly her mother expresses obvious emotion for this man and therefore mother and daughter are for the first time in competition for him. Naturally Pearl wants her mother to resume the cold, asexual identity that would not challenge her possession of Dimmesdale's affection. Consequently, she forces her mother to replace the cap and scarlet letter and thereby withdraw from the competition, but in doing so Pearl also feels the "anxiety" from the potential loss of her mother's love as a result of her desire for father.

Chodorow's conclusions help to illuminate Pearl's conflicts in the forest:

> These psychoanalysts emphasize how, in contrast to males, the female oedipal crisis is not resolved in the same absolute way. A girl cannot and does not completely reject her mother in favor of

men, but continues her relationship of dependence upon and attachment to her. In addition, the strength and quality of her relationship to her father is completely dependent upon the strength and quality of her relationship to her mother. Deutsch suggests that a girl wavers in a "bisexual triangle" throughout her childhood and into puberty, normally making a very tentative resolution in favor of her father, but in such a way that issues of separation from and attachment to her mother remain important throughout a woman's life. (pp. 52–53)

Thus, despite her attraction to father, Pearl's primary loyalty is to mother; and in her fear of mother's withdrawal of love, Pearl shows the affection that will bond her once more to this solemn woman. Pearl in this scene, then, reflects her own conscience as well as her mother's, for she responds not only to Hester's feelings of guilt, but also to her own oedipal fears and anxieties.

In contrast to their ambivalence in the forest, there is no conflict between mother and daughter when Pearl kisses her father in the final scaffold scene. Though Hester holds the minister in her arms as he sinks to the floor, she cannot express her love publicly. Again, with the community as witness, Hester is unable to speak or act for herself, so Pearl is there to act for her. Thus, Pearl's expressive function is part of the structural integrity that marks this novel: as the infant pointed prophetically to Dimmesdale in the first scene, so he is irrevocably identified as her father in the final scaffold scene through both his words and her lips. And as she reached out to him in infancy to reflect her mother's longing and need, she now shows for the last time the love that Hester feels for this weak, tortured man. Yet there is no fear of mother's disapproval or competition here, for with a kiss Pearl says it all for both of them and thus brings the lovers' drama to a close.

With our altered view of Pearl's role in this novel, how and why Hawthorne uses children requires rethinking. Though he has been accused of awkwardness and even incompetence in his depiction of children—and we now see how inaccurate that assessment is—we must consider that his children are not created to stand alone. Rather, in different ways and for different purposes, they function to reflect, or provide a confrontation with, the adult character's conscience or unconscious. Similarly because Hawthorne's perceptive observations and insight regarding identification and interpersonal relationships anticipate the psychoanalytic studies of our century, his work becomes increasingly more relevant to our own concerns. He may have labeled Pearl as a "type" or "symbol" when he used her to externalize his heroine's internal "sphere," but while we use a different vocabulary, our present knowledge verifies the appropriateness of his delineation of this daughter figure and her multiple functions in the book. Indeed, because of Pearl's role in this novel, we are granted new insight into the joys and sorrows, the completion and competition, that define so many relationships between mothers and daughters. Regardless of his feelings about "woman's place," as an artist Hawthorne was able to transcend his personal limitations in this novel and has thereby given us all a gift of lasting value.*

NOTES

1. Nina Baym's study, *The Shape of Hawthorne's Career* (Ithaca, 1976)—in which she describes Pearl as Hester's "id" (p. 138) and "alter ego," "the wild, amoral, creative core" and "the imagination of her sin" (p. 133)—has contributed considerably to our recognition of Pearl's function in relation to Hester.

2. Nathaniel Hawthorne, *The Scarlet Letter*, ed. Millicent Bell (New York, 1983), p. 163.

3. See for example, Michael Vannoy Adams, "Pathography, Hawthorne, and the History of Psychological Ideas," *Emerson Society Quarterly*, 29 (1983), 113–26.

4. For documentation that is readily available, see "Notebooks: Pearl and Una," in *The Scarlet Letter*, ed. Sculley Bradley, et. al. (New York, 1962), pp. 192–94.

5. Barbara Garlitz, "Pearl: 1850–1955," *PMLA*, LXII (September 1957), 697.

6. Theodore Lidz, *The Person* (New York, 1968), pp. 103–04.

7. Adrienne Rich, *Of Woman Born* (New York, 1977), p. 232.

8. René A. Spitz, in collaboration with W. Godfrey Cobliner, *The First Year of Life: A Psychoanalytic Study of Normal and Deviant Development of Object Relations* (New York, 1965), pp. 4, 12. In this paper, I use only the "normal" development of children with regard to Pearl.

9. Anneliese Riess, "The Mother's Eye," *The Psychoanalytic Study of the Child*, 34 (New Haven, 1979), 386, 384.

10. Roy Schafer, *Aspects of Internalization* (New York, 1968), p. 16.

11. Carol Gilligan, *In a Different Voice* (Cambridge, Mass., 1982), pp. 7–8, quotes Nancy Chodorow's 1974 study.

12. T. Berry Brazelton and Heidelise Als, "Four Stages in the Development of Mother-Daughter Interaction," *The Psychoanalytic Study of the Child*, 34 (New Haven, 1979), 354.

13. Signe Hammer, *Daughters and Mothers, Mothers and Daughters* (New York, 1975), p. xiv.

14. Baym, p. 141.

15. See John Demos, *A Little Commonwealth: Family Life in Plymouth Colony* (New York, 1970), p. 139. I am grateful to Elizabeth Peck for sharing this material with me.

16. See Erik Erikson, *Identity: Youth and Crisis*, (New York, 1968), for a description of the developmental stage that applies to Pearl's behavior in this—and every other—scene.

17. Paula J. Caplan, *Barriers Between Women* (New York, 1981), p. 6.

18. Nancy Chodorow, "Family Structure and Feminine Personality," in *Woman, Culture, and Society*, ed. Michelle Zembalist Rosaldo and Louise Lamphere (Stanford, 1974), p. 47, notes: "As Deutsch expresses it, 'In relation to her own child, woman repeats her own mother-child history'."

* I wish to thank Grace Farrell Lee for her time and valuable suggestions.

JANIS P. STOUT

The Fallen Woman and the Conflicted Author:
Hawthorne and Hardy

> Chastity had then, it has even now, a religious importance in a woman's
> life, and has so wrapped itself round with nerves and instincts that to cut
> it free and bring it to the light of day demands courage of the rarest.
> —Virginia Woolf

It is well established in critical commentary that victorian fiction
recurrently, even obsessively, reflects a set of stereotyped assumptions
regarding the social role and the moral nature of women. Such assumptions,
as we might expect, occur most simplistically in popular forms, journalistic
as well as fictional, and adopt the longtime practice of conceiving of women's
nature in extreme terms, either of good or of evil.[1] Women were either
"sexless ministering angels" and moral lights to men and children, or they
were lost creatures, "tempresses" soiled beyond cleansing (Cominos, 167).
The "fallen woman" was labelled with absolute assurance. Though she might
be regarded with some degree of pity, there was no doubt as to what she was
and virtually no expectation that she could ever be regarded any differently.
As Nina Auerbach puts it, in the "popular myth" a woman's fall was
"implacable," and put her "beyond the pale of the family" (Auerback, 158,
153).

At the same time, particularly in the fiction which we would call

From *The American Transcendental Quarterly* 1, no. 3 (September 1987). © 1987 by The
University of Rhode Island.

literature, there occurs a note of ambiguity in the treatment of the fallen woman. Again in Auerbach's words, "admiration mingles with condemnation" in depictions of a simultaneous "fall and apotheosis" (Auerbach, 154, 165). It is not entirely surprising, of course, that this would be true. We expect that in serious literature character will not be utterly swallowed up in stereotype. But this note of ambiguity in some fictional presentations of the fallen woman goes beyond psychological realism to a questioning of the values from which the fiction is itself drawn. The novel becomes, to some degree, subversive. Or, as Tony Tanner puts it, the novel often "writes of contracts but dreams of trangressions" (Tanner, 368). If the sexually sinning woman was perceived as a threat to the very foundations of society, to question that she was altogether sinful was to conspire, to however slight a degree, in that undermining. When the character of the fallen woman is seriously and imaginatively treated, sympathy with her plight becomes a means of questioning not only the correctness of society's moral judgments of her, but the judgmental mentality itself.

As examples of both the radical shaping, or even determining, of a character that results from her being identified as a fallen woman, and, at the same time, the ambiguity or questioning that tends to undermine judgmental categorizing. I will consider three of the most familiar and most celebrated heroines of Victorian fiction—Hester Prynne of *The Scarlet Letter*, Zenobia of *The Blithedale Romance*, and Tess of *Tess of the D'Urbervilles*. Nathaniel Hawthorne, in the early Victorian period and in America, and Thomas Hardy, in England nearly forty years later, both adopted a moralistic stereotype complete with conventions that shaped not only the moral status and social experience of their characters, but even their physical appearance, and challenged the validity of that stereotype. The novels of Hardy and of Hawthorne are of course very different. Working in different places at different times, starting from very different assumptions about the nature of fiction, and treating different kinds of material, they adopt very dissimilar strategies for undermining the simplistic stereotype. Hardy, seemingly much surer of his own attitudes, launches a direct, cuttingly ironic assault.[2] Hawthorne, torn by an inner duality regarding conventional moral standards, questions the apparently simple judgment in his characteristic musing, brooding ironic tones. Hawthorne substitutes for the stereotype a complex object of contemplation, while Hardy sounds a call for change and for justice.

Yet, despite these rather basic and obvious differences, the three novels are curiously similar, both in respect to specific parallels of character and action, and in the final inability of either Hardy or Hawthorne to resolve his own conflicted ambivalence toward the fallen woman and the question of the sexual morality of women. It is this ambivalence, I would propose, that accounts for both Hawthorne's noted uncertainty regarding change and continuity in the two novels considered here and the uncertainty lurking behind Hardy's aggressive subtitle, *A Pure Woman*.

In Zenobia, of *Blithedale*, Hawthorne most clearly follows the romance convention of the dark woman.[3] That Zenobia is indeed "fallen," or sexually experienced, is never directly established but is indicated in a kind of conventional shorthand by her appearance and the suggestiveness of her manner, which is "not exactly maidenlike" but better suited, perhaps, to "a youthful widow, or a blooming matron" (47). She is consistently described in terms of richness or fullness of devleopment, amplitude, exoticism, and "gorgeousness" (164, 16). All of these qualities are joined in the motif of "bloom" or flowers, traditionally a symbol of female sexuality, which is insistently linked to Zenobia's powerful physical presence through the flower she wears in her hair. As Coverdale, the notoriously evasive and at least somewhat autobiographical narrator, points out, the flower is "a subtile expression" of her "character" (45). It is important that Zenobia's flower is not a bud (indicating shyness or maidenliness) or a common wildflower (for humility or simplicity), but a hot-house flower of "exotic" and even "outlandish" beauty, highly colored and fully open (15, 45). Accordingly, Coverdale exclaims of Zenobia in heavily allegorical language, "There is no folded petal, no latent dew-drop, in this perfectly developed rose!" (47).

Upon first meeting Coverdale, Zenobia virtually invites him to think of her sexually by alluding to fig leaves and the possibility of assuming "the garb of Eden" (17). She reinforces the suggestiveness of her words with body language, "shivering playfully." On the basis of this beginning and of her continuing physical allure and free manner, Coverdale becomes obsessed with the question of whether "the great event of a woman's existence had been consummated" (46)—that is, whether she has had sexual experience. His mind so dwells on the idea that she has "given herself away" (48) that he becomes convinced, on no real evidence whatever, that Zenobia had "lived, and loved!" (47). Curiously, though Hawthorne raises serious questions about Coverdale's judgment throughout the novel, he conveys no doubt whatever of the judgment regarding Zenobia's fallen state, but indeed lets its accuracy be assumed without either dramatic evidence or authorial assurance. It is a strangely circular bit of reasoning: if Coverdale thinks she is guilty, she must be guilty, because if she had not been guilty he could not have thought so. Coverdale's response to Zenobia, like his response to virtually every other question, is puzzlingly ambiguous. Auerbach's account of the "dark Madonna's" simultaneous condemnation and "statuesque" majesty (167) might well refer to Coverdale's view of Zenobia. Clearly, he finds her not only fascinating but admirable, recognizing in her a vitality greatly surpassing his own and declaring her "truly a magnificent woman" (44). That this declaration applies to her total character, not just to her allure, is made clear by its context, a passage in which he has acknowledged her intellectual ability, accounted for the meagerness of her achievement by reference to social constraints on women, and established the fact that she is a free-thinking radical. Yet his praise includes indirect expressions of criticism and even condescension:

> Her poor little stories and tracts never half did justice to her intellect: it was only the lack of a fitter avenue that drove her to seek development in literature. She was made (among a thousand other things that she might have been) for a stumporatress. I recognized no severe culture in Zenobia; her mind was full of weeds. It startled me, sometimes, in my state of moral, as well as bodily faintheartedness, to observe the hardihood of her philosophy; she made no scruple of oversetting all human institutions, and scattering them as with a breeze from her fan. A female reformer, in her attacks upon society, has an instinctive sense of where the life lies, and is inclined to aim directly at that spot. Especially, the relation between the sexes is naturally among the earliest to attract her notice.

Zenobia was truly a magnificent woman. (44)

Here, as always, Coverdale finds it necessary to disparage even as he admires. Praising Zenobia, he snidely downgrades her. He desires her sexually but, finding such desires unacceptable, blames her for his own sense of guilt by insinuating that she is morally tainted. As a last defensive gesture, following the same pattern, he insists that he was really in love with Priscilla, Zenobia's blonde foil, all along.

The fact that Hawthorne could conceive so sensuous and so personally forceful a female character as Zenobia shows a powerful strain of unconventionality in his thought and the bent of his imagination. It seems clear, however, that her unconventionality was precisely what he found troubling about her. The conflict reflects the same struggle between change and continuity that forms the motivating tension of *The House of the Seven Gables* and various of his tales and sketches. Zenobia represents the new woman conjoined with the oldest but, in Hawthorne's society, most repressed idea of woman, sexual heat. Although the dramatic statement of the novel at first accords validity to her free ideas, in that it commends the hopes of social reformers and shows the unhealthiness of repressions such as Coverdale's and Priscilla's, finally it simply squashes them when they become too threatening. Hawthorne scapegoats Zenobia no less than Coverdale does. He drains off her potency by having her grovel in unrequited love before the domineering Hollingsworth and then kill herself, leaving the field to the pallid, passive, and utterly conventional Priscilla.[4] Zenobia has complained that women of an age to be regarded as sexual objects "have no rights" or at any rate do not exercise them (141) and has argued persuasively that relations between men and women must be put on a new footing. She has lamented the severity of society's judgment of "the woman who swerves one hair's breadth out of the beaten track" (224). In the end, however, the novel silences her arguments.[5]

Hester Prynne is, of course, drawn along much the same lines as Zenobia, evidencing specific motifs associated with the "fallen woman" stereotype. She, too, is powerfully and alluringly physical, built "on a large scale" (53), or, as Auerbach says, a scale of "regality" (165), with dark hair and eyes. Like Zenobia, again, she is associated with flower imagery, a device which proclaims her sexuality. Even Hester's maternity follows the stereotyped pattern in that Hawthorne depicts her child as being inherently unstable and deficient in moral sense because "a great law had been broken" in her conception (90). Indeed, while Zenobia is identified as fallen only by guesswork and innuendo, Hester is explicitly labelled a "fallen woman" (110). Yet she is never totally contained by that label even to the degree that Zenobia is. Zenobia is a puzzle; Hester is a great mystery.

Though he challenges the stereotype of the fallen woman, Hawthorne never questions the reality of Hester's sin and guilt. His references to her "shame" and her need for "penitence" (59, 263) are direct and untinged by irony. Fully accepting the reality of her fall, Hawthorne nevertheless questions both the adequacy of that view and the severity of her society's judgment of her. His attitude, in Harry Levin's words, is "primly subversive" (73). Puritan society, utterly convinced of its right to pass judgment, is utterly unqualified to do so in any situation involving natural emotions because it is itself emotionally desicated. When Hester is standing on the scaffold with her infant, the faces in the crowd have a "grim rigidity" (49), and in their later treatment of her the townspeople display an appalling insensitivity, using her as an object lesson in the fuits of sin and pronouncing her to her face a "scarlet woman" and a "worthy type of her of Babylon" (110)—that is, the ultimate whore. Even the children greet Hester and Pearl with mudslinging—literal mudslinging. Hawthorne finds such a society fitly symbolized in its prison, the "black flower of civilized society" (48).

In contrast to the "black flower," Hester is the true flower, the rose, an emblem both of beauty and of the vitality and spontaneity of nature. Yet nature is always, for Hawthorne, ambiguous. The wild rose is a remnant of the morally indeterminate forest still looming beyond the edges of the small settlement. Moreover, its vibrant color recalls the scarlet of the phrase "scarlet woman." Thus the rose conveys implications of lasciviousness, even as it conveys the positive values of natural vitality and authenticity. All of these values are fully applicable to Hester. Pearl, too, is linked to the rose-scarlet pattern both through her red dress, a visible sign that she is "the scarlet letter endowed with life" (102), and through her response to the rose she sees when she visits the governor's garden. Another visitor to the garden, a respected minister, suggests that her name might better be Ruby or Red Rose (110). When he seeks to test the piety of her upbringing by asking "who made thee," Pearl replies triumphantly that she "had been plucked by her mother off the bush of wild roses, that grew by the prison-door" (112). In the language of Hawthorne's symbolism, it is an answer of perfect good sense.

The motif of the rose objectifies the deep ambivalence that characterizes Hawthorne's treatment of Hester in every way. He gives her a nunlike garb and mien and offers a cautious and elaborately indirect suggestion of her resemblance to the Virgin Mary, the "image of sinless motherhood, whose infant was to redeem the world," but then adds that the resemblance could only be "by contrast" (56). He challenges the sterotypical notion that the "fallen woman" was irredeemable by showing that after her "fall" Hester not only performs unstinting service to her judgmental community, but also sustains a profound inner growth which includes a very clear vision of the defects of her society. Yet the motif of "regeneration through womanly service" was itself conventional, and still left the repetant Magdalen outside "ordinary society" (Mitchell, 33, x). Hawthorne's final judgment of Hester and of her social vision is uncertain. In her honesty and her practical service to others, she has a strength not accorded to the face-saving Dimmesdale, who, outwardly at least, gets off scot-free until his voluntary confession at the end. But Hawthorne never indicates any doubt of the old idea that sexual license is worse for a woman than for a man.

Finally, Hawthorne cannot accept the radical revaluation of guilt and innocence that he has himself proposed in his treatment of Hester. He cannot leave unchallenged the radical social ideas he attributes to her—much like those he attributes to Zenobia—or even his own stringent castigation of Puritan society. Labelling Hester's vision of "the whole system of society ... torn down and built up anew" (165) a "dark labyrinth of mind" (166), he asserts that such mental rebellion is inappropriate and unhealthy for a woman. Indeed, it shows once again that the fallen woman is a threat to social stability. However strongly he may deplore the narrowness and insensitivity of the self-righteous Puritan system, he must choose law over the trackless wilderness of moral chaos. In the end, he half-accepts the dehumanizing stereotype that he has so beautifully challenged.

In turning to Hardy's *Tess*, we encounter a very different kind of book, but very similar patterns of initial character typing, social experience, and even authorial ambivalence. Like Hawthorne's Hester, Tess is very explicitly a fallen woman, drawn along the lines of romance tradition—dark in coloring, large in stature, and so beautiful as to attract the notice of strangers. Like both Hester and Zenobia, she has a "luxuriance of aspect" or "fullness of growth" (35) indicative of a strongly physical nature.[6] Like Hawthorne, though, Hardy uses these familiar outlines of the fallen woman as the starting point for a sympathetic characterization that both humanizes the stereotype and challenges its validity. For Hawthorne, guilt and innocence, or more precisely guilt and nobility, are deeply intertwined within the individual soul, so that his irony is brooding and pervasive. The effect in Hardy's work is much different. Here, guilt and innocence are more radically disjoined, and irony arises not from the indeterminacy of moral shading but from simple wrongness, calling things one thing which are another. In spite of her obvious nubility and her seduction, Tess is virtually a child, with a child's innocence. The real guilt is not hers but her victimizer's and society's. Thus, Hardy's is the bold irony of clearly defined contrast, located at the forefront of the novel. He produces a fictional effect at once more rounded and more polemical than Hawthorne's.

Hardy insisted in his Preface to the Fifth Edition that "a novel is an impression, not an argument" and that *Tess* was "intended to be neither didactic nor aggressive." Yet the subtitle of the novel, *A Pure Woman*, is an indisputably aggressive challenge to prevailing social standards and assumptions. It is clear from the story line that Tess is not in any usual sense a "pure" woman. She would appear to be, in a very classic sense, a "fallen" one. Indeed, the disparity between the subtitle and the evidence of the novel has occasioned much of the voluminous critical commentary on *Tess*, with pronouncements on the subtitle ranging from "wellmeant but extraneous" to "defiant." Bernard Paris, in particular, has shown that it raises an insoluble logical problem in the novel.[7] There can be little doubt that by affixing the subtitle *A Pure Woman* Hardy created more difficulties than he solved. However, the problem he was setting himself was to invalidate the label "fallen woman" by reducing it to an absurdity. It is not surprising, then, that the opposite label, "pure woman," would also become specious.

At the outset, Hardy elicits our pity for Tess's haplessness. She is seen, as she will continue to be seen throughout the novel, as being caught up in overwhelming forces, and is the victim of her father's shiftlessness and both parent's false hopes even before she becomes the victim of Alec D'Urberville's strategems. She is a victim, too, of her own good nature, her readiness to sympathize with her family's plight and to go along with their foolish schemes for betterment, and indeed a victim of her own body's early maturation, before she has had a chance to develop for herself the wariness that her mother fails to provide her. For all these reasons, as well as the specific circumstances under which Alec takes her, she cannot be held fully responsible for what happens to her. Nevertheless, loss of virginity is absolute, and, fair or not, Tess must bear the social as well as the biological penalty. The effect of her seduction is not to be underestimated. "An immeasurable social chasm," Hardy says would thereafter separate Tess from the self she was before (63). Actually, however, like Hester Prynne, she is separated from her former self not only by disgrace, but also by growth. Her fall becomes in some ways a rise. After her seduction, Tess changes from a virtual child into a sturdy, capable woman, intent on "sweet independence" (77) and rises from pity to respect in the reader's estimation.

After the birth of her child and an initial period of despondency, Tess decides that "the trees were just as green as before," or, in other words, that life goes on, and resolves to "be useful again" (77) by going into the fields to work for pay. It is at this point that she reappears in the novel, after the tactful hiatus of her pregnancy, with a striking new dignity and strength. Keenly aware that she is an object of gossip and a shame to her family, keenly aware of the baby's "offence against society in coming into the world" (78), she stifles her embarrassment and forces herself to look her neighbors "calmly in the face ... even when holding the baby in her arms" (78). At noon, she nurses the child in the field. Already she displays the fortitude that will be so conspicuous a part of her character later in the novel.

Tess's response to her child is rather curious, in that she alternates between a seeming indifference and a torrential excess of affection. However, when it becomes apparent that the sickly infant may not survive, she is roused to a fierce devotion which culminates in her baptism of the dying baby. Tess's action here develops out of two carefully established lines in her character, which will remain prominent to the end: her capacity for devotion and her independence. At this point in the novel, Tess is no disturber of the status quo. She has been schooled in the established teachings concerning salvation and punishment, and she accepts without question "the consideration that if she should have to burn for what she had done, burn she must, and there was an end to it" (78). But she cannot be so resigned where the child is concerned. She is struck by the unfairness of the baby's being damned (as she is convinced it will be, if not baptized) for what it has not done. Like Hawthorne's Zenobia and Hester, out of the experience of her own misfortune she is beginning to develop her own ideas. Denied the services of a clergyman, she conducts her own service of baptism, with her awe-struck brothers and sisters as congregation. This powerful scene is the culmination of the first phase of Tess's rise.

A second phase begins at Talbothays dairy and extends through her marriage to Angel Clare, the scene of their wedding-night confessions, and their initial separation. As this section of the book opens, the self-reliance Tess showed in going into the fields to work has grown into her determination to leave her parents' home and maker her own way. She is no longer in any sense a child, but has "changed from simple girl to complex woman" (84). Clearly enough, such a change is a gain; Hardy does not allow us to prefer innocence over wisdom. It has not come automatically, but as a result of a "reflectiveness" that shows in her face (84), and it has made her "passing corporeal blight" into a "mental harvest" (105). In other words, her fall has been fortunate. At Talbothays, Tess becomes an embodiment of the fertile natural world in which she is immersed. In this respect, the Talbothays phase is only the unfolding of the physicality and passive sensuousness that was evident in her girlhood. At the same time, she gains self-definition through her capability in work, her reflectiveness, and her admiration and desire for knowledge. Indeed, when she first begins to admire Angel Clare it is "as an intelligence rather than as a man" (106). In return, he finds her reflections on the somberness of life "impressive" (105). This awakening of her mind and her admiration for knowledge and clear thinking will contribute to her recognition of the injustice of Angel's (society's) standards of sexual morality.

Tess's behavior during the courtship period is of great significance to her rise in moral stature. Caught between her wish to seize the happiness Angel offers her and her determination not to seize that happiness unfairly by leaving him in ignorance until they are safely married, as her mother has urged, she repeatedly refuses his proposal, insisting that she is "not good enough—not worthy enough" (147) and urging him to choose one of the other girls. Tess's self-abasement here has been seen as evidence of an urge toward self-destruction or "an insidious need to immolate herself under the deceptive guise of benefiting others" (E. Hardy, 234), or what might be called a martyr complex. To be sure, there are times in the story when Tess does seem bent on appropriating the role of victim. However, if Hardy was launching a direct attack on the accepted idea of the "fallen woman," as I have suggested, it was essential that he counter the conventional idea of a pleasure-centered nature. Tess's reluctance to seize the happiness Angel Clare offers is a demonstration that she has motives other than immediate gratification. In spite of her fear of losing him, she writes out her confession, only to have it devoured by a vicious bit of carpet—the notorious incident illustrating Hardy's determination to show how unfair the world is. When she discovers that her letter has gone astray, it seems too late to interrupt the marriage preparations. Only for that reason does she go ahead with the marriage on a basis of untruth.

Against this backdrop of suffering, self-denial, and integrity, and the longer vista which follows, is poised the episode of Tess's wedding-night confession and Angel's astounding, predictable response. (It is one of the little-noted marks of Hardy's mastery that he would make us see Clare's muddled response here as being at once the most normal behavior and the most outlandish.) Her final resolve to go through with the confession springs in part from the generosity that we have observed in her all along. She pities the girls who loved Angel unsuccessfully and reminds herself that she should pay for her own good fortune by undergoing the ordeal of telling all, as she had meant to do before. When Angel solemnly recounts his own sexual impurity in the past, his "eight-and-forty hours' dissipation with a stranger" (189), she perceives, accurately enough, that her confession "cannot be more serious" than his because it is "just the same" (190). In fact, it is less serious, because, as the reader knows, she fell as a deceived child while Angel "plunged" knowingly into depravity. Seeing that her offense is no worse than his and assuming that that fact will be equally evident to him, she is confident he will receive her confession, as she has received his, with forbearance. Instead, he blatantly invokes the double standard. Yes, he says, she has forgiven him, but this is diferent; she is now a different person from the one he loved. What this means, of course, is that he now labels her differently. Angel is trapped in his own judgmental habit of categorizing people. He himself has reassigned her from one category, the one marked "pure ... maidenhood" or "rustic innocence" (199), to another, the category marked "fallen woman." He cannot conceive of loving a member of the latter. Tess is completely accurate and a good deal more reasonable than Clare when she observes, "'It is in your own mind what you are angry at, Angel; it is not in me'" (194).

Tess's submissiveness to Clare's wedding-night demand for a period of separation must strike the modern reader as being at least improbable, if not unworthy,[8] but it is a continuation of the pattern of self-denial seen in her reluctance to accept his proposal. Long after he has proven himself to be either the most cold-hearted prig or the most abject victim of conditioning in false values,[9] Tess defers to his wishes, hoping to expiate her offense and win forgiveness. In so doing, she proves herself possessed of patience, forbearance, and sheer endurance to a degree that indeed belies the self-indulgent image of the fallen woman.[10] Giving her family most of the money

Clare has left for her, she must endure deprivation and hard labor. Even so, she resists the blandishments of Alec D'Urberville, who has diabolically reappeared, offering relief if only she will be his again. Only when Tess's widowed mother and her children are forced out of their home because Tess is not a "proper woman" (294) does she give in to Alec, in exhange for their support. In terms of plot, Tess's prolonged trial after Clare's desertion serves as the final wearing down of her goodness, her will to resist. In terms of the novel's stark contrasts of character, however, it excuses her second sexual fall, her deliberate selling of herself to Alec, and provides the ultimate demonstration of Tess's courage and generosity, hence the injustice of merely labeling her a fallen woman.

As this summary of the novel indicates, Hardy appears to go about the overturning of the stereotype with resolute singlemindedness. At every opportunity, he turns conventional vice to virtue. In the process, he challenges the idea of the double standard, both offering a vindication of Tess's motives and, like Hawthorne, exposing the injustice of the resulting penalties. Both Alec D'Urberville and Angel Clare, like Dimmesdale and like Zenobia's actual or would-be lovers, come away virtually unscathed. But for being seduced through unwariness and then through extremes of hardship and fear for her family, Tess suffers the blighting of her entire life. By piling up the severity of the consequences, Tess must pay, and establishing her dignity and innate goodness, in contrast to Alec's villainy and Clare's hypocrisy, Hardy shows us the injustice of society's labelling of her.

Further, he goes beyond Tess's own case to question the application of such a label to any woman and indeed to question the stereotyping cast of mind altogether. He does this through an argument amounting finally to an appeal to charitable doubt. Our inability fully to fathom Tess's motives, let alone to weigh the balance of motives and deeds or to obviate the semantic slipperiness of language, leaves us uncertain whether she should be called pure, as the subtitle asserts, even while we know she should not be called impure. Yet Hardy's omniscience as narrator has made Tess open to us in a way that real persons seldom are. Considering the inadequacy of our knowledge, his submerged argument runs, and considering the complexity of issues of motive and circumstance, how can we be so confident in our powers of judgment as to affix a destructive label to anyone? Hawthorne would have agreed with this line of reasoning, but would have asked us to consider also our own share in the fellowship of guilt.

Both Hawthorne and Hardy, then, invalidate the stereotype of the fallen woman on grounds of its inhumanity, the limitations of those who would apply that label, and the ultimate mystery of every human being. Their exploration of the human complexity beneath the stereotype becomes a means to undermine the absoluteness of the judgmental mentality. It becomes, as well, an occasion for re-examining common assumptions regarding the nature of women. In particular, notions that sexual liberty is less acceptable for women than for men or that women's characters are defined, simply and absolutely, by their sexual behavior, are shown to be at least questionable, if not absurd.

Nevertheless, for all his seeming certainty as to his convictions, Hardy, after all, shares Hawthorne's uncertainty about the importance of female chastity. As many critics have noted, the subtitle *A Pure Woman* seems at variance with the events of the novel. Granted that Tess is sympathetic, even admirable, how, we wonder, can she be considered pure? There are three major possibilities. Hardy may mean that Tess is pure at the outset, in her innate nature, but is cheated of that purity by others, specifically by Alec D'Uberville. In this case, the subtitle points to the disparity between essence and event, and its import is elegiac, a lament for something lost. In this sense, however, the subtitle not only is ironic, but defends Tess as a victim at the cost of reducing her to nothing more than a victim; it does not adequately reflect the strength and courage evident particularly in the later parts of the novel. Or Hardy may mean that Tess remains pure even after her sexual experience because her intentions were pure, and the actual event has no moral significance. Yet this reading, as Bernard Paris points out, lets stand the idea that her actions were bad, and thus leaves her a fallen woman though it does beg for mercy. A third possibility, a more radical one and completely at variance with both the first and the second, is that the subtitle asserts the essential purity of nature and therefore of sexuality, which is a part of nature. This meaning of the subtitle is sustained mainly by the richly fecund Talbothays chapters. However, it is belied by the anxiousness with which Hardy insists on Tess's childlike state, denying her any mature or overt sexual interest, and by his eagerness to establish a mental awakening that separates her from mere natural process.

In fact, no single meaning of the subtitle can be applied to the novel as a whole. By trumpeting his defiance of conventional morality in a subtitle which is invalidated by the conflicting logic of the work itself, Hardy reveals his uneasiness before the prospect of altogether giving up distinctions based on chastity. Like Hawthorne, he has made a powerful humanitarian statement. Yet, even for so independent a thinker as Hardy, the habit of perceiving women in categorical moral terms and of labelling them according to a set of expectations different from those applied to men is too firmly ingrained to be relinquished without vestiges of anxiety.

NOTES

1. Marina Warner, among others, touches frequently on this double edged sword of moral superiority/inferiority. Tony Tanner stresses the basic importance attached by society to the maintenance of clear distinctions between the good woman and the bad woman (12–13 and 376).

2. Hardy's assurance, however, is in some ways specious. Bernard Paris argues persuasively that *Tess* is "thematically unintelligible" and that Hardy's view "can in no way be unified into a coherent moral vision."

3. Theories relating to the American romance emanate from Richard Chase and have been developed in works such as Porte's. Robert Merill dissents from this widely accepted view.

4. Julian Smith asks "Why Does Zenobia Kill Herself?" and answers that she is pregnant.

5. Nina Baym argues cogently that Zenobia's liberal views have been effectively silenced all along by her "internalization of male values."

6. The word "luxuriant," which is applied to both Tess and Zenobia, is heavily laden with traditional (Biblical) connotations of indulgence and sexual sin.

7. Mary Jacobus terms the subtitle "defiant" and argues that to apply the term "pure" to a woman whose "career ... includes not simply seduction, but collapse into kept woman and murderess taxes the linguistic resources of the most permissive conventional moralist" (320). W. Eugene Davis regards the subtitle as a "well-meant but extraneous authorial commentary" that belies Tess's humanity (400). In Davis's view, although Hardy may, as he later indicated to Edmund Blunden, have been referring to "a certain unassailable virtue, an impregnable goodness that might not be destroyed," Tess is in fact memorable because "her impurity makes her human and makes her actions in the novel credible" (401). Maggie Humm, following a very different line of reasoning, finds that Tess "gain[s] purity at the end of the novel" by ridding herself of the "images" fastened on her by a masculine society (82). Bernard Paris sums up, "The argument of Tess's purity from the goodness of her intentions implies that her sexual relations with Alec were bad: the argument for Tess's purity from nature as moral norm regards her relations with Alec as innocent" (64).

8. Katharine Rogers writes that Tess's submissive loyalty to Angel "would be more appropriate to a lower animal than to a rational human being" (250).

9. To James T. Hazen, who reads the novel as the tragedy of Tess's scapegoating by a "sick" society whose "attitudes toward the 'fallen' woman and toward sexuality in general" are "unnatural and harmful," Angel Clare represents the ordinary person who cannot escape his society's assumptions and who falls into error and inadequacy. Hazen's reading is a good corrective, but excessively merciful toward Angel.

10. In her provocative study of Hardy's revisions made for the sake of minimizing the novel's offense to his reading public, Mary Jacobus counts Tess's submissiveness to Clare's plan among the evidences of Hardy's bowdlerization of his more subtle original characterization, which produced in the final version a Tess of exaggerated goodness, an Alec of exaggerated villainy, and an Angel of exaggerated heartlessness.

WORKS CITED

Auerbach, Nina. *Woman and the Demon: The Life of a Victorian Myth*. Cambridge, Massachusetts: Harvard University Press, 1982.

Baym, Nina. "Hawthorne's Women: The Tyranny of Social Myths." *Centennial Review* 15 (1971): 250–272.

Chase, Richard. *The American Novel and Its Tradition*. New York: Doubleday, 1957.

Cominos, Peter T. "Innocent Femina Sensualis in Unconscious Conflict." *Suffer and Be Still: Women in the Victorian Age*. Ed. Martha Vicinus. Bloomington and London: Indiana University Press. 1972. 155–172.

Davis, W. Eugene. "Some Ambiguities about a Pure Woman." *Nineteenth Century Fiction* 22 (1968): 397–401.

Hardy, Evelyn. *Thomas Hardy, A Critical Biography*. London: Hogarth Press, 1954.

Hardy, Thomas. *Tess of the D'Urbervilles*. Ed. Scott Ellege. New York: Norton, 1979. This edition follows the Wessex Edition of 1912.

Hawthorne, Nathaniel. *The Blithedale Romance. The Centenary Edition of the Works of Nathaniel Hawthorne*. Columbus: Ohio State University Press, 1961-1968. Volume III.

_____. *The Scarlet Letter. The Centenary Edition of the Works of Nathaniel Hawthorne*. Columbus: Ohio State University Press. 1961–1968. Volume I.

Hazen, James T. "The Tragedy of Tess Durbeyfield." *Texas Studies in Literature and Language* 11 (1969): 779–794.

Humm, Maggie, "Thomas Hardy and Women: A Psycho-Social Criticism of Tess D'Uberville and Sue Bridehead." *Massachusetts Studies in English* 6 (1979): 77–89.

Jacobus, Mary. "Tess's Purity." *Essays in Criticism* 26 (1976): 318–338.

Levin. Harry, *The Power of Blackness*. New York: Knopf, 1958.

Merrill, Robert. "Another Look at the American Romance." *Modern Philology* 78 (1981): 379–392.

Mitchell, Sally. *The Fallen Angel: Chastity. Class and Women's Reading*, 1835–1880. Bowling Green, Ohio: Bowling Green University Popular Press, 1981.

Paris, Bernard. "A Confusion of Many Standards: Conflicting Value Systems in *Tess of the D'Urbervilles*." *Nineteenth Century Fiction* 24 (1969): 57–79.

Porte, Joel. *The Romance in America: Studies in Hawthorne, Melville, and James*. Middletown. Connecticut: Wesleyan University Press, 1969.

Rogers, Katharine. "Women in Thomas Hardy." *Centennial Review* 19 (1974): 249–258.

Smith, Julian. "Why Does Zenobia Kill Herself?" *English Language Notes* 6 (1968): 37–39.

Tanner, Tony. *Adultery in the Novel: Contract and Transgression*. Baltimore: Johns Hopkins University Press. 1979.

Warner, Marina. *Alone of All Her Sex: The Myth and the Cult of the Virgin Mary*. New York: Knopf, 1976.

MONICA M. ELBERT

Hester and the New Feminine Vision

Hester is the only protagonist in *The Scarlet Letter* who has the courage to live after "stand[ing] denuded and see[ing] the intolerable abyss of [herself]." The landscape of her mind is described in terms of this abyss: she wanders "without a clew in the dark labyrinth of mind; now turned aside by an insurmountable precipice; not starting back from a deep chasm. There was wild and ghastly scenery all around her, and a home and comfort nowhere" (261). Hester, precisely because she stands outside the realm of the religious and scientific law and cannot find a home outside her own psyche, is able to confront her self honestly and to work creatively with her existence. Some traditional critics, among them Crews (135), think that it is through Dimmesdale that that reader gains access to Hawthorne's masterpiece; I feel that Hester offers the key to understanding, as she resists all those negative traits which Hawthorne denounces in his portrayal of Dimmesdale.

It is not so much Hester's sin of "passion" as her motherhood which gives her latitude in this society of patriarchs. Pearl, the stigma of her sin, and her badge, the scarlet letter, stay with her until the end, and both baby and badge become a good part of her personality. As Hester fells the council of elders, Pearl "is the scarlet letter, only capable of being loved" (214). In becoming a mother on her own terms, as she does, and in investing the child and the emblem "A" with her own meaning, she displaces patriarchal

From *Encoding the Letter "A": Gender and Authority in Hawthorne's Early Fiction.* ©1990 by Haag + Herchen.

authority.[13] Her creative mothering and her creative artistry (the ornate embroidery of her letter, for example) separate her from both male and female authority in this society. In fact, she quietly but defiantly mocks authority from the start, with her unconventional appearance. Moreover, the "fantastically embroidered and illuminated" scarlet letter "had the effect of a spell, taking her out of the ordinary relations with humanity, and inclosing her in a sphere by herself" (164). Hawthorne repeatedly alludes to Hester's realm as an isolated sphere; even in the end, she stands in the "magic circle of ignominy" (331).

Since she cannot express her private self publicly, Hester uses Pearl as a vehicle to convey her repressed feelings. Hester spends much of her free time "lavishing ... morbid ingenuity, to create an analogy between the object of her affection [Pearl], and the emblem of her guilt. But, in truth, Pearl was the one, as well as the other" (204–05). To an extent, Pearl is the public expression of Hester's feelings. Thus, while she attempts to pacify the authorities who judge her, by dressing in subdued hues and coarse materials, she dresses her daughter in clothes "distinguished by a fanciful, or ... a fantastic ingenuity" (189). Pearl's "bright and sunny" appearance is in sharp contrast to Hester's appearance, but the former "owed its existence to the shape of gloomy gray" (314; cf. the ending where the meanings on the tombstone coexist by virtue of their opposites). Hester's fancy is "at once so gorgeous and so delicate" as to create the child's dress, but it also is "the same that had achieved a task more difficult, in imparting so distinct a peculiarity to Hester's simple robe" (314). This complex luxuriance and natural simplicity are the two impulses which characterize Hester's imagination: neither impulse is more genuine than the other, as each has its source in the same mind.[14]

In this novel where the protagonists are constantly seeking self-affirmation through mirror images,[15] it is significant that Hester searches for a sense of self through Pearl. Indeed, Pearl mirrors her repressed passions and moods, and through Pearl's sensitive and rebellious nature, she comes to understand herself: as the narrator explains, "Children have always a sympathy in the agitations of those connected with them; always, especially, a sense of any trouble or impending revolution, of whatever kind, in domestic circumstances" (314). With Pearl at her side, Hester cannot lose touch with herself.

> Once ... while Hester was looking at her own image in [her child's eyes], as mothers are fond of doing ... she fancied that she beheld, not her own miniature portrait, but another face in the small black mirror of Pearl's eye. It was a face, fiend-like, full of smiling

malice, yet bearing the semblance of features that she had known full well, though seldom with a smile, and never with malice, in them. It was as if an evil spirit possessed the child, and had just then peeped forth in mockery. Many a time afterwards had Hester been tortured, though less vividly, by the same illusion. (201)

Hester is terrified of losing her maternal sense of self, as translated through her child Pearl's eyes, and her fears and delusions prompt her to see a fiendish and distorted version of Chillingworth reflected in Pearl's eyes; it is surprising that she detects the vindictive husband and not the cowardly lover, who is, after all, Pearl's father, in this image of the child. She cannot bear the thought of her reality being absorbed or eclipsed by the patriarch's authoritarian presence (in whatever form the patriarch may take), nor can she bear the thought of having the Governor take the child out of her custody. This hallucination, in which Hester is haunted by the patriarch's possession of her daughter, is followed immediately by Hester's trial of maternity in the Governor's mansion, where Dimmesdale and Chillingworth will act the part of jurors.

This question of child custody which comes up in "The Governor's Hall" brings the conflict between patriarchal oppression and Hester's type of maternal nurturing to a climax. The leading citizens of the town, who cherished "the more rigid order of principles in religion and government," head a campaign to "deprive her of her child" (203). The reactions of the secular and spiritual fathers, as well as those of Chillingworth and Dimmesdale, are telling. The theocratic government, viewing the child (in theological terms) as a demon offspring, feels it their duty "to remove such a stumbling-block from her [Hester's] path" (203) in order to "save" Hester's soul and secretly to punish her further, since she is not suffering enough for them. If they discover that the child is amenable to Christian doctrine and possesses "the elements of ultimate salvation," they will transfer her "to wiser and better guardianship than Hester Prynne's" (203).

Dimmesdale, still working within the patriarchal tradition, diplomatically changes the town council's gospel truth around and preaches a message of New Testament humility and guilt as well as Old Testament severity:

"This child of its father's guilt and its mother's shame hath come from the hand of God, to work in many ways upon her heart, who pleads so earnestly, and with such bitterness of spirit, the right to keep her. It was meant for a blessing; for the one blessing of her life! It was meant, doubtless, as the mother herself hath told us, for a retribution too; a torture, to be felt at many an unthought of moment; a pang, a sting, an ever-recurring agony, in the midst of a troubled life!" (215)

Chillingworth, of course, is merely concerned with the child's physiognomy as a clue to discovery of the child's paternity:

"A strange child! ... It is easy to see the mother's part in her. Would it be beyond a philosopher's research, think ye, gentlemen, to analyze the child's nature, and, from it make and mold, to give a shrewd guess at the father?" (217)

This type of scientific thinking (a forerunner to genetics, though popular parents' guides of the time suggested that "parents transmitted moral as well as physical traits through heredity" Ryan 54) naturally goes against the teachings of the Church Fathers, who view the mystery of birth as something sacred. Reverend Wilson attacks Chillingworth's stand, "... it would be sinful, in such a question, to follow the clew of profane philosophy.... Better to fast and pray upon it; and still better ... to leave the mystery as we find it" (217). Hester appeals to the sacred bonds between mother and child; moreover, she realizes that the child is the only human connection she has in life. She appeals to Dimmesdale's sympathies, rightly so, for Dimmesdale knows all about a child's bonds to the mother, for he longs for his own primal bonds to the mother.

"Thou knowest—for thou hast sympathies which these men lack—thou knowest what is in my heart, and what are a mother's rights, and how much the stronger they are, when the mother has but her child and the scarlet letter! ... I will not lose the child!" (215).

Hester instinctively knows that she has the backing of nature, but not of the iron framework of the law: she is "so conscious of her own right, that it seemed scarcely an unequal match between the public, on the one side, and a lonely woman, backed by the sympathies of nature, on the other" (204). It is this fierce natural quality which separates Hester from the Puritan matrons.

As we have seen, the Puritan "iron-visaged" women are almost more severe than the men, and they delight in making Hester an outcast. They attend her scaffold humiliation all the while taking "a peculiar interest in whatever penal infliction might be expected to ensue" (161). This public spectacle allows the repressed women to feel the courage and power denied to them by the male rulers: the spokeswoman argues that the group of assembled women should "have the handling of such malefactresses as this Hester Prynne" since they are "of mature age and church-members of good repute" (161). This is not the soft, maternal order of women which appeals to Hawthorne so much in this and in his later works and which Hester prophesies in the end, but rather, a masculine group of power-hungry women who want to give a harder sentence than "the worshipful magistrates. One woman, "the ugliest as well as the most pitiless of these self-constituted judges" (162; cf. Chillingworth's deformity, which makes him insecure and pitiless also), is so envious of Hester's beauty and liberty that she calls for the death penalty: "This woman has brought shame upon us all, and ought to die. Is there no law for it? Truly there is, both in the Scripture and the statute-book" (162). Ironically, she relies, in her condemnation, on the same patriarchal texts that have imprisoned her. Rather than feminizing and personalizing religion, as Hester does, she attempts to gain access to their power by persecuting one of her sisters. Hawthorne, who knew much about woman's nature (however much amiss), is astute in making these harsh women middle-aged, menopausal, rheumatic matrons, who have lost their mothering function and thus know no other way of gaining power in this closed society than to be as critical as their men. Hawthorne is not attacking these women per se; rather, he is attacking the patriarchal system which makes motherhood a commodity. As Evelyn Fox Keller points out, mothers become intrusive, harsh, or possessive because of their feelings of inadequacy and impotence in the patriarchal family structure, and reflects men's own inability to come to terms with the mother: "their actual behavior can and often does reinforce fathers and sons in their own confusion about maternal power and love and hence in their defensive preoccupation, first with autonomy and finally with power and dominion" (112). Significantly, the only woman who is sympathetic to Hester is another young mother with a child in hand, and yet this mother dies shortly after, as the harshness of the system destroys her. Hester can certainly find no support in this system, and so she subversively becomes the most feminine, least patriarchal, but strongest individual by becoming a sister of mercy, on her own terms as we shall see.

It is to Hester's credit that she does not join the counter-culture of women in this repressed society; she does not ally herself with the likes of Mistress Hibbins, the reputed witch, who certainly is as much out of the mainstream of life as Hester (Mistress Hibbins dresses in the same ornate way as Hester initially and she finds herself at home with those on the periphery of society). This counter-culture of witches and wizards is merely an offshoot of the patriarchal society which Dimmesdale represents; the repressed outsiders are still in the same power struggle of demons and angels, only they seek power in exploring forbidden underworld forces. Baym describes their predicament appropriately: "The witches are rebels, but their rebellion arises from accepting the Puritan world view and defining themselves as evil.... Because they view themselves as society views them, the witches indirectly validate the social structure" (*The Shape of Hawthorne's Career* 134). Thus, these witches, unlike Hester, cannot transcend the moral system of the patriarchs. (This is reminiscent of Young Goodman's Brown search for an alternative to Christian patriarchy; he cannot escape it: he merely finds its reflection in the devil.) In opposition to the prevailing theological values, Mistress Hibbins practices witchcraft and black magic, and if read in this manner (the narrator vacillates between a psychological and a theological reading, often questioning whether the encounters with Mistress Hibbins are authentic or parables), Hester's brand of maternity has saved her from eternal damnation: she tells the witch-lady, "Had they taken her [Pearl] away from me, I would willingly have gone with thee into the forest, and signed my name in the Black Man's book too, and that with mine own blood!" (217). Once again, it is evident that Pearl is Hester's vehicle for self-affirmation.

On a psychological level, Mistress Hibbins is merely another variation of the frustrated, repressed matrons in the opening scene. Significantly, she is described as "Governor Bellingham's bitter-tempered sister, and the same who, a few years later, was executed as a witch" (217). Throughout the novel, the reader has the feeling that she is locked up within the spacious mansion of her powerful brother and dying to escape (another version of the mad woman in the attic):

> At another window of the same house, moreover, appeared old Mistress Hibbins, the Governor's sister, also with a lamp, which, even thus far off, revealed the expression of her sour and discontented face. She thrust forth her head from the lattice, and looked anxiously upward. (247)

The narrator then adds that after she detects the gleam of her brother's lamp, Mistress Hibbins "quickly extinguished her own, and vanished" (247). The narrator subversively suggests that she "went up among the clouds" in search of her sister witches, but then he undercuts the fantastical reading by saying that the minister and Governor Bellingham could observe nothing in the darkness (the empirical reading). Most likely, Mistress Hibbins is a bit paranoid living under the same roof as her patriarchal brother, and thus, she extinguishes her light. Nonetheless, Hawthorne makes a point of emphasizing her ill humor, her "sour and discontented face." In the end, it is even suggested that Mistress Hibbins is "eccentric" and "insane" as she dares to speak with Hester in public: "the crowd gave way before her, and seemed to fear the touch of her garment, as if it carried the plague among its gorgeous folds" (326). Mistress Hibbins is probably no more than an outcast spinster or moody menopausal woman, but she is later hanged as a witch, as the narrator reports. How much more repressive can the patriarchal authority get? These three negative stereotypes that go together (the spinster, the menopausal woman, and the hag) are the products of the patriarchal imagination, and they are all contrasted to the fertile mother image of Hester.

Yet Hester and Mistress Hibbins are uncannily allied, even though they remain in their separate spheres. They both possess a highly evolved intuition, which can detect sin and hypocrisy in other people's breasts. Hester's badge of shame gives her "a sympathetic knowledge of the hidden sin in other hearts" (192), and she is united with others through this mystic bond. Mistress Hibbins, reputed to be of "infirm mind," knows of the townspeople who have been to the forest and communed with the devil. She knows of the hypocrisy of the authority figures; about Dimmesdale, she tells Hester, "Who, now, that saw him pass in the procession, would think how little while it is since he went forth out of his study,—chewing a Hebrew text of Scripture in his mouth, I warrant,—to take an airing in the forest" (326). Whereas the townspeople become progressively more frightened of Mistress Hibbins' antics and prophecies, they gain respect for Hester and even feel kindly towards her. Even though it is "the darkened house that could contain" Hester (257), the community soon takes pride in her deeds: "Do you see that woman with the embroidered badge? ... It is our Hester,—the town's Hester,—who is so kind to the poor, so helpful to the sick, so comfortable to the afflicted!" (258). They claim her as their public property, but at the same time, they still whisper about her personal transgression; in so doing, they still do not allow any intimacy with Hester. Because Hester has made no demands on the community for acceptance, they accept her conditionally and conventionally, by transforming the badge of shame into a holy badge: "the scarlet letter had the effect of the cross on a nun's bosom. It imparted to the wearer a kind of sacredness, which enabled her to walk securely among all peril" (258). Thus, they make her into another safe stereotype, the nun, by refusing to acknowledge the natural woman. So Hester still remains isolated and alone.

Hester's acceptance of herself as a woman saves her; moreover, as a woman, she does not have to contend with the patriarchal system which defines the self by one's career, social standing, and politics (thus neglecting the private self). Hester does not have to compromise herself because she has nothing left to lose, and she is not participating in the power struggle, which drives Chillingworth and Dimmesdale. She can no longer be hurt because she is an outlaw and lives literally on the periphery of civilized life (in her cottage by the sea). In a perverse sense, Dimmesdale is correct in saying that Hester has been luckier than he: "Happy are you, Hester, that wear the scarlet letter openly upon your bosom! Mine burns in secret!" (283). There is never the threat of hypocrisy or a breakdown between a private and public self in Hester's mind because they are not contradictory. She evades the categorization with which the public attempts to define her; the inner self remains elusive to the public. The only two instances where Hester feels that madness is a real threat occur early in the book, when she is forced to confront the civil and religious authorities: first when she is on the scaffold, adjusting to the collapse of her public image ("under the leaden infliction which it was her doom to endure, she felt, at moments, as if she must needs shriek out with the full power of her lungs, and cast herself from the scaffold down upon the ground, or else go mad at once," 167), and then when she is faced with losing Pearl, her last link to humanity ("Hester Prynne's situation had provoked her to little less than madness" 214). Once secure in her position as a mother, she becomes self-sufficient.

Natural landscapes, the forest and the sea, typify Hester's psyche, and so she is linked with Mother Nature, who knows no rules outside of her own. (It should be recalled that Dimmesdale is relegated to the stuffy study and Chillingworth to a sterile laboratory.) The sea and the forest are her natural habitats; she lives "on the outskirts of the town, within the verge of the peninsula, but not in close vicinity to any other habitation ... [in a] small thatched cottage" (187). It is removed from the civilizing influence of the town of Boston: "it is out of the sphere of that social activity which already marked the habits of the emigrants" (187). Her cottage, which is situated neither in the town nor in the forest wilderness, represents the no-man's land which allows her mobility from the civilized to the natural sphere; her being is characterized by this state of flux (cf. her extremes of "fancy"), which is in sharp contrast to the fixed meaning imposed upon the townspeople by the civilizing enclosure of Boston. Yet here in this realm of ambiguities there is freedom for Hester; significantly, it stands on the shore but it looks "across a basin of the sea at the forest-covered hills, toward the west" (187).

Symbolically Hester has access to both the realms of the sea and of the forest. It should be remembered that Hester is at home with both the seafarers and the Indians who roam the forest. In the chapter "The New

England Holiday" the narrator shows Hester's alliance with the sailors, who are allowed a certain license not granted to the men on land (it recalls also the need for men in *Moby Dick* to escape the strict categorization of life on the land for the freedom and imagination of the sea):

> But the sea, in those old times, heaved, swelled, and fumed very much of its own will, or subject only to the tempestuous wind, with hardly any attempts at regulation by human law. The buccaneer on the wave might relinquish his calling, and become at once, if he chose, a man of probity and piety on land ... (319)

Another feminine landscape representative of Hester is the forest, where she feels at home with her passionate nature. "The mother-forest" (295) also "recognized a kindred wildness in the human child [Pearl]," where Hester has put her displaced passions. Pearl, too, is more obviously described as a creature of nature: her ornate dress is compared to "the many-hued brilliancy from a butterfly's wing, or the painted glory from the leaf of a bright flower.... her garb was all of one idea with her nature" (314). However, the forest is a place of freedom as well as of danger: "She [Hester] had wandered, without rule or guidance, in a moral wilderness; as vast, as intricate, and shadowy, as the untamed forest" (290; the "moral wilderness" is a Puritan trope, but the "untamed forest," morally neutral, is an apt description of Hester's psyche). Pearl, as "the effluence of her mother's lawless passion" (260), also represents nature gone astray: "The child's own nature had something wrong in it, which continually betokened that she had been born amiss ..." (260).

If we compare Hester with the men in her life, we see that she is both similar to and different from them in her attitudes towards authority. She shares with Chillingworth the desire and latitude to roam freely among the Indians and the sailors, and both she and Chillingworth have a speculative nature. However, Chillingworth is an exacting man (however much the narrator attempts to exonerate him for being a wronged husband), and this is most evident in his unwillingness to forgive Hester and Dimmesdale. Dimmesdale also suffers from his unchristian attitude towards forgiveness. One instance in which he allows his passionate (and uncharacteristically egoistic) self to erupt is when he scolds Hester in the forest for not having disclosed Chillingworth's identity: "... the shame!—the indelicacy! ... Woman, woman, thou art accountable for this! I cannot forgive thee!" (285). Hester is the most Christian in her humanity, and she reminds Dimmesdale that it is not for him to judge: "Let God punish! Thou shalt forgive!" (285). However, Hester does share some of Dimmesdale's dogmatic nature; this comes about, in part, because of her role as a mother (as the narrator and Dimmesdale suggest, this role is both a blessing and a blight, liberating and limiting): she feels compelled to catechize the child and to give her a sense of paternity, "Hester Prynne, the daughter of a pious home, very soon after her talk with the child about her Heavenly Father, had begun to inform her of those truths which the human spirit, at whatever stage of immaturity, imbibes with such eager interest" (213). As a mother, she feels the need to give her child some basic moral training, though it is not exactly to the Governor's liking, as he demands a more rigorous catechism. Finally, when Hester is most tormented by her lonely position in society or by the wiles of her daughter, she, like Dimmesdale, interprets the world as comprised of angels and demons. But her acceptance of this male mythology is merely a manifestation of her desperation.

Ultimately, however, Dimmesdale and Hester are more different than alike: this is shown clearly in their forest encounter, "But Hester Prynne, with a mind of native courage and activity, and for so long a period not merely estranged, but outlawed from society, had habituated herself to such latitude of speculation as was altogether foreign to the clergyman" (290). Again, the narrator associates her with the Indians, in her lack of respect "for the clerical band, the judicial robe, the pillory, the gallows, the fireside, or the church" (290). She has essentially rebelled against all patriarchal institutions, whether established by "priests or legislators" (290). Hawthorne, however, shows the other side of this freedom, as he has shown the negative side of Dimmesdale's foundation, the Church. Although "the scarlet letter was her passport into regions where other women dared not tread" (290), it also led her into a labyrinth of doubt: "Shame, Despair, Solitude! These had been her teachers,—stern and wild ones, and they had made her strong, but taught her much amiss" (290). This authorial condemnation, that she has learned "much amiss," is reminiscent of Dimmesdale's moralizing voice which tells Hester to "Hush!" (286). It also shows the narrator's own ambivalence towards Hester's freedom: he reveals the dark side of her individualism and freedom which is at odds with the ordering process of civilization (whether that be embodied in the "judicial robe," the domestic hearth, or "the church"). However, it must not be forgotten that Hester's experience has also made her strong, a degree of strength to which Dimmesdale can never hope to aspire.

Of course, she obtains this freedom at a price; in essence, she becomes the embodiment of an inner self, and that makes her a specter of a woman in society. She has no public voice and no obvious bonds, so that in the end, the narrator says that her face has frozen into a mask, which no one can decipher: the "marble quietude" of her face is like "like a mask, or rather, like the frozen calmness of a dead woman's features; owing this dreary resemblance to the fact that Hester was actually dead, in respect to any claim of sympathy and had departed out of the world with which she still seemed to mingle" (313). This is not really true, in that Hester still connects, but only to the "unworthy" people of society, not to the public officials, like Dimmesdale and Chillingworth.

The reader is reminded of an earlier description by the narrator in "Another View of Hester": "Much of the marble coldness of Hester's impression was to be attributed to the circumstance that her life had turned, in a great measure, from passion and feeling, to thought" (259). Interestingly, the "marble coldness" of reason would be construed as positive in man, but negative in woman: somehow the narrator feels that passion and emotion are woman's province. Both of these times where the narrator mentions Hester's transformation, he tries to desex her, implying that a woman bereft of passion is only part woman and doubting Hester's success as a woman: there was "nothing in Hester's form, though majestic and statuelike, that Passion would ever dream of clasping in its embrace" (259). Robbing Hester of the earlier romantic or seductive powers, he then condemns Hester to a passionless existence: "Some attribute had departed from her, the permanence of which had been essential to keep her a woman" (259). He figures that the only salvation for Hester would be the touch of a man, "the magic touch" would "effect the transformation" to womanhood (259). Ironically, though, the narrator subverts even this judgment, which after all belongs to the stereotypical notions of his day, by pronouncing that woman, "If she be all tenderness ... will die" (259), and then, with his next breath, he even compliments Hester, by noting her speculative nature: "She assumed a freedom of speculation...." (259). It seems positive, in the long-run, that Hester has re-invested her energy in discovering herself alone (after all, the Emersonian ideal of self-reliance promotes this) than in getting involved with relationships which would make her a love addict to men. Indeed, this "cold" exterior is proof that she has grown: she still possesses her early sympathies and passions, only she has rechanneled them into her work with women and invalids—those on the periphery. If anything, her ability to resist male definitions of female passion (as men dictate its existence only in relationship to men) and to integrate the two sides of her personality (reason with emotion), she has succeeded in subverting the letter "A" one more time: "A" as androgyny.

What is alarming about the narrator's treatment of Hester is that he finally "hushes" her public self in the same way Dimmesdale and Chillingworth have attempted to do with her (Dimmesdale in the forest and on the scaffold, Chillingworth by making her vow silence about his identity).

Of course, all the voices of his protagonists are hushed (the patriarchs' voices in a grand, dramatic way) by the end of the narrative, but her voice becomes fainter gradually and takes on meaning only in the personal realm, as she mothers wayward women. Everyone in this repressed patriarchal society is hushed; as Michael Ragussis explains it, "the ban of silence lies on everyone in *The Scarlet Letter*" (59), and he shows the dangers which threaten the family structure. However, Hester is enveloped in a type of protective silence, very early on:

> In all her intercourse with society, however, there was nothing that made her feel as if she belonged to it. Every gesture, every word, and even the silence of those with whom she came in contact, implied, and often expressed, that she was banished, and as much alone as if she inhabited another sphere, or communicated with the common nature by other organs and senses than the rest of human kind. She stood apart from mortal interests, yet close beside them, like a ghost that revisits the familiar fireside, and can no longer make itself seen or felt ... (190)

When she encounters Dimmesdale in the forest ("The Parish and His Parishioner"), Hester is described as specter-like. She appears "statue-like" (328) at the foot of the scaffold when Dimmesdale gives his Election Day Sermon. In the end, too, Hester is seen gliding "shadow-like" into her cottage by the sea (343; cf. the earlier image of her "gliding silently through the town" 191). The ultimate hushing of Hester comes when the narrator literally buries her in the grave; even there, though, her tombstone, a "simple slab of slate" quietly defies the self-importance of those patriarchs buried in "monuments carved with armorial bearings" (345), tributes to their meaningless show of power in life, for they are now dead. (Actually, Dimmesdale and Chillingworth are also hushed, since the subversive narrator does not disclose whose body is buried next to Hester's!)

Hester's silence need not be regarded as negative; perhaps it shows a way of existence requiring the least deference to patriarchal rule and authority. Moreover, this silence is also defiant (note her poised, quiet demeanor when she is interrogated) as it eludes the many words which characterize the sermons of the ministers and Governor. The silence need not be construed as imposed by the narrator but as self-imposed. In the opening scene Hester quietly resists the beadle's authority, and her haughty attitude affronts the crowd. The townspeople interpret her impenetrable silence as arrogance and insolence. Hester herself never imposes her needs or lifestyle on others, the way the minister Dimmesdale or the scientist Chillingworth does. She lives by her own code when she remains silent, when she refuses to disclose Dimmesdale's identity as the adulterer, as the father of her child (cf. Ragussis 59). She also abides by her own standards when she finally breaks her vow of secrecy to Chillingworth and reveals to Dimmesdale that Chillingworth is his tormentor.

Recently, feminist linguists, such as Deborah Cameron and Dale Spender, have suggested that women who are left outside the experience of male discourse, find themselves mute or alienated when they attempt to internalize the male meanings. However, I see Hester's silence as her refusal to participate in male discourse and thus as a sign of triumph over the male reality. My reading of Hester's silence as a sign of defiance is in keeping with Leland S. Person's basic premise about the power of Hester's silence in a loud male world, but I disagree with his notion that Hester is being manipulative or vindictive in maintaining silence. His statement that "her vengeful silence" has "the effect of action" ("Hester's Revenge" 470) is a typically male-biased one which cannot embrace the maternity of silent language, a maternity which is far removed from male power dynamics of revenge.

In the opening scaffold scene, Hester hugs the baby to her "maternal bosom," and immediately traces the letter "A": from that point on, the baby and the "A" become "her realities" (168). Motherhood is on trial here in the public arena of the marketplace, but because Hester does not feel the schism between private and public selves which Dimmesdale experiences, she does not experience his type of cultural schizophrenia imposed on men. She is privately and publicly a mother, and proud of it. By investing her letter "A" with personal meaning, Hester removes the social stigma and ultimately hushes the community, who begin to lose interest in her emblem, "this worn-out subject" (330). The meaning is transformed from that which the narrator and Chillingworth have assigned to it earlier: Hester is no longer a living sermon against sin whose infamy would live beyond the grave. The narrator's prediction that Hester would give up her individuality in becoming "the general symbol at which the preacher and moralist might point, and in which they might vivify and embody their images of women's frailty and sinful passion" (185) is proven wrong. The community softens as "Hatred, by a gradual and quiet process, will even be transformed to love, unless the change be impeded by a continually new irritation of the original feeling of hostility" (256). Hester, however, retains pride in her isolation, even emphasizing the presence of her badge, when it is no longer necessary: "If they [the community] were resolute to accost her, she laid her finger on the scarlet letter, and passed on. This might be pride, but was so like humility, that it produced all the softening effect of the latter quality on the public mind" (257). Even when the "sternest" magistrate would have granted her the right to remove the letter (344), she continues wearing it, as if affirming the identity she has woven into it and rebelling against and mocking the old meaning assigned to it by her judges. She returns "of her own free will" to her realm in the cottage by the sea, as she accepts the consequences of her past actions. Moreover, her mothering role continues until the end: she is seen "embroidering a baby-garment" (343, presumably for Pearl's child, thus linking the three generations together), and in her role of sister of mercy, she helps misguided women (whose passions have led them astray, taught them much amiss). She remains independent as she transfers her nurturing and maternal guidance from Pearl to wayward girls.

In this analysis of Hester's maternal nature, it is also necessary to point out that she is religious, but in the most subversive ways (she creates her own personalized religion). She becomes a deity in the most pagan sense and embodies the many faces of the Great Mother. The narrator initially compares her to "the image of Divine Maternity," but only in contrast to "that sacred image of sinless motherhood" (166).[16] This distorted comparison brings Hester down to the level of a pagan goddess of motherhood (Demeter, for example): "she had in her nature a rich, voluptuous, Oriental characteristic" (189). This passionate, voluptuous quality makes her more akin to Aphrodite than to Divine Maternity; Hester embodies two irreconcilable traits in the public's and narrator's perspective— maternity and sensuality (hence, also, the striking image of Hester as a fallen madonna). As the book progresses, Hester becomes like Artemis (Diana): she is less passionate, almost chaste, as she ties her hair up under a cap, and she is likened to a sister of mercy and even a nun. As the narrator suggests, Hester's life "had turned, in a great measure, from passion and feeling, to thought" (259). She moves from earthy voluptuousness to Sophia-like wisdom.[17] As man has tried to repress the goddess in him and the goddess in every woman, so too do Chillingworth and Dimmesdale attempt to repress Hester's maternity, to hush her being. Erich Neumann has pointed out that "In the patriarchal development of the Judeo-Christian West, with its masculine, monotheistic trend toward abstraction, the goddess, as a feminine figure of wisdom, was disenthroned and repressed" (331). However, Neumann asserts that this feminine principle is the eternal spirit of growth for all of mankind, and thus, needs to be heard: "The Great Goddess—if under this name we sum up everything we have attempted to represent as the archetypal unity and multiplicity of the feminine nature—is the incarnation of the Feminine Self that unfolds in the history of mankind as in the history of every individual woman; its reality determines individual as well as collective life" (336). A society which suppresses or eradicates its Hesters is doomed to self-destruct, and the man, who attempts to repress the mother within, is also heading towards self-destruction or a fragmented consciousness, as we have seen in the case of all of Hawthorne's questers.

Hester pursues no religious orthodoxy: she tries to formulate a personal, feminine religion, much in the vein of feminist theologians today. Hester despairs of men's earthly power, and asserts, in rather conventional terms, that if her child does not seek a heavenly Father, "she shall never know an earthly one" (176). From the start, then, we see that Hester is spiritually inclined. However, she does not adhere dogmatically to a faith which represses or feigns feelings: "she forbore to pray for her enemies, lest, in spite of her forgiving aspirations, the words of the blessing should stubbornly twist themselves into a curse" (193). She is often plagued by doubts: she questions any type of providential order when she asks "in bitterness of heart, whether it were for ill or good that the poor little creature had been born at all" (260). She doubts a divine purpose for women's lives: "Was existence worth accepting, even to the happiest among them? As concerned her own individual existence, she had long decided in the negative ..." (260). Hester even contemplates suicide: "At times, a fearful doubt strove to possess her soul, whether it were not better to send Pearl at once to heaven, and go herself to such futurity as Eternal Justice should provide" (261). It is her role as a mother which once again saves her and humanizes her. The narrator says that Hester would have become a saint or martyr, or a prophetess and foundress of a religious sect (cf. Hibbins stereotype at the other end of the spectrum), in the vein or Anne Hutchinson (another rebel of sorts, whose image is evoked in connection with Hester in the opening scene of the novel), had she not borne Pearl, i.e., had she not been a natural woman. The narrator suggests that it would have been folly to take on the whole Puritan system, for it surely would have meant death (260).

Her unconventional relationship to Pearl allows her to rebel against Puritan norms in a smaller way, "... in the education of her child, the mother's enthusiasm of thought had something to wreak itself upon" (260). It is her redefinition of motherhood, and single motherhood at that, which gives her the most power and freedom. Mary Ryan and Anne L. Kuhn have discussed the prominence of the mother's role in the nineteenth-century cult of domesticity, at a time when man's professional interests and duties were taking him out of the home. Hester does not simply have control over the realm of child-care, she revels in maternal nurturing and emotional discourse. And her maternity, inevitably, is the strongest weapon against the patriarchs. As one mother's magazine of the time expressed it, "Compared with maternal influence, the combined authority of laws and armies, and public sentiment, are little things" (*Parent's Magazine*, 1:33, October 1840, qted. in Kuhn, xiii). Maternal energies save the day; as Baym puts it, "The great liberation of *The Scarlet Letter* comes not only from its celebration of a woman, but of a woman who is centrally a mother" ("Thwarted Nature" 75).

When she has accepted the limitations of her existence "on the periphery," a no-man's land between forest and sea, and when she has won custody of Pearl, Hester can get on with her life confidently. She criticizes Dimmesdale's unrelenting harshness, which is a sign of his lack of personal identity: "Your sin is left behind you, in the days long past. Your present life is not less holy, in very truth, than it seems in people's eyes. Is there no reality in the penitence thus sealed and witnessed by good works?" (283). Religion to Hester includes good works and humanitarian service. In the end, Hester is described somewhat as a high priestess: "as [she] had no selfish ends, nor lived in any measure for her own profit and enjoyment, people brought all their sorrows and perplexities, and besought her counsel, as one who had herself gone through a mighty trouble" (344). She counsels these desperate women with the hope that the system of authority will change in the future: "... at some brighter time, when the world should have grown ripe for it, in Heaven's own time, a new truth would be revealed, in order to establish the whole relation between man and woman on a surer ground of mutual happiness" (344). She no longer feels that she is the destined prophetess who will effect the change; rather, "the angel and apostle of the coming revelation must be a woman," who is lofty, beautiful, and wise (a new type of goddess?), and her wisdom will stem from joy and not from sin and suffering (the basis of Dimmesdale's theology).

Although this prophecy is optimistic, we should recall that much of Hester's power lies within her silent and visionary nature.[18] The narrator himself (who is known to withhold praise) celebrates Hester's revolutionary spirit, even if it is limited to her thinking:

> The world's law was no law for her mind. It was an age in which the human intellect, newly emancipated, had taken a more active and wider range than for many centuries before. Men of the sword had overthrown nobles and kings. Men bolder than these had overthrown and rearranged—not actually, but within the sphere of theory, which was their most real abode—the whole system of ancient prejudice, wherewith was linked much of ancient principle. Hester Prynne imbibed this spirit. She assumed a freedom of speculation, then common enough on the other side of the Atlantic, but which our forefathers, had they known of it, would have held to be a deadlier crime than that stigmatized by the scarlet letter. In her lonesome cottage by the sea, by the sea-

shore, thoughts visited her, such as dared to enter no other dwelling in New England. (259)

Hester's freedom exists in the latitude of her mind; she is like the "bold" men who change the world with their theories, not with their swords. Her freedom of speculation goes beyond even Chillingworth's for she can imagine a totally new way of thinking and living (Chillingworth has lost the vision to empiricism distorted by egotism). The narrator suggests that thoughts are often more liberating than deeds, and that Hester's seeming conformity to the outworn laws of her time is insignificant because an inner self governs her:

> It is remarkable, that persons who speculate the most boldly often conform with the most perfect quietude to the external regulations of society. The thought suffices them, without investing itself in the flesh and blood of action. So it seemed to be with Hester. (258)

At this point the narrator seems to celebrate the refuge of the mind over the power of the sword to effect change. However, in the next instance, he recognizes the obstacle, that man is a social animal after all. During one of his long commentaries, in which he takes up the cause of Hester and of women in general, the narrator discusses the trials and tribulations of women in the nineteenth century. Hawthorne suggests that unless a revolution in the social structure takes place, the self will not be adequately fulfilled. There are three steps in the process: "the whole system of society is to be torn down, and built anew" (260), "the very nature of the opposite sex, or its long hereditary habit ... is to be essentially modified" (260), and finally women's nature will have to be changed so that "the ethereal essence, wherein she has her truest life, will be found to have evaporated" (260). Until that time, women will be made "quiet" and "sad" by being forced to speculate instead of act. The latter requisite for change sounds chauvinistic on the narrator's part only if the reader does not consider that the male protagonists in this novel suffer as a result of their deficiency in "the ethereal essence" (260). This is one of the many paradoxes which the narrator proffers the reader. Thus, even though Hester appears "to conform with the most perfect quietude to the external regulations of society" by taking on the role of the sister of mercy, an image approved by the community, her private self remains hidden to the public. However, she is still acknowledging her speculative and passionate nature by becoming a revolutionary on a small scale, by helping wayward girls, who resemble her and Pearl at an earlier stage.

The narrator does not endorse the view of any one of his three protagonists. He depicts each positively and negatively: Dimmesdale is a man oppressed by the bonds which give him identity, hence he is a hypocrite and a coward; Chillingworth is a brilliant scholar and scientist, a "man of skill" (181), but he uses his knowledge for personal and vicious ends; Hester is strong and free, but she has learned much amiss. He cleverly takes on various voices in the telling of his tale: [19] thus, the letter "A" in the second scaffold scene is alternately read as having theological mystique (as a message to Dimmesdale) or scientific purport (as it would appear as natural phenomenon to the empiricist Chillingworth). Similarly, Chillingworth's science (alchemy) can only be construed as diabolical from the perspective of a Dimmesdale, and thus, the narrator's ranting and raving about demons is suspect. Perhaps most brilliantly (in that this predates the Lacanian theory of the mother's communication as pre-verbal), the narrator takes on the ethereal voice of the female protagonist, only in the silences, in the fleeting flash of mind, which cannot be explained or verbalized, or in the symbolic depiction of Hester's "A" and child. The narrator's eclectic voice not only shows the limitations of one individual perspective, but it shows how one's perception of authority can suppress or hide the private self. There are apparent inconsistencies in the narrator's voice because he takes in a wide array of human perspectives. He has no place to stand outside the fleeting perception of the persona whom he portrays at any given moment. And he fluctuates between the public and private selves of each of the three protagonists. The writer Hawthorne is a compendium of these three figures: Dimmesdale is Hawthorne the idealist, Chillingworth is the all-knowing, objective writer, and Hester in her freedom is a better "man" than Hawthorne ever thought of being.

The last chapter of the novel is the most splendidly paradoxical because all the negations and affirmations are taken into account at once; the narrator's final word is uncertainty. The reader is left hanging during the entire chapter: many questions, e.g., about Dimmesdale's end (was there really an "A" inscribed on his chest) or about Pearl's fate, are left unanswered. [20] The narrator has also (through an alchemical technique of his own) merged the love and hatred of Dimmesdale and Chillingworth by viewing the relationship or considering it "philosophically" (342) through the medium of both "celestial radiance" and "a dusky and lurid glow": "In the spiritual world, the old physician and the minister—mutual victims as they have been—may, unawares, have found their stock of hatred and antipathy transmuted into golden love" (34, we are back in the realm of feminine ether!). Dream and reality converge as Hester returns in the end, a mere shadow of a person. We are left with the uncertainty of reality which characterizes much of the fiction of Virginia Woolf. What is presented is internality, which is more real than what the realists thought could be real. Before this time, the externality of empirical science and natural phenomena was real, or the self-contained mythology of religion was plausible. Hawthorne shows that what the individual perceives subjectively and imperfectly (in its fragmented form) is the ultimate reality. The epigraphs at the start of this chapter reflect the nineteenth-century obsession with and anxiety about knowledge and authority: there is a dual impulse to validate and negate individual and institutionalized truths. Hawthorne's non-authoritarian narrator releases the reader from any conclusive, authoritative notions of truth by leaving him with unresolved questions and irreconcilable tensions.

The last paragraph of *The Scarlet Letter* capsulizes every tension within the work. It suggests a panoramic view which encompasses and simultaneously denies all possibilities; this narrative technique reflects the Hegelian dialectic of truth. As Hegel points out in the introductory epigraph, true and false, like good and evil, are relative and comprise one reality. A "new grave" is dug "near an old and sunken one." The lovers lie together in the earth, but their dust is not allowed to mingle. Syntactically analyzed, the duality of vagueness and clarity is effected through the use of subordinate conjunctions (as all possibilities and truths are conjoined): "It was near that old and sunken grave, *yet* with a space between, as if the dust of the two sleepers had no right to mingle. *Yet* one tombstone served for both" (345, my emphasis). Hester and Dimmesdale are together yet separated even in death. We have merely the "*semblance* of an engraved escutcheon" (345, emphasis mine), vague hieroglyphics, since time has blurred the tombstone's motto and heraldic device.[21] The tomb is dark (with its sable background), and the only illumination comes from "one ever-glowing point of light gloomier than the shadow" (345). This again is misleading as dark and light cancel each other out. The "motto and brief description of our now concluded legend" undercuts itself: "On a field, sable, the letter A, gules." There are no colors here in reality: we cannot distinguish between the red of the letter and the black of the tombstone (there is no light, no perspective). The words say one thing, but the reality is something else. We cannot see anything: the eclectic voice of the non-authoritarian narrator leaves us with nothingness and formlessness, both terrifying and liberating.

NOTES

13. Hester's subversive activity in the narrative and Hawthorne's art in "The Custom-House" have their source in rebellion against the fathers. For other readings which focus

on the connections between the characters and the narrator in "The Custom-House" and the narrative proper, see Baym ("The Romantic Malgré Lui: Hawthorne in the Custom House"); Cox; Franzosa ("Hawthorne's Separation from Salem"); Johnson (46–66); Macshane; McCall; Van Deusen; and Weldon. Most of these essays discuss Hawthorne's narrative stance, his aesthetic principles (romance as compared to novel), and his relationship to the characters (as fragments of the narrator's artist personality), as they relate to the "Custom-House" sketch.

For another reading which views art as a rebellious activity in Hawthorne's American romances, see Michael Davitt Bell (*The Development of the American Romance*): Hawthorne saw "the connection between the unleashing of fantasy and the unleashing of revolutionary violence" (171).

14. Neither impulse is more genuine than the other, as each develops from the same imagination. Moreover, the blasphemous (free) imagination must not be construed as wrong. In the end, the narrator asks, "What imagination would have been irreverent enough to surmise that the same scorching stigma was on them both" (331)? The implication is that the knowing imagination, which encompasses all possibilities (Hester's), is evil or irreverent, but ultimately true!

15. Much has been made of the mirror imagery in Hawthorne, as a reflection of his aesthetic principles and also as a key to the characters' self-concept. Waggoner was one of the first critics to discuss the mirror imagery. Unlike artificial mirrors, "natural mirrors ... especially those formed by water ... normally tell the truth in Hawthorne, especially the hidden truth of the heart" (*Hawthorne: A Critical Study* 147). More recently, Irwin (257–72) has done a Lacanian reading of *The Scarlet Letter* which focuses on the mirror image as a structuring device—to emphasize the doubling of characters, as well as the doubling of the narrator. Sundquist also discusses the mirror image, and its more complex version, the daguerreotype in Hawthorne's novels (104–142). What Sundquist says about the daguerreotype in *HSG* reveals Hawthorne's fear of fixity (permanent truths or traditional authority), as I have shown in this chapter. The daguerreotype, "the mirror *with* a memory," "makes the mirror *of* memory lasting: it executes a sign of revenge and conquest, and a reminder of submission to the forms of the past" (141). Sundquist goes on to compare the daguerreotype symbol to the letter "A."

16. Gervais focuses on this scene of Hester as the Divine Maternity and asserts that the struggle in the novel is "between an older Anglo-Catholic pictorial symbolism that encourages mutability and ambiguity, and the newer Puritan linguistic logic that attempts to fix definite meanings" (11).

17. For a psychological (Jungian) reading of the archetypal goddesses which constitute women, see Bolen, who views Hester Prynne as the Aphrodite archetype.

18. Prophecy is an important motif in *The Scarlet Letter*. Dimmesdale prophesies "a high and glorious destiny for the newly gathered people of the Lord" (332–33) during his Election Day Sermon. Hester is equally optimistic when she predicts the dawning of a new age, with the coming of a pure prophetess. These predictions are uncharacteristically optimistic for Hawthorne. This optimism may be attributed to the nineteenth-century sense of millennialism; that feeling of well-being, however, was more common to Emerson (see Bercovitch, chapter five; and Peacock).

In the context of my second chapter on science in Hawthorne, it is significant that Francis Bacon's writings have an "apocalyptic thrust" (Guibbory 341). Bacon, however, views the potential for man's perfectibility through knowledge.

19. Cf. J. Hillis Miller on narrative voice: "A novel is a structure of interpenetrating minds, the mind of the narrator as he beholds or enters into the characters, the minds of the characters as they behold or know one another...." (2). This describes Hawthorne's oscillating perspective and his compendium of voices.

20 In the end, we are uncertain of the characters' meaning and the symbol "A" 's meaning. Critics have always pondered the meaning of the letter "A": D.H. Lawrence wrote the seminal essay on multiple perspectives. I agree with Feidelson that Hawthorne's subject is "meaning in general; not only *what* the focal symbol means, but *how* it gains significance" (10). Most critics in the 70's and early 80's have approached Hawthorne's oscillating meanings through an analysis of genre. For an analysis of the tensions between the romance and the novel, see Bell (*The Development of the American Romance*), Brodhead (*Hawthorne, Melville, and the Novel*), and Stubbs.

I disagree with Brodhead's assessment that Hawthorne gives the reader authority to choose his own version of Dimmesdale's end:

> Hawthorne releases us from his narrative authority and allows us to choose among these [alternate versions], or to adopt whatever other explanation we like. ... Our final moment of direct confrontation with the scarlet letter ... leaves us alone to complete the novel by determining its reality and its meaning as we think best, and to be conscious of our imaginative procedure as we do so (68).

I don't believe that Hawthorne gives the reader a choice. It is not that he is an authoritarian narrator, but rather that to offer personal choices to his audience would be as deceptive and illusory as to validate Hester's, Dimmesdale's, or Chillingworth's individual visions of reality. Hawthorne's vision encompasses all and nothing—that is the nature of reality, and that is what the reader is left with in the end. Thus, I strongly disagree with Brodhead's belief that "we are left alone to complete the episode's [the "A" in the sky] reality and meaning as we may ..." (59). I also disagree, for the same reasons, with Dauber's pronouncement that Hawthorne "invites us to be as subjective as we may" (17). Dauber sees Hawthorne's appeal for intimacy with his reader (in the prefaces) as sincere, while I see it as another narrative pose. Dauber seems to want a traditional authoritative narrator; he accuses Hawthorne of abdicating an author's authority: "he even surrenders his proper authority to the vision of his characters. No longer is he responsible for anything that occurs" (115). Franzosa is more astute when he recognizes that Hawthorne understands the audience's need for some "final truth" (with which to "make sense of our reading") but that he ultimately withholds its expression ("A Psychoanalysis of Hawthorne's Style" 401).

21. The meaning of the tombstone and its heraldic device has been as controversial as the meaning of the letter "A" during the course of the narrative. Greenwood and Jenkins believe that there is no epitaph on the tombstone at all, but that Hawthorne's words merely describe the heraldic device on the tombstone. Robert and Marijane Osborn discuss the relationship between Hester's crest and its source in Marvell's poem; they suggest that in both cases "the heraldic device is an ironic reduction" (279).

It is obvious that the final scene is a scene parallel to the first scene; the blackness of the tomb corresponds with the darkness of the Puritans (their somber dress as well as their prison, "the black flower of civilized society" and cemetery) and the redness of the letter corresponds with the wild rose growing outside the prison (though the rose is not specifically described as red, the color red is later evoked, by comparison, as Pearl begs for a red rose in the Governor's Garden). These colors embody the impulses of authority and freedom. Significantly, these were the colors of the dual-complexioned insurgent in "My Kinsman, Major Molineux."

For one of the best readings of the meaning of the tombstone and its colors, see Waggoner (*The Presence of Hawthorne*), who discusses the ambiguity of "the still dominant colors, red and black" on the tombstone: "The red has been associated with nature and life and beauty—the rose beside the prison. Hester's vivid coloring, her beautiful needlework—but also with sin. Black has been associated with both sin and death—the prison and the cemetery" (31–32; see also Waggoner's chapter on *The Scarlet Letter* in *Hawthorne: A Critical Study*).

WORKS CITED

Anderson, Quentin. *The Imperial Self: An Essay in American Literary and Cultural History.* N.Y.: Alfred A. Knopf, 1971.

Arac, Jonathan. *Commissioned Spirits: The Shaping of Social Motion in Dickens, Carlyle, Melville, and Hawthorne.* New Brunswick, N.J.: Rutgers Univ. Press, 1979. 94–114.

———. "Reading the Letter." *Diacritics* 9 (1979): 42–52.

Arner, Robert D. "The Legend of Pygmalion in 'The Birth-mark'." *ATQ* 14 (1972): 168–171.

Asimov, Isaac. "The Eureka Phenomenon." *The Norton Reader.* N.Y.: Norton & Company, 1984. 202–211.

Auerbach, Nina. *Woman and the Demon: The Life of a Victorian Myth.* Mass.: Harvard Univ. Press, 1982.

Augros, Robert M., and George N. Stanciu. *The New Story of Science: Mind and the Universe.* N.Y.: Bantam, 1986.

Bacon, Francis. "The Great Instauration." *The English Philosophers from Bacon to Mill.* Ed. Edwin A. Burtt. N.Y.: Modern Library, 1967. 5–25.

———. "Novum Organum." *The English Philosophers from Bacon to Mill.* Ed. Edwin A. Burtt. N.Y.: Modern Library, 1967. 28–123.

Bailyn, Bernard. "Puritan Social Ideals and the Dilemma of the New England Merchant." *Tensions in American Puritanism.* Ed. Richard Reinitz. N.Y.: John Wiley and Sons, 1970. 55–65.

Bales, Kent. "Hawthorne's Prefaces and Romantic Perspectivism." *ESQ* 23 (1977): 69–88.

Bauer, Wolfgang, Irmtraud Dümotz, and Sergius Golowin. *Lexikon der Symbole: Mythen, Symbole, und Zeichen in Kultur, Religion, Kunst, und Alltag.* München: Wilhehlm Heyne Verlag, 1989.

Baym, Nina. "Hawthorne and His Mother: A Biographical Speculation." *AL* 54 (1982): 1–27.

———. "The Head, the Heart, and the Unpardonable Sin." *NEQ* 40 (1967): 31–47.

———. "Passion and Authority in *The Scarlet Letter.*" *NEQ* 43 (1970): 209–230.

LELAND S. PERSON

The Dark Labyrinth of Mind:
Hawthorne, Authorship, and Slavery

> If a pastor has offspring by a woman not his wife, the church dismiss him,
> if she is a white woman; but if she is colored, it does not hinder his
> continuing to be their good shepherd.
> —Harriet Jacobs, *Incidents in the Life of a Slave Girl*

"Explicit or implicit, the Africanist presence informs in compelling and inescapable ways the texture of American literature," argues Toni Morrison. "It is a dark and abiding presence, there for the literary imagination as both a visible and an invisible mediating force. Even, and especially, when American texts are not 'about' Africanist presences or characters or narrative or idiom, the shadow hovers in implication, in sign, in line of demarcation."[1] In this essay I want to accept the challenge Morrison issues to American literary scholars and to explore the "dark labyrinth of mind," as Hawthorne calls it, that constitutes Hester Prynne's subjectivity and subject position in *The Scarlet Letter*.[2] With some uncanny inspiration from the epigraph I have taken from Harriet Jacobs's *Incidents in the Life of a Slave Girl*,[3] I want to examine Hester within a historical context formed by the intersection of motherhood and race and to ask some questions about how discourses of motherhood, slavery, miscegenation, abolition, women's rights, child custody, and so on contend with one another at the site of Hester's character.

From *Studies in American Fiction* 29, no. 2 (Spring 2001). © 2001 by Northeastern University.

Hawthorne referred to the importation of slaves as a "monstrous birth," and in this essay I wish to see how and what Hester's maternal behavior signifies within a racial context of "other," if not monstrous, mothering.[4]

Hester Prynne's adulterous behavior and the scarlet letter that initially represents it also deform her motherhood. Examined within a nineteenth-century context, moreover, Hester's deviant mothering can be understood more particularly within a framework of slave motherhood. Sociologist Patricia Hill Collins, for example, describes a "distinctly Afrocentric ideology of motherhood" that slave women adapted to the oppressive conditions of slavery: community-based childcare, informal adoption, reliance on "*othermothers*"—traditions, she emphasizes, rooted in very different life experiences from the prevalent cult of true womanhood, with its dependency on a world of separate male and female spheres.[5] Hazel Carby points out, in this respect, that Harriet Jacobs's *Incidents in the Life of a Slave Girl* contradicts and transforms an ideology of true womanhood and motherhood "that could not take account of her experience."[6] Linda Brent abandons her children in order to save them—convinced that they have better chances of survival and success with "others." In Carby's view, "Jacobs developed an alternative set of definitions of womanhood and motherhood in the text which remained in tension with the cult of true womanhood."[7] Deborah Gray White, furthermore, documents cases from the 1830s and 1840s of slave mothers who actually killed their children. Some "claimed to have done so because of their intense concern for their offspring." One mother claimed that "her master was the father of the child, and that her mistress knew it and treated it so cruelly that she had to kill it to save it from further suffering."[8] Whether or not a mother actually commits infanticide, as Cassy does in *Uncle Tom's Cabin* or as the slave mother does in Frances Harper's poem of that title, slavery radically altered motherhood—inverting or ironizing it.[9] "I made up my mind," Stowe's Cassy explains. "I would never again let a child live to grow up! I took the little fellow in my arms, when he was two weeks old, and kissed him, and cried over him; and then I gave him laudanum, and held him close to my bosom, while he slept to death."[10] Converting the maternal breast into a source of poison rather than nourishment—being a good mother in the deforming context of slavery can actually mean killing, not nurturing, one's child. Killing the child to save it, giving it up to ensure it a better life: both forms of ironic mothering suggest a perverse inversion—what Jean Wyatt, referring to Sethe's murder of Beloved in Toni Morrison's novel, calls the "ultimate contradiction of mothering under slavery."[11]

If not quite in such terrible terms, the question of bad and even infanticidal mothering arises in *The Scarlet Letter*. After the opening scene in the market place, when Pearl is newborn, Hester returns from the scaffold "in a state of nervous excitement that demanded constant watchfulness, lest she should perpetrate violence on herself, or do some half-frenzied mischief to the poor babe" (*CE* 1:70). Later, at the Governor's Hall, when Pearl is three, Hester vows to kill herself before allowing the magistrates to remove Pearl from her care (*CE* 1:113). Later still, when Pearl is seven, a "fearful doubt strove to possess [Hester's] soul, whether it were not better to send Pearl at once to heaven, and go herself to such futurity as Eternal Justice should provide" (*CE* 1:166). This last thought proceeds directly out of the "dark labyrinth of mind" in which Hester has wandered during her seven years of ostracism from the Puritan community, and this infanticidal impulse leads directly into Hawthorne's observation that the "scarlet letter had not done its office" (*CE* 1:166). Among other features of her character, in other words, Hawthorne makes Hester's motherhood and its deviant tendencies— over the entire seven-year period of the novel—issues for careful observation.

Hawthorne could have found numerous examples of infanticidal mothers in the Puritan sources from which he composed *The Scarlet Letter*, including several that occurred during the period that comprises the novel's historical setting. Peter Hoffer and N. E. H. Hull cite the case of Dorothy Talbie of Salem, who was hanged in 1638 for murdering her three-year-old daughter. Recording this incident in his journal, John Winthrop noted that Talbie was "so possessed with Satan that he persuaded her (by his delusions, which she listened to as revelations from God) to break the neck of her own child, that she might free it from future misery."[12] Winthrop's explanation and the motive he attributes to Talbie anticipate Hester's thoughts of saving Pearl and herself from earthly pain. In another case Allice Bishop was executed in Plymouth in 1648 for murdering her four-year-old daughter, whom she had apparently conceived in an act of adultery.[13] In the same year another Massachusetts court condemned Mary Martin to death for killing her newborn daughter. The circumstances of the case bear some similarities to those in *The Scarlet Letter*. As recorded by Winthrop, Mary Martin's father had returned to England without arranging for proper supervision for his two daughters. Mary, the elder, promptly committed adultery with the married Mr. Mitton of Casco and, "her time being come, she was delivered of a woman child in a back room by herself." Martin attempted to kill the child by kneeling upon its head and then ultimately "put it into the fire."[14] Abandonment by a father (Martin) or father-like husband (Chillingworth), followed by adultery, the birth of an "illegitimate" child, and thoughts of infanticide—the resemblances seem compelling. Cotton Mather, moreover, preached two sermons inspired by the execution of Margaret Gaulacher, an

Irish servant who had murdered her illegitimate newborn child. Mather
cared less about the details of Gaulacher's case, which he scarcely mentioned,
than about the frequency of bastard neonaticide. "I cannot but think," he
concluded, "That there is a *Voice of God* unto the Country in this Thing; That
there should be so many Instances of Women Executed for the Murder of
their *Bastard-Children*. There are now Six or Seven such unhappy
Instances."[15]

One of the most striking was the case of Esther Rodgers of Kittery,
Maine, who confessed to being "defiled by a *Negro* Lad" at the age of
seventeen, to murdering the resulting child, and to giving it a "Private Burial
in the Garden."[16] Some time after committing this infanticide, which she did
"in Secret" and without being caught, Rodgers moved to Newbury, where
she repeated the crime. In her own words:

> And there I fell into the like Horrible Pit (as before) *viz.* of
> Carnal Pollution with the *Negro* man belonging to that House.
> And being with Child again, I was in as great concern to know
> how to hide this as the former. Yet did not so soon resolve the
> Murdering of it, but was continually hurried in my thoughts, and
> undetermined till the last hour. I went forth to be delivered in the
> Field, and dropping my Child by the side of a little Pond,
> (whether alive, or still Born I cannot tell) I covered it over with
> Dirt and Snow, and speedily returned home again. (124)

Rodgers was caught immediately and ultimately executed (on July 31, 1701)
for both crimes, and the remainder of her brief confession, like the three
sermons John Rogers preached upon the subject of her sinfulness, recounts
her repentance and conversion. I cannot tell if Hawthorne knew this text, but
Esther Rodgers' situation certainly bears some similarities to Hester's.
Rogers emphasizes Rodgers' public presence in and for the Puritan
community—the visitors she receives in prison, the round of visits she makes
to "private Meetings of Christians in the Town" (131), the freedom and
openness with which she discusses her situation (132), the "invincible
Courage" she maintains on the verge of her execution (144), the public
spectacle of the execution itself, which draws a crowd of 4,000–5,000 (153),
and even her insistence to the High Sheriff that she be allowed "the liberty
to walk on Foot" to the gallows rather than being carried in a cart (143). In
his preface to Rodgers' "confession" Samuel Belcher calls her a "poor
wretch, entering into Prison a Bloody Malefactor, her Conscience *laden with
Sins of a Scarlet Die*" (italics added, 118). Whether or not this scarlet Esther
inspired Hawthorne's Hester, Esther Rodgers' case does evidence an

Africanist presence in the seventeenth-century background of *The Scarlet Letter*. Whereas Rodgers resorts to infanticide, of course, Hester Prynne rejects that final solution and chooses instead to raise Pearl by herself.

Nineteenth-century as well as seventeenth-century materials comprise Hester's character, of course. While these seventh-century examples of fornication, adultery, and infanticide offer important evidence that Hawthorne had ample material to underwrite the Puritan features of Hester's maternal situation, the most striking examples of maternal infanticide in nineteenth-century literature involve slave mothers killing (or some times simply abandoning) their children in order to save them from enslavement. *The Scarlet Letter* has increasingly been examined in its nineteenth-century context, and its participation in a conversation about slavery and abolition has become almost axiomatic. For the most part, however, critics such as Jonathan Arac, Sacvan Bercovitch, Jennifer Fleischner, and Deborah Madsen have revealed Hawthorne's historicism in order to confirm his conservatism—his failure to oppose slavery and embrace abolition. Arguing that Hester's scarlet A resembles the United States Constitution as a contested text, Arac, for example, considers the "indeterminacy" of the letter's meaning a strategy on Hawthorne's part for avoiding political action and change. *The Scarlet Letter*, he believes, is "propaganda—*not* to change your life."[17] Bercovitch makes a more abstract case, but he too considers *The Scarlet Letter* to be "thick propaganda," and he cites Hawthorne's "ironies of reconciliation" and laissez-faire "strategy of inaction" as key ingredients in the liberal ideology that sponsored numerous compromises with slavery, especially in 1850, the year of *The Scarlet Letter*'s publication.[18]

Jean Fagan Yellin has gone furthest in exploring the novel's inscription by slavery and abolitionist discourses and convincingly established Hawthorne's knowledge of anti-slavery feminism.[19] She has linked Hester iconographically to female slaves as sisters in bondage even as she stresses Hawthorne's refusal to let Hester function as a full-fledged anti-slavery feminist. "*The Scarlet Letter* presents a classic displacement," Yellin points out: "color is the sign not of race, but of grace—and of its absence. Black skin is seen as blackened soul." When "'black' is read as describing skin color and not moral status, the text of *The Scarlet Letter* reveals the obsessive concern with blacks and blackness, with the presence of a dangerous dark group within society's midst, that is characteristic of American political discourse in the last decades before Emancipation."[20] Even though she explicitly links Hester to slave womanhood, Yellin ignores one of the key parallels. She focuses briefly on Hester's single motherhood but only in order to link her to other "fallen women" in nineteenth-century life and letters.[21] Complaining of Hester's erstwhile feminism obscures her position on the "other" side of the slavery/abolition equation—as a single mother whose racial identity helps illustrate the politics of racial mothering.

Jay Grossman offers an even more particularized reading of race in *The Scarlet Letter* by arguing that, in its fixation on the figure of the black man, the novel becomes "profoundly implicated" in "antebellum discourses of miscegenation." The "novel's depiction of miscegenation does not merely reproduce the terms of the Southern confrontation between a white master and a female slave," he argues. "Rather, the novel shifts the genders of that equation, with the effect ultimately of revealing the white fears that linked North and South: a shared belief in the unbridled sexuality of African men and the vulnerability of white women, a shared panic when confronted with the possibility of racial mixing."[22] In the allegorical terms that Grossman uses, Hester is a "victimized woman and Pearl the illegitimate child of a father-master"—Dimmesdale, whom the text obsessively figures as black.[23] Although he does not say so explicitly, Grossman seems to recognize the ambiguities, or doubleness, of Hawthorne's symbolic representation of race in *The Scarlet Letter*. Hester and Dimmesdale can be both black and white.

Similarly, I am not interested in identifying Hester Prynne as a slave mother or a black woman who has "passed" as white all these years. To be sure, our current critical interest in the representation of race and gender in literary texts provides a lens through which previously invisible textual features, such as Morrison's "Africanist presence," come to light. But the issue is not Hester's blackness or the Africanist "shadow" (to use another of Morrison's suggestive terms) that may "hover" over her character. The question is Hester's connection as a woman and a mother to other nineteenth-century female "characters"—in particular, to slave mothers and anti-slavery feminists. That connection is tricky. Hazel Carby, for example, has cautioned that "any feminist history that seeks to establish the sisterhood of white and black women as allies in the struggle against the oppression of all women must also reveal the complexity of the social and economic differences between women," so I want to be careful in examining how Hawthorne's representation of Hester as a mother engages and addresses contemporary issues of slave motherhood.[24] While Hester's motherhood, constructed discursively and intertextually, does link her with slave mothers, she also enjoys some privileges by virtue of her white racial identity. Insofar as she embodies racial identities, Hester represents an amalgam, or amalgamation. Hawthorne does link her situation closely enough with that of slave mothers that he tacitly invites us to discover an Africanist "presence" in her character. Describing the Puritans' expectations outside the prison door in the opening scene of *The Scarlet Letter*, Hawthorne observes that it might be that a sluggish bond-servant, or an undutiful child, whom his parents had given over to civil authority, was to be corrected at the whipping post. It might be, that an Antinomian, a Quaker, or other heterodox religionist, was to be scourged out of town, or an idle and vagrant Indian, whom the white man's fire-water had made riotous about the streets, was to be driven with stripes into the shadow of the forest. It might be, too, that a witch, like old Mistress Hibbins, the bitter-tempered widow of the magistrate, was to die upon the gallows. (*CE* 1:49)

Hawthorne's catalog makes clear the Puritans' conflation of various outlaw groups into a single figure of alterity—Hester herself. As an object of the Puritans' collective gaze, Hester embodies multiple forms of otherness, certainly including race. As a subject, therefore, Hester finds it difficult to escape her objectified being. Contemplating the "entire track along which she had been treading, since her happy infancy," she finds herself focusing on the scarlet letter and all that it signifies: "these were realties,—all else had vanished!" (*CE* 1:59).

This is not to say that Hester's objective status entirely eclipses her subjectivity—or, in the terms that concern me here, that her objectified status as an "other" woman colors her character completely in racial terms. Hester carries ambiguous racial markings, and I think Hawthorne exploits that ambiguity—the whiteness of her blackness—to shine an interesting and ironic light on the presumptions of white female abolitionists like Margaret Fuller and his sister-in-law, Elizabeth Peabody. In arguing the case for women's emancipation, for example, Fuller links women and slaves, effectively commandeering the subject position of black women for her own rhetorical and political purpose.[25] Elizabeth Peabody had long irritated Hawthorne with her abolitionist views. When she sent the Hawthornes an abolitionist pamphlet she had written, Hawthorne returned it to her without even showing it to Sophia. "No doubt it seems the truest of truth to you," he told his sister-in-law, "but I do assure you that, like every other Abolitionist, you look at matters with an awful squint, which distorts everything within your line of vision."[26] Three months later, after Peabody apparently sent him the same pamphlet, Hawthorne returned it again with a curt note:

I read your manuscript abolition pamphlet, supposing it to be a new production, and only discovered afterwards that it was the one I had sent back. Upon my word, it is not very good; not worthy of being sent three times across the ocean; not so good as

I supposed you would always write on a subject in which your mind and heart were interested.[27]

This correspondence occurred in 1857 while the Hawthornes were living in Liverpool and, thus, years after publication of *The Scarlet Letter*, but the Hawthornes' arguments with Peabody over slavery and abolition were longstanding.[28] To whatever extent he was aware of it, then, Hawthorne had personal reasons to criticize the feminist antislavery position and to situate Hester Prynne within the ideological context that discourse created. Considered as both subject and object, Hester occupies a symbolic position, it seems to me, on the dividing line between black and white feminism—the line that some white nineteenth-century feminists either ignored or erased. Objectified in a way that associates her with slave mothers, Hester retains some privileges of her status as a white feminist who, like Fuller and Peabody, presumed to occupy the subject position of slave women.

When he referred to slavery as a "monstrous birth" in "Chiefly about War-Matters," Hawthorne was playing upon the odd fact that, some time after carrying the Pilgrims to Plymouth, the *Mayflower* had become a slave ship. "There is an historical circumstance, known to few," he observed, "that connects the children of the Puritans with these Africans of Virginia in a singular way. They are our brethren, as being lineal descendents from the May Flower, the fated womb of which, in her first voyage, sent forth a brood of Pilgrims upon Plymouth Rock, and, in a subsequent one, spawned slaves upon the southern soil;—a monstrous birth, but with which we have an instinctive sense of kindred, and so are stirred by an irresistible impulse to attempt their rescue, even at the cost of blood and ruin."[29] We "must let her white progeny offset her dark one," Hawthorne concludes, and I would like to speculate further on the black and white doubleness to which he refers by suggesting that he had already explored the "singular" connection between Puritans and Africans—that in Hester he had discovered a vehicle for letting the "white progeny" of the *Mayflower* "offset her dark one." Hester Prynne embodies the racial doubleness that Hawthorne cites. Objectively and subjectively considered, she may be considered both black and white, and the challenge Hawthorne poses for the reader is how to deal with the Africanist presence (in Morrison's term) that shadows the white feminist subject.

Yellin has demonstrated conclusively that Hawthorne "became intimately acquainted with the essential facts of chattel slavery, as well as with the debate raging around it."[30] The Peabody sisters' Cuba Journals describe the sexual exploitation of slave women, for example, and even the frequency of infanticide—twenty or thirty deaths on the plantation where they stayed.[31] Hawthorne's 1835 sketch "Old News" not only mentions the slave population of Salem, but also includes the observation that "when the slaves of a family were inconveniently prolific, it being not quite orthodox to drown the superfluous offspring, like a litter of kittens, notice was promulgated of a 'negro child to be given away.'"[32] Although Yellin concludes that Hawthorne "deliberately avoided thinking about black slavery in antebellum America," I want to argue that, in identifying Hester with slave motherhood, Hawthorne interrogates and critiques the familiar identification of women and slaves—the conflation in nineteenth-century victimology of white mothers and slave mothers.[33] Illustrating the ironies of racialized maternal signification, Hawthorne undermines an anti-slavery feminist discourse that pretends to occupy the subject position of the slave woman and mother.

Dimmesdale's impregnation of Hester—after the "middle passage" that separates her from her husband—resembles a white master's miscegenetic coupling with a slave woman, at least in its analogous imbalance of power. Hester and Dimmesdale's action, even as it recalls the seventeenth-century predicaments catalogued by Mather and Winthrop, places Hester in a position that was beginning to register with nineteenth-century readers of abolitionist tracts and fugitive slave narratives. "Thou hadst charge of my soul," Hester reminds Dimmesdale at the Governor's Hall (*CE* 1:113), as she implores him to intercede with the Puritan magistrates and convince them to let her retain custody of Pearl. In *Incidents in the Life of a Slave Girl* (1861) Harriet Jacobs comments that "there is a great difference between Christianity and religion at the south.... If a pastor has offspring by a woman not his wife, the church dismiss him, if she is a white woman; but if she is colored, it does not hinder his continuing to be their good shepherd."[34] Much like a slave mother, whose only hope for keeping her child resided in her ties to white male authority, Hester must plead her case at secondhand. Harriet Jacobs maintains some leverage over Dr. Flint by threatening to expose his licentiousness to his wife and to the community. Similarly, Hester has gained leverage over Dimmesdale by refusing to name him as Pearl's father. According to a similar, absolute authority that separated slave mothers from their children and converted children into property subject to sale by the very fathers who denied their blood ties, Hester and Pearl remain subject to patriarchal law. Ultimately, however, Hester's feminist victory at the Governor's Hall offers a model that slave mothers like Jacobs were hard-pressed to emulate. Jacobs's many appeals to Mr. Sands, the biological father of her two children, repeatedly fall on deaf ears. Indeed, when she finally gets safely to New York, she is astonished to learn that, instead of freeing the daughter whose freedom she pressured him into buying, he has given Ellen to the daughter of a friend.

Like the mulatto children of slaveholders, Pearl follows the condition of her mother, and the parental triangle Hawthorne describes around Pearl resembles the common triangle on southern plantations if "Good Master Dimmesdale" occupies the position of the slave master, who fathers an illegitimate child upon one of his slaves, cuckolding her husband and then denying the child whom he fathers—even as, in his role as magistrate, he retains the power to remove her from her mother. In the terms that Hortense Spillers uses about fatherhood under slavery, "a dual fatherhood is set in motion, comprised of the African father's *banished* name and body and the captor father's mocking presence."[35] Not unlike a paranoid slave owner, determined to erase all traces of his miscegenetic paternity, furthermore, Dimmesdale worries about Pearl's maturing appearance. His refusal to acknowledge Pearl in any way, his dread that his "own features were partly repeated" in her face (*CE* 1:140), parallels the paradoxical relation between fatherhood and master-hood that writers such as Frederick Douglass and Harriet Jacobs describe. Douglass explains that slave women's children "in all cases follow the condition of their mothers," in order to make the slave-owning father's "wicked desires profitable as well as pleasurable; for by this cunning arrangement, the slaveholder, in cases not a few, sustains to his slaves the double relation of master and father."[36] And Jacobs tells the story of a Congressman who insists that his six mulatto children be sent away from the "great house" before he visits with his friends. "The existence of the colored children did not trouble this gentleman," she observes; "it was only the fear that friends might recognize in their features a resemblance to him."[37]

In the scaffold scene that opens *The Scarlet Letter* Hester seems uncannily linked to her sisters in bondage through a similar relationship to patriarchal power. Yellin notes the iconographic link to anti-slavery emblems of women on the auction block: "Hawthorne's book begins by presenting a woman publicly exposed, a figure made familiar by the abolitionists."[38] The narrator himself wonders before Hester's entrance if a "sluggish bond-servant" is about to appear (*CE* 1:36). Hester's stubborn refusal to name her child's father, furthermore, links her uncannily, if ironically, with slave mothers. Monika Elbert celebrates this refusal as a feminist gesture of defiance, a defiant "sin against patriarchy" along the lines Julia Kristeva marks out in "Stabat Mater."[39] The "Virgin assumes her feminine denial of the other sex (of man) but overcomes him by setting up a third person," Kristeva says: "I do not conceive with *you* but with *Him*."[40] For Hester, compared if "only by contrast" to the "image of Divine Maternity" (*CE* 1:56), denial of Dimmesdale promises transcendence—for Pearl—of the mother's condition. "My child must seek a heavenly Father," Hester insists; "she shall never know an earthly one!" (*CE* 1:68). Hester's refusal to name Pearl's father highlights the ironies of racial mothering, however, for in the inverted world of slavery, as Harriet Jacobs notes, "it was a crime for a slave to tell who was the father of her child."[41] While Hester's repeated refusals to name the father link her with the black sisterhood Jacobs identifies, such refusals signify very differently within different discursive and legal communities. The sort of heroic feminist action that Elbert celebrates signifies a *slave* mother's compliance *with* rather than rebellion *against* slave law. Parthenogenesis—Kristeva's feminist ideal, a male slaveholder's economic strategy. The condition and race of the mother make the difference.

While "Good Master Dimmesdale" may not be a *slave* master, his repudiation of Pearl resembles a slave master's behavior and subjects his daughter, as the Governor's Hall scene makes clear, to a similar patriarchal authority. Fatherhood, in Douglass's terms, gives way to "masterhood." Slave owners "controlled virtually all dimensions of their children's lives," Patricia Hill Collins observes; "they could be sold at will, whipped, even killed, all with no recourse by their mothers. In such a situation, simply keeping and rearing one's children becomes empowerment."[42] The Puritan magistrates, "Good Master Dimmesdale" included, claim a similar authority to dispose of Pearl. Hester claims a mother's power not to let them, and as her desperation increases in the face of her powerlessness her subjectivity and her subject position resemble those of nineteenth-century slave mothers like Harriet Jacobs. The "fact that slave society did not condemn 'illegitimacy' indicates the centrality of the mother role," observes Deborah Gray White, "a role which was presumed legitimate independent of the father's or husband's role."[43] Hester's situation in *The Scarlet Letter*, of course, tests the legitimacy of her maternal role. She does not commit infanticide, choosing heroically to live apart from her husband and to be the single mother of an "illegitimate" child, but she still confronts many of the same issues faced by slave mothers.

"What are a mother's rights," Hester asks Dimmesdale at the Governor's Hall, and "how much stronger they are, when that mother has but her child and the scarlet letter!"—that is, no husband/father and no political or legal standing (*CE* 1:113). Although Hester has successfully marked out a marginal space of her own in which to *be* a mother, the Puritan magistrates remind her that she mothers, so to speak, at the pleasure of the patriarchs; for they retain the power, *in loco Parentis*, to take Pearl away from her in much the same way that slave owners—fathers or not—possessed that absolute power. Michael Grossberg has shown that custody rulings in the nineteenth-century, however, "increasingly devalued paternally oriented, property-based welfare considerations and emphasized maternally biased child nurture ones."[44] Interpolating such changes anachronistically into his Puritan setting, Hawthorne conducts a "custody trial" (in Elbert's terms) at the Governor's Hall.[45] The Massachusetts legislature, in fact, enacted a law in the 1840s instructing the courts that "the rights of the parents to their children, in the absence of misconduct, are equal and the happiness and welfare of the child are to determine its care and custody."[46] As if quoting the statute—albeit for selfish as much as altruistic reasons—Dimmesdale argues that, "for Hester Prynne's sake, and no less for the poor child's sake, let us leave them as Providence hath seen fit to place them!" (CE 1:115). But even as the Governor's Hall scene dramatizes changes in nineteenth-century custody law, it addresses itself—if only in ironic contrast—to scenes of slave mothers begging for their maternal rights before intransigent slave owners, who had no legal obligation to care about the welfare of mothers or children. Harriet Jacobs, therefore, in contrast to Hester, must prevent her children from following their mother's condition—ironically, by giving them up or sending them away. "Poor little ones! fatherless and motherless!" she exclaims, as she bends over her sleeping children at the moment she leaves them for her solitary hiding place; "I knelt and prayed for the innocent little sleepers. I kissed them lightly, and turned away."[47]

Hester's admission to Mistress Hibbins that, had the magistrates taken Pearl from her, she would "willingly" have gone into the forest and signed her name—in her "own blood"—in the "Black Man's book" acquires an uncanny new meaning in this context, as if Hester acknowledges her racial difference, her narrow escape from the horrors of black slave motherhood—the privilege she has been granted, as it were, to *pass* as a white mother. Surely this scene and its threat to single motherhood might have struck a responsive emotional chord in a readership of anti-slavery feminists who might have appreciated the ironies of racial mothering Hawthorne highlights—the ironic signification of similar maternal acts. Following the condition of even the single mother means different things. In nineteenth-century America, Hawthorne instructs us, maternal differences are rooted in race.

Sacvan Bercovitch links the ending of The Scarlet Letter to the Liberian solution (the repatriation of slaves) promoted at the end of Uncle Tom's Cabin—largely, however, for its enactment of political gradualism or denial.[48] He might have found a more particularized similarity by following, if you will, the condition of the mothers. For like Linda Brent or Stowe's Eliza and George Harris, Hester flees America with her daughter. In the wake of the Fugitive Slave Law of 1850, Linda Brent feared that she and her children could be kidnapped on the streets of New York and returned to the South. Indeed, "many a poor washerwoman who, by hard labor, had made herself a comfortable home," she comments, "was obliged to sacrifice her furniture, bid a hurried farewell to friends, and seek her fortune among strangers in Canada."[49] Hester, too, considers a kind of Underground Railroad journey to freedom from white men's power. Deeper and deeper goes the path into the wilderness, she tells Dimmesdale, "less plainly to be seen at every step; until, some few miles hence, the yellow leaves will show no vestige of the white man's tread. There thou art free" (*CE* 1:197). After Dimmesdale's death, however, Hester seeks asylum in England, much as Jacobs—ironically—leaves New York for New England to avoid the likelihood of capture and then travels to England with her mistress's daughter Mary. "For the first time in my life," Jacobs observes, "I was in a place where I was treated according to my deportment, without reference to my complexion. I felt as if a great millstone had been lifted from my breast" and experienced for the first time "the delightful consciousness of pure, unadulterated freedom."[50] Even Pearl's inheritance from Chillingworth rather than from Dimmesdale makes a kind of sense—if Dimmesdale, with his exaggerated paleness, plays the role of slave-owning father. While Dimmesdale seems to acknowledge his paternity, his death enables Pearl's repatriation away from her father's world. She follows the condition of her mother. Linda Brent's children receive nothing from their white father, Mr. Sands. In bypassing her biological father in favor of her mother's legal husband, Pearl (despite her generous behavior to Dimmesdale on the scaffold) can be liberated from a "slave" economy and can return to her "step" father's estate—to a patrimony associated with the Black Man in the forest.

The case I have been making for reading Hawthorne's representation of Hester Prynne within a context of slave mothering does not mitigate recent criticism of his politics—his gradualist, providential views on slavery and its abolition. His interest in the experience and psychology of motherhood has its own political dimensions. If only through instructive analogy, Hawthorne situates Hester's maternal behavior within a context in which mothering signifies in racial terms. Refusing to name her child's father, resisting the efforts of the good masters to take her child away, planning an escape to freedom—Hester resembles slave mothers like Harriet Jacobs even as her actions signify and thereby underline the politics of racial difference. Situating Hester in a complex subject and object position in which slave motherhood and antislavery feminism come together, he represents the dangers of a presumption—the identification of black and white women's experiences and politics—that cuts as sharply today as it would have in the nineteenth century. Hester's abject dependence upon patriarchal sufferance for her mothering rights links her to her slave sisters, but her ability to mother at all marks her feminist difference from slave mothers like Harriet Jacobs. Hester Prynne is not a slave mother, but in representing her maternally, Hawthorne shows more sympathy and ironic understanding of the politics of her motherhood than his nineteenth-and twentieth-century detractors have allowed.

NOTES

1. Toni Morrison, *Playing in the Dark: Whiteness and the Literary Imagination* (Cambridge: Harvard Univ. Press, 1992), 46–47.

2. Nathaniel Hawthorne, *The Scarlet Letter,* ed. William Charvat et al., *The Centenary Edition of the Works of Nathaniel Hawthorne,* Vol. 1 (Columbus: Ohio State Univ. Press, 1962), 166. Hereafter cited parenthetically by volume and page number.

3. Harriet Jacobs, *Incidents in the Life of a Slave Girl* (1861), ed. Jean Fagan Yellin (Cambridge: Harvard Univ. Press, 1987). 74.

4. Nathaniel Hawthorne, "Chiefly about War-Matters," *Miscellaneous Prose and Verse,* ed. Thomas Woodson, Claude M. Simpson, and L. Neal Smith, *The Centenary Edition of the Works of Nathaniel Hawthorne,* Vol. 23 (Columbus: Ohio State Univ. Press, 1994), 420.

5. Patricia Hill Collins, "The Meaning of Motherhood in Black Culture and Black Mother/Daughter Relationships," *SAGE* 4, no. 2 (Fall 1987), 3, 5.

6. Hazel V. Carby, *Reconstructing Womanhood: The Emergence of the Afro-American Woman Novelist* (New York: Oxford Univ. Press, 1987), 49.

7. Carby, 56. In Stephanie Smith's felicitous terms, Jacobs' "desertion will translate into devotion." *Conceived by Liberty: Maternal Figures and Nineteenth-Century American Literature* (Ithaca: Cornell Univ. Press, 1994), 146.

8. Deborah Gray White, *Ar'n't I a Woman? Female Slaves in the Plantation South* (New York: W. W. Norton, 1985), 88.

9. Frances Harper, "The Slave Mother," *A Brighter Coming Day: A Frances Ellen Watkins Harper Reader,* ed. Frances Smith Foster (New York: Feminist Press, 1990), 85:

> Then, said the mournful mother,
> If Ohio cannot save,
> I will do a deed for freedom,
> She shall find each child a grave.
>
> I will save my precious children
> From their darkly threatened doom,
> I will hew their path to freedom
> Through the portals of the tomb.
>
> A moment in the sunlight,
> She held a glimmering knife,
> The next moment she had bathed it
> In the crimson fount of life.
>
> They snatched away the fatal knife,
> Her boys shrieked wild with Dread;
> The baby girl was pale and cold,
> They raised it up, the child was dead. (ll. 41–56)

10. Harriet Beecher Stowe, *Uncle Tom's Cabin,* ed. Elizabeth Ammons (New York: Norton, 1994), 318.

11. Jean Wyatt, "Giving Body to the Word: The Maternal Symbolic in Toni Morrison's *Beloved*," *PMLA* 108 (May 1993), 476.

12. Quoted in Peter C. Hoffer and N. E. H. Hull, *Murdering Mothers: Infanticide in England and New England 1558–1803* (New York: New York Univ. Press, 1981), 40.

13. Hoffer and Hull, 42.

14. Hoffer and Hull, 43.

15. Cotton Matter, *A Sorrowful Spectacle*, in *Two Sermons Occasioned by the Just Sentence of Death, on a Miserable Woman, for the Murder of a Spurious Offspring* (Boston: T. Fleet & T. Crump, 1715), 90.

16. Esther Rodgers, "The Declaration and Confession of Esther Rodgers," in John Rogers, *Death the Certain Wages of Sin to the Impenitent: Three Lecture Sermons; Occasioned by the Execution of a Young Woman, Guilty of Murdering Her Infant Begotten in Whoredom* (Boston: Green and Allen, 1701), 122. Hereafter cited parenthetically.

17. Jonathan Arac, "The Politics of *The Scarlet Letter*," *Ideology and Classic American Literature*, ed. Sacvan Bercovitch and Myra Jehlen (New York: Cambridge Univ. Press, 1986). 251.

18. Sacvan Bercovitch, *The Office of* The Scarlet Letter (Baltimore: Johns Hopkins Univ. Press, 1991), 89, 109, 110. Fleischner also argues that *The Scarlet Letter* reflects an "ideology that is related to the belief in compromise toward slavery adopted by Hawthorne and other Northerners at mid-century who, although anti-slavery, were above all pro-union." See "Hawthorne and the Politics of Slavery," *Studies in the Novel* 23 (1991), 97. Deborah L. Madsen, "'A for Abolition': Hawthorne's Bond-servant and the Shadow of Slavery," *Journal of American Studies* 25 (1991), 255–59, focuses on Governor Bellingham's bond-servant to claim that Hawthorne "complicates the vision of American liberty by representing, in 'typical' form, the entire generation of Founding Fathers who were slave owners" (257).

19. Jean Fagan Yellin, "Hawthorne and the American National Sin," *The Green American Tradition: Essays and Poems for Sherman Paul*, ed. H. Daniel Peck (Baton Rouge: Louisiana State Univ. Press, 1989). 75–97, and *Women and Sisters: The Antislavery Feminists in American Culture* (New Haven: Yale Univ. Press, 1989).

20. Yellin, *Women and Sisters*, 138. Yellin goes on, however, to argue that Hester's refusal to become a prophetess at the end of the novel reflects Hawthorne's repudiation of the "antislavery feminists who were defying social taboos in an effort to move other women to action"(149).

21. Yellin, *Women and Sisters*, 142.

22. Jay Grossman, " 'A' is for Abolition?: Race, Authorship, *The Scarlet Letter*," *Textual Practice* 7 (Spring 1993), 14, 15.

23. Grossman, 14, 17.

24. Carby, 53. See also Margaret M. R. Kellow, "The Divided Mind of Antislavery Feminism: Lydia Maria Child and the Construction of African American Womanhood," *Discovering the Women in Slavery: Emancipating Perspectives on the American Past*, ed. Patricia Morton (Athens: Univ. of Georgia Press, 1996), 107–26. Kellow concludes that the "discourse of independence and self-reliance as constructed by Child, crucial though it was to undermining the defense of slavery, had very little to do with black women" (113).

25. Fuller asserts, for example, that "there exists in the minds of men a tone of feeling towards women as toward slaves," and makes her case for women's emancipation by placing women in the same position as "Negroes": "As the friend of the negro assumes that one man cannot by right, hold another in bondage, so should the friend of woman assume that man cannot, by right, lay even well-meant restrictions on woman," *Woman in the Nineteenth Century*, ed. Larry J. Reynolds (New York: Norton, 1998), 18, 20.

26. Nathaniel Hawthorne, *The Letters, 1857–1864*, ed. William Charvat et al., *The Centenary Edition of the Works of Nathaniel Hawthorne*, Vol. 18 (Columbus: Ohio State Univ. Press, 1987), 89.

27. *The Letters, 1857–1864*, 115.

28. In his biography of Peabody, Bruce Ronda discusses the conflict between Hawthorne and Peabody, as well as Hawthorne's "hostility to antislavery advocates." See *Elizabeth Palmer Peabody: A Reformer on Her Own Terms* (Cambridge: Harvard Univ. Press, 1999), 265.

29. Hawthorne, "Chiefly about War-Matters," 420.

30. Yellin, "Hawthorne and the American National Sin," 76.

31. Yellin, "Hawthorne and the American National Sin," 84.

32. Nathaniel Hawthorne, "Old News," *The Snow-Image and Uncollected Tales*, ed. William Charvat et al., *The Centenary Edition of the Works of Nathaniel Hawthorne*, Vol. 11 (Columbus: Ohio State Univ. Press, 1974), 139.

33. Yellin, "Hawthorne and the American National Sin," 89.

34. Jacobs, 74.

35. Spillers, "Mama's Baby, Papa's Maybe: An American Grammar Book," *diacritics* 17, no. 2 (Summer 1987), 80.

36. Douglass, *Narrative of the Life of Frederick Douglass* (New York: Penguin, 1982), 49.

37. Jacobs, *Incidents in the Life of Slave Girl*, 142.

38. Yellin, *Women and Sisters*, 126.

39. Monika M. Elbert, "Hester's Maternity: Stigma or Weapon?" *ESQ* 36 (1990), 179.

40. Julia Kristeva, "Stabat Mater," *The Kristeva Reader*, ed. Toril Moi (New York: Columbia Univ. Press, 1986), 180.

41. Jacobs, 13. "The secrets of slavery are concealed like those of the Inquisition," Jacobs observes. "My master was, to my knowledge, the father of eleven slaves. But did the mothers dare to tell who was the father of their children? Did the other slaves dare to allude to it, except in whispers among themselves? No, indeed! They knew too well the terrible consequences" (35).

42. Collins, "Shifting the Center: Race, Class, and Feminist Theorizing about Motherhood," *Representations of Motherhood*, ed. Donna Bassin, Margaret Honey, and Meryle Mahrer Kaplan (New Haven: Yale Univ. Press, 1994), 66.

43. White, 159.

44. Michael Grossberg, "Who Gets the Child? Custody, Guardianship, and the Rise of a Judicial Patriarchy in Nineteenth-Century America," *Feminist Studies* 9 (1983), 240–41.

45. Elbert, 194.

46. Grossberg, 241.

47. Jacobs, 96.

48. Bercovitch, *The Office of* The Scarlet Letter, 89.

49. Jacobs, 191.

50. Jacobs, 183.

Character Profile

Before Hester Prynne appears, we learn what others think about her. The older matrons of the Puritan New England colony where Hester lives (approximately during the 1640s) call her a "hussy" and believe the punishment inflicted on her by the authorities has been too weak. Instead, one of the matrons says, Hester should have been branded with a hot iron, while yet another woman, "the ugliest," calls for Hester to be put to death. Yet when Hester emerges from her jail cell into the public eye, she comes into the light and shows her beautiful face, her dark shining "abundant" hair, and deep dark eyes. She is elegant, tall, lady-like, and almost Madonna-esque as she holds her baby; this is quite a juxtaposition to the matrons' perspectives. We do not know Hester's age, only that she is in her child-bearing years. Aside from her beauty and grace, there is something else startling in her physical appearance. The letter "A," which has been ordered to stay attached to her breast for the rest of her life, is there, "fantastically embroidered and illuminated" in gold thread.

One's physical appearance is some reflection of one's personality, and we see the beautiful bold letter as an indication not only of Hester's artistic ability but perhaps of her rebellion against the dark, merciless Puritans. Indeed, Hester's first utterance in the book is clearly defiant: "Never!" She tells the crowd that she will never reveal the name of her fellow adulterer, even if it means the authorities may lessen her own punishment. Her cry, though, is not just against their rules but indicative of her sympathy and love for Arthur Dimmesdale, the conflicted reverend who has sinned with her.

Her exclamation also proves her steadfastness and determination, for it indicates that she will never reveal the name now.

As the book progresses, Hester become stronger; she is independent, courageous, active, and thinking, as well as humble, penitent, giving, and sympathetic. Early in the book, we see her humble side. She admits to her husband, Roger Chillingworth, that she has prayed for death, but she also questions whether she is fit to pray for anything at all. She admits, also, that she "greatly wronged" him. Hester lives a life of misery, ostracized, quietly accepting of the townspeople's horrible treatment, and even at times enduring the scorn of the very poor for whom she makes clothing.

At the same time, though, just as she acts on the scaffold in the book's opening, Hester can be bold. For example, at one point we are told that she doesn't pray for her enemies, just in case "in spite of her forgiving aspirations, the words of the blessing should stubbornly twist themselves into a curse." Similarly, when she later realizes the wicked psychological torture her husband has inflicted on Dimmesdale, we read of her feelings for her husband: "'Be it sin or no,' said Hester Prynne bitterly, as she still gazed after him, 'I hate the man!' She upbraided herself for the sentiment, but could not overcome or lessen it.... 'Yes, I hate him!' repeated Hester, more bitterly than before."

Hester is also a woman of action. When she hears that her child, Pearl, may be taken away from her, Hester pleads directly with the governor at his own home. When she fears he is not agreeing with her perspective, she cries, "'Ye shall not take her! I will die first!'" And then, "raising her voice almost to a shriek," she adds, "'I will not give her up!'" While on the scaffold in the opening she suffered tremendously while struggling to uphold her dignity, here she starts speaking calmly but is pale, and, finally, she loses some self-control.

Later, Hester takes action once again but in a more controlled manner, when she realizes how Dimmesdale's guilt is destroying him. Again, this is seven years after the accusation against her and now she is "[s]trengthened by years of hard and solemn trial.... She had climbed her way, since then, to a higher point." She is now bold enough to confront Chillingworth. When she speaks to him, he, too, sees her strength. "'Woman, I could wellnigh pity thee!' said Roger Chillingworth, unable to restrain a thrill of admiration too; for there was a quality almost majestic in the despair which she expressed."

Aside from Chillingworth's admiration, Hester, during this seven-year period, has also provoked a new response from the townspeople. Because she has never complained about her punishment, because she has given to the poor, offered help in many calamities and cared for the sick, and has been a "well-spring of human tenderness," many people now see the "A" on her breast differently. "They said it meant Able; so strong was Hester Prynne, with a woman's strength," the narrator tells us.

There is also another change that has taken place in Hester. Her life has turned:

> from passion and feeling, to thought....The world's law was no law for her mind. It was an age in which the human intellect, newly emancipated, had taken a more active and a wider range than for many centuries before. Men of the sword had overthrown nobles and kings. Men bolder than these had overthrown and rearranged—not actually, but within the sphere of theory, which was their most real abode—the whole system of ancient prejudice.... Hester Prynne imbibed this spirit.

The narrator explains that had Hester not been responsible for Pearl's upbringing, Hester would have acted on her rebellious thoughts. "Then, she might have come down to us in history, hand in hand with Ann Hutchinson, as the foundress of a religious sect. She might, in one of her phases, have been a prophetess. She might, and not improbably would, have suffered death from the stern tribunals of the period, for attempting to undermine the foundations of the Puritan establishment."

Years later, Hester returns to the small town where she endured so much. Pearl is now a grown woman, no longer, then, a reason for Hester to hold back her rebellion. The scarlet letter is again seen differently by the townspeople, who have since seen the results of its torture on their beloved priest as well. Now it is "something to be sorrowed over, and looked upon with awe, yet with reverence too." Yet, Hester still holds back her rebellion. The narrator tells us that earlier Hester had "vainly" imagined herself as the prophetess of a new vision but that now she realizes such a mission must be reserved for one who is not "stained with sin, bowed down with shame, or even burdened with a life-long sorrow." Her sin has indeed altered her destiny. While there is hope, it will not be transformed into action by Hester.

Contributors

HAROLD BLOOM is Sterling Professor of the Humanities at Yale University and Henry W. and Albert A. Berg Professor of English at the New York University Graduate School. He is the author of over 20 books, including *Shelley's Mythmaking* (1959), *The Visionary Company* (1961), *Blake's Apocalypse* (1963), *Yeats* (1970), *A Map of Misreading* (1975), *Kabbalah and Criticism* (1975), *Agon: Toward a Theory of Revisionism* (1982), *The American Religion* (1992), *The Western Canon* (1994), and *Omens of Millennium: The Gnosis of Angels, Dreams, and Resurrection* (1996). *The Anxiety of Influence* (1973) sets forth Professor Bloom's provocative theory of the literary relationships between the great writers and their predecessors. His most recent books include *Shakespeare: The Invention of the Human* (1998), a 1998 National Book Award finalist, *How to Read and Why* (2000), *Genius: A Mosaic of One Hundred Exemplary Creative Minds* (2002), and *Hamlet: Poem Unlimited* (2003). In 1999, Professor Bloom received the prestigious American Academy of Arts and Letters Gold Medal for Criticism, and in 2002 he received the Catalonia International Prize.

One of the great novelists of the early twentieth century, D.H. LAWRENCE also wrote short stories, poems, plays, essays, and travel books. Two of his most well-known novels are *Sons and Lovers* and *Women in Love*.

EDWARD STONE has taught at Ohio University. He is the author of *Voices of Despair: Four Motifs in American Literature*.

CHARLES FEIDELSON, JR. is the author of *Symbolism in American Literature* and the editor of *Herman Melville: Moby Dick*.

AUSTIN WARREN was a Professor of English at the University of Michigan. A critic of the New England literary tradition, he edited International Thomson Publishing's edition of *The Scarlet Letter*. He also wrote *New England Saints*, *The Elder Henry James*, and was the joint author of *Theory of Literature*.

WALTER SHEAR has been a Professor of English at Kansas State College of Pittsburgh, where he was also the director of the graduate program. He is the author of *The Feeling of Being: Sensibility in Postwar American Fiction*.

PRESTON M. BROWNING, JR. teaches at the University of Illinois at Chicago. He has written on Flannery O'Connor.

MICHAEL J. COLACURCIO has taught English at Cornell University and the University of California at Los Angeles. He is the author of a book on Hawthorne's early tales and the editor of *New Essays on* The Scarlet Letter.

NINA BAYM has been director of the School of Humanities at the University of Illinois, Urbana-Champaign, where she is a professor. She is one of the editors of *The Norton Anthology of American Literature* and is the author of *The Shape of Hawthorne's Career*, The Scarlet Letter: *A Reading*, and several other titles.

LOIS A. CUDDY teaches at the University of Rhode Island. A specialist in nineteenth- and twentieth-century American literature, she has written a book on T. S. Eliot and has been on the editorial board of *Modern Language Studies*.

JANIS P. STOUT is the Dean of Faculty at Texas A&M University. She is the author of several books covering such authors as Willa Cather, Jane Austen, and Katherine Anne Porter.

MONICA M. ELBERT teaches English at Montclair State College. She is the author of *Encoding the Letter "A": Gender and Authority in Hawthorne's Early Fiction*.

LELAND S. PERSON teaches at the University of Cincinnati. He is the joint editor of *Roman Holidays: American Writers and Artists in Nineteenth-Century Italy*.

Bibliography

Anderson, Douglas. "Jefferson, Hawthorne and 'The Custom-House.'" *Nineteenth-Century Literature* 46, no. 3 (December 1991): 309–26.

Barlowe, J. "Rereading Women: Hester Prynne-ism and the Scarlet Mob of Scribblers." *American Literary History* 9, no. 2 (Summer 1997): 233–37.

———. "Response to the Responses." *American Literary History* 9, no. 2 (Summer 1997): 238–43.

———. *The Scarlet Mob of Scribblers: Rereading Hester Prynne.* Carbondale, Ill.: Southern Illinois University Press, 2000.

Baym, Nina. "Hester's Defiance." In Morey, Eileen, ed. *Readings on* The Scarlet Letter. San Diego: Greenhaven Press, 1998.

Bercovitch, Sacvan. "Hawthorne's A-Morality of Compromise." *Representations* 24 (Fall 1988): 1–27.

Bewley, Marius. *The Complex Fate: Hawthorne, Henry James and Some Other American Writers.* London: Chatto and Windus, 1952.

Boewe, Charles, and Murphey, Murray G. "Hester Prynne in History." *American Literature* 32 (1960): 202–204.

Bridgman, Richard. "As Hester Prynne Lay Dying." *English Language Notes* 2 (1965): 294–96.

Budick, Emily Miller. "We Damned-If-You-Do, Damned-If-You-Don't Mob of Scribbing Scholars," *American Literary History* 9, no. 2 (Summer 1997): 233–37.

Carpenter, Frederic I. "Scarlet A Minus." *College English* 5 (1944): 173–80.

Colacurcio, Michael J. "'The Woman's Own Choice': Sex, Metaphor, and the Puritan 'Sources' of *The Scarlet Letter.*" In Colacurcio, Michael J., ed. *New Essays on* The Scarlet Letter. Cambridge: Cambridge University Press, 1985.

Cottom, Daniel. "Hawthorne versus Hester: the Ghostly Dialectic of Romance in *The Scarlet Letter.*" *Texas Studies in Literature and Language* 24, no. 1 (Spring 1982): 47–67.

Cowley, Malcolm. "Five Acts of *The Scarlet Letter.*" *College English* 19 (1957): 11–16.

Davis, Sarah I. "Another View of Hester and the Antinomians." *Studies in American Fiction* 12 (1984): 189–98.

Doubleday, Neal F. "Hawthorne's Hester and Feminism." *PMLA* 54 (1939): 825–28.

Dunne, Michael. "Hawthorne, the Reader, and Hester Prynne." *Interpretations* 10 (1978): 34–40.

Elbert, Monika M. "Hester's Maternity: Stigma or Weapon?" *ESQ: A Journal of the American Renaissance* 36, third quarter (1990): 175–207.

Erlich, Gloria C. "Deadly Innocence: Hawthorne's Dark Women." *New England Quarterly* 41 (1968): 163–79.

Fiedler, Leslie. *Love and Death in the American Novel.* New York: Dell, 1960.

Foster, Dennis. "The Embroidered Sin: Confessional Evasion in *The Scarlet Letter.*" *Criticism* 25 (1983):141–63.

Fryer, Judith. *The Faces of Eve: Women in the Nineteenth-Century American Novel.* New York: Oxford University Press, 1976.

Gartner, Matthew. "*The Scarlet Letter* and the Book of Esther: Scriptural Letter and Narrative Life." *Studies in American Fiction* 23, no. 2 (Autumn 1995): 131–51.

Gerber, John C. "Form and Content in *The Scarlet Letter,*" *The New England Quarterly* 17 (1944): 25–55.

———. *Twentieth-Century Interpretations of* The Scarlet Letter: *A Collection of Critical Essays.* Englewood Cliffs, N.J.: Prentice-Hall, 1968.

Gross, Seymour. "'Solitude, and Love, and Anguish': The Tragic Design of *The Scarlet Letter.*" *College Language Association Journal* 3 (1968): 154–65.

Hardwick, Elizabeth. *Seduction and Betrayal: Women in Literature*. New York: Random House, 1974.

Hart, James D. "*The Scarlet Letter*: One Hundred Years After." *New England Quarterly* 23 (1950): 381–95.

Houston, Neal B. "Hester Prynne as Eternal Feminine." *Discourse* 9 (1966) 230–44.

———. "Hester Prynne as Eternal Feminine." *Real: The Journal of Liberal Arts* 21, 1 (Spring 1996): 29–39.

Howells, William D. *Heroines of Fiction*. New York: Harper, 1901.

Kalfopoulou, Adrianne. "Hester's Ungathered Hair: Hawthorne and 19th Century Women's Fiction." *Gramma: Journal of Theory and Criticism* 1 (1993): 40–61.

Kaul, A. N. "Character and Motive in *The Scarlet Letter*." *Critical Quarterly* 10 (1968): 373–84.

Kim, Young-hee. "Hester Prynne's Tragedy." *Journal of the English Language and Literature* 31 (May 1990): 1–20.

Lane, Lauriat, Jr. "Allegory and Character in *The Scarlet Letter*." *Emerson Society Quarterly* 25 (Fourth Quarter, 1961): 13–16.

Leverenz, David. "Mrs. Hawthorne's Headache: Reading *The Scarlet Letter*." *Nineteenth-Century Fiction* 37, no. 4 (March 1983): 552–75.

Li, Haipeng. "Hester Prynne and the Folk Art of Embroidery." *University of Mississippi Studies in English* 19 (1992): 80–85.

Lloyd-Smith, Allan Gardner. *Eve Tempted: Writing and Sexuality in Hawthorne's Fiction*. London: Croom Helm, 1984.

Male, Roy R. "Transformation: Hester and Arthur." *Hawthorne's Tragic Vision*. Austin: University of Texas Press, 1957, 102–117.

Mellard, James M. "Pearl and Hester: A Lacanian Reading." In Kesterson, David B., ed. *Critical Essays on Hawthorne's* The Scarlet Letter. Boston: G. K. Hall, 1988, 193–211.

Milliman, Craig. "Hester Prynne as the Artist of the Beautiful." *Publications of the Mississippi Philological Association* (1995): 82–87.

Parulis, Cheryl. "Hawthorne's Genre of Romance: The Seduction of Betrayal in *The Scarlet Letter*." *Collages and Bricolages: The Journal of International Writing* 5 (1991): 108–116.

Pearce, Roy Harvey. *Hawthorne Centenary Essays*. Columbus: Ohio State University Press, 1964.

Sandeen, Ernest. "*The Scarlet Letter* as a Love Story." *PMLA* 77 (1962): 425–35.

Tassi, Nina. "Hawthorne's Hester: Female History into Fiction." *CEA Magazine* (Fall 1995): 5–14.

Trollope, Anthony. "The Genius of Nathaniel Hawthorne." *The North American Review* 129 (1879).

Van Doren, Mark. *Nathaniel Hawthorne*. New York: William Sloane Associates, 1949.

Waggoner, Hyatt H. *Hawthorne:A Critical Study*. Cambridge: Harvard University Press, 1955, 1963.

Warren, Robert Penn. "Hawthorne Revisited: Some Remarks on Hell-firedness." *Sewanee Review* 81 (1973).

Young, Virginia Hudson. "D. H. Lawrence and Hester Prynne." *Publications of the Arkansas Philological Association* 13, no. 1 (Spring 1987): 67–78.

Acknowledgments

"Nathaniel Hawthorne and 'The Scarlet Letter'" by D.H. Lawrence. From *Studies in Classic American Literature*: 121–147. © 1923 by Thomas Seltzer, Inc. Reprinted by permission.

"The Antique Gentility of Hester Prynne" by Edward Stone. From *Philological Quarterly* 36, no. 1 (Jaunuary 1957): 90–96. © 1957 by The State University of Iowa. Reprinted by permission.

"*The Scarlet Letter*" Charles Feidelson, Jr. From *Hawthorne Centenary Essays*, edited by Roy Harvey Pearce: 31–35, 46–63. © 1964 by Ohio State University Press. Reprinted by permission.

"*The Scarlet Letter*" by *Austin Warren*. From *Connections*: 45–69. © 1970 by The University of Michigan. Reprinted by permission.

"Characterization in *The Scarlet Letter*" Walter Shear. From *The Midwest Quarterly* 12, no. 4 (July 1971): 437–454. © 1971 by *The Midwest Quarterly*. Reprinted by permission.

"Hester Prynne as Secular Saint" by Preston M. Browning, Jr. From *The Midwest Quarterly* 13, no. 4 (July 1972): 351–62. © 1972 by *The Midwest Quarterly*. Reprinted by permission.

Colacurcio, Michael J. "Footsteps of Ann Hutchinson: The Context of *The Scarlet Letter*." From *ELH* 39, no. 3 (September 1972): 459–85. © 1972 by The Johns Hopkins University Press. Reprinted by permission of The Johns Hopkins University Press.

231

"Who? The Characters" by Nina Baym. From *The Scarlet Letter: A Reading*: 52–53, 62–67, 73–82. © 1986 by G.K. Hall. Reprinted by permission of The Gale Group.

"Mother-Daughter Identification in *The Scarlet Letter*" by Lois A. Cuddy. From *Mosaic* 19, no. 2 (Spring 1986): 101–115. © 1986 by *Mosaic*. Reprinted by permission.

"The Fallen Woman and the Conflicted Author: Hawthorne and Hardy" by Janis P. Stout. From *The American Transcendental Quarterly* 1, no. 3 (September 1987): 233–246. © 1987 by The University of Rhode Island. Reprinted by permission.

"Hester and the New Feminine Vision" by Monica M. Elbert. From *Encoding the Letter „A": Gender and Authority in Hawthorne's Early Fiction*: 219–245. © 1990 by Haag + Herchen. Reprinted by permission.

"The Dark Labyrinth of Mind: Hawthorne, Authorship, and Slavery" by Leland S. Person. From *Studies in American Fiction* 29, no. 2 (Spring 2001): 33–48. © 2001 by Northeastern University. Reprinted by permission.

Index